Never to be Forgotten

Joe Mière

Never to be Forgotten

First Published in 2004 by

CHANNEL
ISLAND
PUBLISHING

We acknowledge with thanks permission to
reproduce photographs and material supplied by:

Channel Island Publishing
Jersey Evening Post
Jersey Archives Services
Jersey Heritage Trust
Jersey War Tunnels Archives
States of Guernsey Archives Service
The Joe Mière Collection
Frank Le Quesne
Dr Paul Sanders
Jurat P.J. de Veulle FCA
Frederick Cohen
Robert Pallot
Frank Keiller
Frank Falla
Paul Simmonds
Chris Addy
Le Pennec Family

ISBN 0-9542669-8-6

Contents...

This book is dedicated to:

THE MEMORY OF THOSE WHO DID NOT RETURN -
THE SURVIVORS - AND THOSE WHO FOUGHT BACK.

IT IS BETTER TO PERISH IN BATTLE THAN TO LOOK UPON THE
OUTRAGE OF OUR NATION AND OUR ALTARS.

LET THE GODS SO SPARE ME AS I LOVE THE NAME OF HONOUR MORE
THAN I FEAR DEATH.

A YOUNG JERSEY LAD, COLD, HUNGRY AND ALONE IN A DARK, DAMP
CELL AWAITING HIS TENTH NIGHT OF BRUTAL INTERROGATION BY
THE GERMAN SECRET FIELD POLICE.

AS JACKBOOT STEPS APPROACH HIS SMALL CELL DOOR HE KNEELS
AND A CHILDHOOD PRAYER HE HAD LONG FORGOTTEN PASSES HIS
SWOLLEN, CUT LIPS.

O GOD, LET ME NOT TURN COWARD BEFORE THE DIFFICULTIES OF
THE DAY OR PROVE RECREANT WHEN FACING ITS DUTIES.
LET ME NOT LOSE FAITH IN MY FELLOW MEN,
KEEP ME SWEET AND SOUND OF HEART IN SPITE OF INGRATITUDE,
TREACHERY OR MEANNESS. PRESERVE ME FROM MINDING LITTLE
STINGS OR GIVING THEM.

THE KEY TURNS IN THE LOCK "MITKOMMEN SCHNELL." AS HE PASSED
THROUGH THE CELL DOOR HE WAS NO LONGER A YOUTH BUT A
MAN.

PRISONER 12503 / 27638 ak. German Military Prison,
St Helier, Jersey, Channel Islands.
November 1944.
Joe Mière. 17 year old Jerseyman.

FORGOTTEN PEOPLE

Quote from ex-prisoner Frank Falla in his book, "The Silent War."

It was not a case of active co-operation or fraternisation "But" in the subsequent statements of those in authority. It was their intention that it should be and prove a model "Occupation" and that everyone's behaviour should be correct.

In subsequent statements it was made clear that anyone who stepped out of line could expect no sympathy, understanding or help from the local civil government, and this was carried out to the letter in most instances. In other words if you offended the Germans and got punishment for it, that was your own fault and the local authorities had no intention of helping you in your troubles.
This was the right impression to give the Nazis, but it should not have been practiced by the local authorities on its own people.

Not such a quiet "Occupation" as some people would have you believe.
Judge for yourselves!

START OF THE GERMAN OCCUPATION OF THE CHANNEL ISLANDS

In 1938 the clouds of war were starting to drift over Europe. The British officials in London sent out feelers to the States of Jersey to ascertain if the Island could accommodate 12 to 14 Jewish children, refugee children who had arrived in England to escape persecution by the Nazi regime in Germany. But the shame of it was that some leading old dyed-in-the wool Jerseymen were against giving refuge to what they called "foreign children" being thrust on them. So these little children never came to these Islands, but were sent to kind homes in England. I often wonder what such mean old sods who called themselves good Jerseymen thought when in June 1940 thousands of our Jersey people arrived in England as refugees, and the English took them in with open arms. (Thank you, dear old England.)

In June 1940, just before the Germans arrived, panic set in. People were fleeing the Island and thousands were queued all along at the St Helier Town Hall for the evacuation from Jersey to England by boat. By the 20th/21st June, 1940, 23,062 people had registered at the Town Hall, about half the population of Jersey.

Some States of Jersey members were not very kind in their remarks about the people who had left, or were leaving the Island. Some of these States' members were calling people "rabbits, rats and cowards." It was okay for these States' members; most of them owned large properties or farms but what about the ordinary man in the street and his family? If the Island was to be occupied by the Germans the little man would be the first to suffer if shortages came, such as food, and no employment. It was these States' members who shouted the loudest who let the people down. They should have organised the evacuation to England a week before, and they should have informed the public of what was going on and explain to them the choice of evacuating to England or remaining in Jersey. To be fair, these States' members had never before had to cope with invasion by enemy troops, let alone evacuation. We think that the Police Court Magistrate, J.E. Pinel hit the nail on the head when on 25th June, 1940, he stated in Court; 'It is a very sad state of affairs to see the muddle the whole Island is in now, and the blame for most of the muddle must be born by responsible people in office.' If the matter had been properly handled all this would never have happened and we would not have seen thousands of people leaving their homes, their cattle and their pets, thinking that they were about to be murdered. There was something rotten in the administration of this Island. Some heads of departments, even though they were staying in the Island, lost their heads and were to blame for not explaining to the public what was intended. If that had been done we would not have seen officials and hospital nurses in some cases leaving everything. When the rest of the people saw that many of them followed like sheep.

'I say this publicly: Jersey is about the safest place people can live in, in comparison with others for the time being,' Judge Pinel said. 'It has saddened my heart to see how many cowards there are in this Island but they are not to blame, they were encouraged to leave when they were told women and children first.' Then the States voted £1,000 for the evacuation of those who could not pay. 'If all that is not creating panic I do not know what is,' stated our leading Police Judge in Jersey.

10,798 people were evacuated to England from Jersey.
20,202 people was evacuated to England from Guernsey.

Total population remaining in the Channel Islands

Jersey   41,101
Guernsey   24,429
Sark   470

Total remaining in the Channel Islands; 66,000

In the summer of 1940, the British Government evacuated 25,000 people from Gibraltar to England, most were billeted in small hotels in Kensington, London.

START OF MY LIFE: 27 JULY 1926

So many people over the years have approached me and asked 'When are you going to write that book, Joe, on your experiences during the German Occupation of Jersey 1940-1945?'

Well for better or worse, here goes. But where to start, the German Occupation of Jersey is very well recorded in many books, films, T.V and radio, but there are parts of the German Occupation that need to be recorded.

There is the human side of the Occupation, the history of our people, young and old, the little people, with true facts that can be checked out. I am not so interested in the German view of the German Occupation because when Hitler was on top many of the Germans were all for their beloved Führer, but when he was losing the war it seemed as if none of them belonged to the Nazi party. Hitler was right about one thing - his Generals. When one reads their memoirs they give you the impression that they were with us against Hitler. Well, who the hell were our people fighting against, and to give the Germans their due they could fight, even to the end of the war.

It seems that I am always doing research work for other people, so they can write about the Occupation, so at last I am writing for myself. I do want to put the facts on paper about our very loyal and brave Jersey people. I love our Jersey people so will try to show that it was not such a quiet Occupation as many writers state in their books.

I was born at 29 Hilgrove Street (now Boots the chemist). I was born a black baby (really blue). I was in a mess, my feet were turned inward and when I was very young I had to wear leg braces. Later on in life, I could not speak properly and I still lisp badly sometimes. Two days after my birth the doctor told my father he could do no more for me and advised him that being Roman Catholics it was better to get a priest. The priest gave me the last rites and also baptised me. I however lived to tell the tale. We moved to Midvale Road in 1928 but sold our old home to Boots the chemist. My first school was the little Roman Catholic school next to St Thomas' church, then Vauxhall school but only a short stay. Then on to de la Salle College. I left this college in 1940 when the German Occupation started.

Brother Edward, our head teacher, was not very pleased with me to be leaving his school and tried very hard for me to change my mind but I have always been a country boy at heart and always wanted to be a farmer like my grandfather who farmed at St John's. He lost two sons, William and Joe, both killed in the 1914-1918 war. Part of my young life was spent at my uncle's and aunt's farm at St Peter's. The farm was next to a pig farm (now the Mermaid Hotel). In those days there was no airport until later.

I was for a short time an altar boy at St Thomas' Roman Catholic Church. One day I was very late for the service, and it was my duty to fill and carry to the alter the small pot that contained the incense to refill the censer (the incense burner which is swung) but being so late I dropped the incense pot on the floor and all the contents spilled all over the floor. I could not find the tin which contained the incense powder so I tried to pick up what was on the floor and blew the rest under a table. I went through to the altar with the empty pot.

Later during the service the old priest signalled to me to come forward with the incense pot to refill the incense burner. The priest opened the pot and on seeing it was empty got very angry and slapped me across the face, and it was a very hard slap. My natural instinct made me hit back very fast by kicking him in his lower parts. He was shocked and the congregation let out a cry of disapproval. I ran into the vestry, threw off my gown and did a runner.

After seven in the evening I thought I had better head for home and face the music. When I opened our parlour door I could see Mother and Father and the priests from St Thomas' and priests from St Mary's and St Peter's (also the nuns from the convent,) and the old priest who had slapped me across the face. Mother went for me and they all joined in, with the old priest pointing at me. This went on for over half an hour. In the end my father told the old priest 'You, Father, should have reported the boy to me if he had done wrong and you should not have slapped him! I would have punished him.' In the end I was kept in after school for four weeks and no pocket money for two months. And I was no longer an altar boy.

It was a different story six months before this incident at the altar of St Thomas' church. My mother had promised me to the church when I was born, (that's if I lived), so when I was 12 years old I had to attend Highlands Jesuit College after school on Saturday afternoons. I did not like all this and I thought to myself this is not right promising me to the church to be a priest. There were a number of young Frenchmen learning to be priests or Jesuits. After a few weeks one of the very kind Jesuit fathers took me into a big room to ask me questions (he knew I was not set on being a priest). 'Joseph, do you smoke?' I stated that I did smoke. Question No 2: 'Do you talk to and go out with girls?' I again stated "yes." 'Have you ever kissed girls?' Again the answer was "yes" He asked me many other questions. I knew that if I gave the Jesuit priest answers he did not like it was a way out from learning to become a priest (I was really shy when it came to girls).

The kind Jesuit priest and four other Jesuits that were in the room sent me home with a note to my mother and father. Before handing the note to my mother, I steamed it open. The note stated that I was very intelligent but at this date I was not suitable for the priesthood. And when I was older then I could learn the priesthood.

My mother cried all day but I was over the moon. No Father Joseph for me, thank God. In 1940 my father took me away from the farm life I loved and put me to learn engineering at the Axis Engineering works in Hilgrove Street, and I did not do so bad at engineering.

RESISTANCE GROUPS IN JERSEY

The following facts in this book about our wartime Occupation history are not recorded here to get at any person or family, or to attack this Island of Jersey which we all love deeply. There is no axe to grind, this old Jerseyman, Joe, is not anti-States, or anti-police, having family in the local uniformed police, uncle and cousins in the Occupation years. They have always helped with the true facts and filled in the missing part of our Occupation police history. Many writers of our Occupation history keep off the subject of our wartime local police or anything that touches on collaboration by some of our Jersey authorities during the German Occupation of these Islands. In private they tell you that there was some collaboration with the Germans but they never put it in print. They seem to draw a line when it comes to anything so sensitive a subject. I do not blame them in one way because the press and the TV people seem to blow up any little story about collaboration into a big front page story. They seem to not want to know about all our 4,000 Channel Islanders arrested by the Germans and the 621 who were deported to German penal prisons and concentration camps in France and Germany. And they do not want to know, it seems, about the 22 people from Jersey who did not return from the German prisons or concentration camps.

But could you sleep peacefully, knowing you had not respected the memory of dear friends and fellow Channel Islanders who died under brutal conditions in German prisons or concentration camps?

We old Jersey Occupation people do know that some of our officials bent the knee to the might of the Nazi forces. We also know that these officials had no choice but to obey the German orders, otherwise they and their families would have ended up in German concentration camps. But there should have been at least one among them with enough courage to lead and organise the dozens of little resistance groups that had formed in Jersey over the five years of the German Occupation. If the British forces had landed on the Island, and a battle to liberate us had started, look at the help a well organised resistance group would have been to our troops. Woelfe was one of the well known German Secret Field Police, and after an unusually quiet morning being interrogated by him and his boss Bode, I realised he was in a good mood and trying slyly a new tact of being or trying to be a friend to me (it did not last) I did ask him why had he arrested so many young people and why so many people were imprisoned by his say so. He replied 'We are going to sort you people out and don't think for one moment that we are going to let your leaders stab or shoot our troops in the back if the Americans or British try to land in these Islands. We do know that you are not groups on your own, and that you are led by older ex-service men but we intend to find them in the end.' I kept a straight face but was smiling inside. No wonder the German police kept on about leaders and a secret headquarters. On my return to the prison I told the lads all about it all and it made them laugh.

Collaborators in Jersey were spared prosecution because the Island authorities blocked plans for a tribunal to examine scandalous conduct during the German Occupation. The Jersey loyalists wanted collaborators brought to trial but a committee of Island authorities (same authorities from the Occupation Local Government) decided in February 1946, that it would not be in the best interests of the Islanders to have a public tribunal. You the reader of this book must judge for yourself. But please remember that as every year the TV and press come to Jersey to try and dig up stories about collaboration, it would have been better all round if we could have had the public tribunal in 1946 and be done with it.

We were not the only little resistance group trying to steal German weapons. People must understand that there were dozens of little resistance groups in Jersey. All trying to arm themselves with German weapons and ammunition stolen from German stores and billets. And some of these groups were much more successful than our little group. Our idea of stealing German arms was quite simple (but it was not simple to steal the weapons). If our Allied Forces invaded the Island we would be armed and act as guides for our troops to where the German bunkers and strong points were.

If only we could have found some ex-soldier or officer to organise all our little groups into one Island organisation. We did approach two old army majors and one colonel to try and organise our group but they were of no use at all when it came down to modern underground warfare. All they wanted to do was to teach us how to march and how to salute, and to listen to their 1914-18 war history. These dear old ex-officers were a bunch of old farts, god bless them.

I do wish more of the old resistance groups would write and publish their Occupation histories before it's too late. I can well assure you that some of their adventures would make your hair stand on end.

The people who spread the lie that there were no resistance groups in Jersey are mostly people who did nothing to oppose the Germans. They obeyed German orders to the letter and submitted to German rule. These rumour mongers have a guilty conscience and they wish they could put the clock back and be counted among the 2,600 people who were arrested and imprisoned by the Germans in Jersey 1940-1945.

The German Secret Field Police did think that in Jersey there was a big well organised resistance movement lead by well known people. You have only to ask anyone in Jersey who had been arrested for acts of sabotage, and they will tell you that the very first question by the German police was always 'Who is your top leader? What is their name and address, and where is their headquarters, what are their plans?' etc. No wonder many a lad or girl did not know what the police were on about. The German Secret Field Police were being close to neurotic about this mythical resistance headquarters.

It was not as quiet or as passive a German Occupation of the Channel Islands as many would have you believe. Many writers and historians of the Occupation years, press and TV people for some reason or other seem to pass over the fact that over 4,000 Channel Islanders and British residents were arrested and imprisoned by the German Occupation Forces 1940-1945. Even our own past States of Jersey played down the numbers of political prisoners who were imprisoned by the Germans. The political prisoner of the Occupation years seemed to be an embarrassment to our wartime local government. But things have changed for the better, thanks due to our present Bailiff, Sir Philip Bailhache. One of his first duties as Bailiff was to unveil a plaque to the courage of those imprisoned by the Germans in Jersey 1940-1945. The plaque is set in the wall next to the main gate where the old prison stood in Gloucester Street, St. Helier. Sir Philip at the unveiling stated 'We salute the courage of all who defied the invaders and showed the sturdy spirit of independence which beats in every true Jersey heart.'

(Comment by ex-prisoner Joe Mière)

I am sure that the ghosts of many of the old political prisoners kept watch and nodded in satisfaction. And the spirit of the brave young Frenchman François Scornet taken from this prison and shot at St Ouen's Manor 17 March 1941 was also there. Also the spirits of the German service men who were also taken from this prison and executed at Fort Regent, Queen's Valley, La Moye, St. Saviours etc. And without shame I thought of them all, and the days and months we spent under the same prison roof. We all shared a common enemy, the brutal Nazis.

JAMES COLGAN, JERSEY POLICE COURT

The Germans had only arrived in Jersey three days, and already they were showing that they were the masters. And some of our officials were either very frightened old men, or ready to obey German orders to the letter.

The Colgan Police Court case was followed with great interest by young Jerseymen and women and after it was over, we knew that acts against the Germans would not be tolerated by our local authorities, and we could find ourselves not only in a German Military Court but a good chance of being tried in our own police court.

Police Court, before J.E.Pinel Esq, Magistrate, Friday 5th July 1940

James Colgan of County Westmeath, Eire. 30 year old ex-Irish Guardsman. 1st Battalion Irish Guards, London, was charged by the Connétable of St Helier with assaulting a German soldier, Fritz Scholle, at a cafe in Seaton Place, St Helier, on 3rd July 1940.

The Connétable of St Helier said that on Wednesday about 11.30 Centenier Tostevin telephoned him and informed him of a disturbance which had occurred at 18 Seaton Place at a cafe. He was informed that a soldier had been struck by an Irishman who had afterwards got away. The witness heard no more until yesterday morning when he was informed that the Irishman, Colgan, had been apprehended by a police constable at a house in Seaton Place. The witness went into the matter and elicited that Colgan and the soldier were in the cafe and the civilian had, for some reason unknown, struck the soldier. Colgan had no police record against him. When questioned by witness, Colgan stated he had no recollection of the affair and had been drinking.

Centenier Tostevin said he received the complaint and telephoned to the Connétable. The witness later interviewed the German soldier and the German Kommandant and was instructed to find the civilian concerned and eventually at 7am next day, Colgan whose description was given, was detained at 17 Sand Street.

James Colgan, the ex-Irish Guardsman, had as much chance in the Police Court as a snowball in hell. Lined up against him in the court were;

The Magistrate, (who had a bias against the Irish and for some unknown reason hated them.)

The Jersey Attorney General
The Connétable of St Helier
St Helier Centenier Tostevin
Three uniformed police constables
Four German Officers
Three German soldiers

And to top it all, two Englishmen who had come into the cafe with the German soldier who had been assaulted. So what chances did the is ex-guardsman have - none !

James Colgan stated in court that he was sitting smoking after his meal when the soldier came in with the two Englishmen. He, Colgan, was wearing his hat and the German soldier took it off and threw it on a chair. He, Colgan, picked it up and put it on his head again and sat down, whereupon the soldier repeated the action. The accused admitted striking the soldier but he did not strike the soldier then as he was sitting down. The first blow was struck at the door of the cafe. Colgan's blood was up and he could not stand it any more so he hit the soldier when he stood up.

The soldier, Fritz Scholle, said it was not true. He stated that he was hit at the table. The Magistrate told Colgan he had done his best to give him a fair trial and asked him if he had any other statement to make. Colgan said 'Every statement I have made is true, Sir.'

The Attorney General, addressing the Judge, then made the following statement 'I take a very serious view of this case. This Island is under German Occupation. That Occupation has been carried out by the German forces with the utmost consideration for and courtesy towards the civil population of the Island. It is therefore intolerable that any member of these forces should be treated with less consideration or courtesy. The offence which is alleged against the prisoner is one in respect of which, if found guilty, he is liable to be punished under German Military Law or under Jersey Criminal Law. The penalties of the former are very much more severe than those of the latter. The Connétable of St Helier and I have investigated this case in collaboration with the German Kommandant and it is at the special request of the latter that as this is the first and I hope the last incident of this kind it is being dealt with by the civil and not the military jurisdiction. I wish it to be clearly understood however by the public that to assault a German officer or soldier in Occupation here is a very grave offence which will not be tolerated and will in future be dealt with as a military crime and punished accordingly.

'It is the wish of the Kommandant that in this case leniency should be shown and in these circumstances you may feel that you can dispose of the matter here. I hope that you will do so.'

The Magistrate said that Colgan should be very grateful indeed that the Kommandant had agreed that the case should be dealt with under Jersey civil law and not under German Military Law. He was pleased it was neither a British or a Jerseyman who had committed this assault. Since they had been here the German troops, to his personal knowledge, had been most courteous and well behaved to the civil population.

'Colgan was an Irishman and an alien on these shores,' The Magistrate continued. 'The only proper place for people was in their own country and if they could not get there they should be placed in an internment camp for they were no use in Jersey . The accused's statements were entirely uncorroborated whereas that of the soldier was correct whereas Colgan's was not and could not be tolerated. Colgan was here in a strange land yet could not behave himself. He should be thankful for the leniency shown to him by the Kommandant but the least punishment which the Court could inflict was one month with hard labour.'

Colgan was then removed to serve his month, and the German Officers and interpreter left the Court after punctiliously saluting the Magistrate.

Comment by Joe Mière: I well remember this ex-Irish Guardsman who was a very quiet and steady man. He was the first test case between the German Occupying Forces and the the Jersey Legal Authorities. But never again would a civilian be tried in a Jersey Court for a German Military offence, except for breaking the German curfew order. Then if you broke the German curfew order and had been arrested by the local police you were tried in the Royal Court.

CURFEW DURING THE GERMAN OCCUPATION OF JERSEY
1940-1945

In some cases of curfew breaking when people were caught out by the local uniformed police or by the honourary police, you were arrested by the local police and sent before the Royal Court and before the Bailiff of Jersey. You were either fined or given a sentence of three to seven days imprisonment in the public prison. What a terrible job the Bailiff of Jersey had. It must have hurt him deeply to have to sentence his own people to prison. Men, women, boys and girls were sent by him in some cases to remand homes. All because they broke the German curfew laws.

The Bailiff must have had very strong nerves and great willpower to face on one hand the German demands and yet to fight hard for his own people. He had to face his own Government, half of whom were old men who were out of touch with the ordinary man in the street. When things were right and all was well in Jersey the Bailiff got no praise but when things got tough we all blamed him. We were lucky that he was a strong minded man who did not suffer fools gladly, be it German or local. Ex-officers from the German Occupation forces I have spoken with since the war have told me: "Your Bailiff was a shrewd man but tough and fair to deal with, always ready to battle and argue the point over the smallest matter like the professional lawyer which he was."

Mind you, the Bailiff could look you up and and down with that long face of his as if you had just fallen out of the dustbin. He had to be in charge, the boss. He was never as keen to take second place. You could not mistake who the Bailiff was at any States meetings. Like all of us he made mistakes, but when he made a mistake it was mostly recorded for all to see.

Taking an all round view of him after all these years since the Liberation of Jersey in 1945, there were not many of our top people who would have faced up to the Germans as he did. Bailiff Alexander Coutanche and deputy Edward Le Quesne were the two top men of the Superior Council in Jersey 1940-1945 who stood up to the Germans.

When reading and researching the Occupation issues of the Evening Post which recorded how many of our people were arrested and charged by our Royal Court for breaking the German curfew order, one finds that sometimes our own officials went over the top in arresting and charging their own people with this German Occupation military law.

On the orders of the German Military Commander the Jersey authorities registered the German Curfew Orders for the civil population in the Royal Court on 2nd July 1940. This made the Curfew Order a civil offence.

This order was read out by H.M. Attorney General and this registration was ordered and published in the Evening Post.

To prosecute your own people was the right impression to give the Germans but should not have been practiced with such real authority on our own people. If one was caught out after the curfew hour by the German Military patrols, or the German Military Police your details were taken down, your address, name etc and you had to report at a given date to the German administration headquarters at College House. There you were fined mostly about 10 marks and warned about any future breaking of the curfew hour. These cases were never published in the Evening Post so no record at this date exists of how many people were charged and fined by the German Military for these infractions of the curfew order .

The cases of people charged in the Royal Court for breaking the German curfew order were people arrested by our own uniformed St Helier Police and by the Honourary Police - mostly Centeniers. There were many decent and loyal uniformed St Helier policemen who would not bend the knee or become lap dogs to the Germans, and those good men had no intention of doing the German's dirty work for them.

Many times I had been out after the curfew hour, and been stopped by our local uniformed police, told off by them and told to get home fast because a German patrol was two streets away. Remember if these local policeman were caught helping you their job and pension were on the line, and they would have been arrested and imprisoned. Several uniformed policemen were imprisoned by the Germans.

One of the policemen arrested by the Germans and imprisoned for helping three Jersey lads to escape from Jersey to England was the late Albert (Bert) Chardine (passed away in November 1998). Bert risked getting the sack because he refused to patrol outside the prison in St Helier to stop political prisoners attempting to escape.(See inset)

Another case of breaking the curfew order but smelling more of collaboration and giving our police a bad name concerns a brother-in-law of ours. One evening he had reached the Parade from First Tower when, looking at his watch, he was horrified to discover he had only three minutes to get home in Don Road before the curfew. He knew he would never make it home in three minutes so being a sensible and law abiding young man he went into the police station at the Town Hall which was near and reported to a St Helier uniformed policeman. He told the police the situation he was in and asked if a policeman could escort him home. 'Take a seat lad, and we will sort something out for you,' the policeman told him. He heard the policeman telephone someone or other and twenty minutes later a German military police car pulled up outside the Town Hall and in came two German military policemen, and he was handed over to them and taken away. After taking down details, name, address etc, he was taken

POLICE REPORT.

DATE .... 15-2-1945 ....

TIME .... 6-50 P.M. ....

SUBJECT .... Re. Patrolling of Gloucester St. & Newgate St. ....

.... Re. escaping of Political Prisoners. ....

SIR,

I beg to report that at the above stated time I was instructed by P.Sgt. Griffin to patrol Gloucester St. & Newgate St. re. Political Prisoners attempting to escape from prison.

On receiving the instructions I refused to carry them out because I don't think it is the duty of a civilian Policeman, and I have friends who have been put in prison by the Germans for very little little reason, and I would not like them to know that I was outside waiting to catch them if they tried to escape; and as you know I, and several other Policemen have been in prison for the Germans, and I am sure if any of us were in their today we would not like to know that our own workmates were waiting to try and stop us from escaping.

A. A. Chardine

I certify that the above is a genuine copy of a Police Report by P.C. Chardine and copied by me as Town Clerk of St. Helier in 1945.

W. H. Marshall

home and warned to report at College House the next day. At College House he was fined 10 marks . To this day he still has the receipt the Germans gave him when he paid the fine.

The following two examples taken from Evening Post reports of Royal Court cases of 1941 infractions of the German Curfew Order are classic instances of our people going over the top with the curfew cases. However, judge for yourselves !

Taken from the Jersey Evening Post 8th March 1941.
The Royal Court. 8th March 1941. Before A.M. Coutanche Esq., Bailiff, the Jurats Le Feuvre and Luxon. Gaol for septuagenarian offender.

Pierre François Fossey (72) was charged by H.M. Attorney-General with an infraction of the German Curfew Order on Thursday 27th February 1941 being out after hours. Advocate Valpy for the accused admitted the facts.

H.M. Attorney-General, in view of the accused's age, moved for 48 hours imprisonment and not the four days imprisonment as was usually asked for. The court imposed 48 hours imprisonment on the accused and he was escorted to His Majesty's Prison in St Helier.
(acknowledgments to the Jersey Evening Post)

JEP . Friday 28th February 1941
The German Curfew Order. Four cases of alleged infraction of the German Curfew Order are to come before the Royal Court tomorrow. Those concerned are :

Mr P. W. Hoar who is to be charged with the alleged riding of a cycle without a light after curfew on Saturday last (22 February 1941) and Mr Rolland George Le Tavernier, Mrs Le Tavernier (née Le Filliastre) and Mrs Stella Turner (née Le Filliastre) who are to be charged with being out after hours.

These cases were first reported to Centenier A.E.A. Tostevin of St Helier at the weekend and the prosecutions were ordered today. (The above four people were caught out of curfew by a St Helier uniformed policeman who reported them to the Centenier).

JEP Saturday 1 March 1941
The Royal Court. Saturday 1 March 1941. Before A.M. Coutanche Esq, Bailiff and Jurats Baudains and Dorey.   Weeks delay for inquiries.
Mr Rolland George Tavernier (33)
Mrs Hilda Le Tavernier, 46 (née Le Filliastre)
Mrs Stella Arthur (née le Filliastre) 46, widow of F Arthur, were charged with wheeling

their bicycles toward the Parade at 11.50pm on 2 February 1941 near Cheapside without being in possession of a permit authorising them to be out of doors after 11pm.

Accused who surrendered to bail in the sum of £1 each were remanded from Saturday late in order that their statements regarding a punctured tyre whilst returning from St Peter might be investigated. The Attorney-General said the accuracy of the statements made last week had been ascertained. The parties did leave Mr Tressards residence at St Peter and the tyre of one of the cycles was punctured. There was a delay in an attempt to effect repairs, and they were thus out after the curfew hour. The fact remained there had been a technical offence, so The Attorney General moved for a fine of ten shillings on each person.

Advocate Bois expressed thanks to the Attorney General for the way he had presented the facts. He left the matter in the hands of the court. The court granted the Attorney General's conclusions and each of the accused was fined ten shillings. If the fine was not paid the accused would have been sent to the prison for four days. The fines were paid.

In one year alone, 1941, there were over 72 cases before the Royal Court with Jersey people charged with breaking the German Curfew Order. Some were fined, some sentenced to 2 days, some 4 days, some 7 days imprisonment. We think that this proves beyond doubt that Jersey people did resist and defy German rule and orders. With more than 2,600 people imprisoned by the Germans over the five years of the Occupation 1940-45 and the 621 deported from the Islands to German prisons and concentration camps in Germany, plus the 10,000 Islanders in the forces, what a proud record for these loyal little Channel Islands.

The German Curfew Order, Jersey, Channel Islands

This is the uncompleted list of persons in Jersey who were arrested, imprisoned or fined for breaking the German Curfew Order of July 1940. On orders of the German Military Commander of Jersey, the Royal Court of the Island registered the German Curfew Order for the civil population. Having been registered this made breaking the German Curfew Order a civil offence.

At the Royal Court of Jersey, cases of breaking the German Curfew Order came before A.M. Coutanche, Esq., Bailiff of Jersey. Accused persons were charged by His Majesty's Attorney General, C.W. Duret Aubin, with infractions of the German Curfew Order.

29-09-1940	William Wallser	2 days imprisonment
08-12-1940	Denis Murphy (22), Dublin	£3 fine
08-12-1940	Clarence Henry, Dudley	8 days imprisonment
09-12-1940	John Lewis (42), Pembrokeshire	4 days imprisonment
09-12-1940	Patrick Joseph Donoghue (22), Cork	4 days imprisonment
17-12-1940	Doreen Eva Gautier, (17), First Tower	Probation
17-12-1940	Roselle Mary Gourdin (21), First Tower	Probation
17-12-1940	E.G. Morrissey (Red Lion Hotel)	Fined
17-12-1940	John Downey, Conway Street	14 days imprisonment
19-12-1940	Vernon Le Monnier (18)	2 days imprisonment
30-12-1940	Walter Renouf Marett	8 days imprisonment
01-01-1941	John Smith (39) Bristol	4 days imprisonment
05-01-1941	Clarence Whelan (34)	4 days imprisonment
14-01-1941	Nicholas Brendon, Eire	8 days imprisonment
14-01-1941	Michael Doyle, Eire	4 days imprisonment
14-01-1941	Timothy O'Donoghue (28), Killarney	4 days imprisonment
22-01-1941	Mrs Florence Eunice Guinard	8 days imprisonment
26-01-1941	Timothy Kerns, Eire	1 months imprisonment
26-01-1941	P. W. Hoar	4 days imprisonment
28-01-1941	Herbert Alfred De La Perrelle	4 days imprisonment
28-01-1941	Mrs Marcel (née Le Moine) Bagot	Fined
01-01-1941	Patrick Sweeney (Cork), (2nd time)	4 days imprisonment
10-02-1941	Mrs Phyllis May Bone (née Rowe)	Fined
10-02-1941	Adeline May Rowe (18)	Fined
24-02-1941	Ronald George Le Tavernier (33)	Fined
24-02-1941	Mrs Hilda Le Tavernier (46)	Fined
24-02-1941	Mrs Stella Turner (46)	Fined
27-02-1941	Pierre François Fossey (72)	2 days imprisonment
27-02-1941	Emma Jane Tredan	Fined
01-03-1941	Oliver John Baker, Guernsey	4 days imprisonment
11-03-1941	François Albert Huet (53), St Martins	2 days imprisonment
11-03-1941	Charles Walter John Le Sueur (43)	2 days imprisonment
17-03-1941	Martin Curtis, Cork	8 days imprisonment
17-03-1941	Michael Hurley, Cork	8 days imprisonment
29-03-1941	Joseph Uffret (39), Guernsey	7 days imprisonment
31-03-1941	Florence Eunice Guinard (née Hervè)	8 days imprisonment
31-03-1941	Dorothy Alice Georgelin (20) St Mary	2 days imprisonment
31-03-1941	Mavis Kathleen Jackson (19), St Helier	Probation

01-04-1941	Doreen Amanda Langford (22)	Fined
03-04-1941	William Stack (34), Cork	7 days imprisonment
08-04-1941	Florence Margaret Marriott, Grouville	Fined
14-04-1941	Honour Bowker (16), Warwickshire	Probation
14-04-1941	Elsa Bowker (14), St Peter	Probation
15-04-1941	Margaret May Hansford (née Jackson)	Fined
17-04-1941	Philip James McAllen (39), Burnley	Fined
17-04-1941	Winifred Cavill Batchelor (née Renouf)	Fined
04-05-1941	Henry Francis Botel (39), St Peter	7 days imprisonment
05-05-1941	Evelyn May Drelaud (née Kermarec)	Probation
06-05-1941	Mavis Kathleen Jackson, St Clements	2 days imprisonment
06-05-1941	Doreen Maud Ewens (17), St Saviour	Probation
06-05-1941	Mavis Françoise Perrot (46), France	2 days imprisonment
07-06-1941	Marther Berthe Le Cuirot, Guernsey	Fined
15-06-1941	Hilda May Vaudin (33), St Saviour	Fined
19-06-1941	Doris Pauline Alice Le Long	Fined
24-07-1941	Madeleine Simmons Le Gros, St Helier	4 days imprisonment
25-07-1941	Donald Robert Corfield (17), M/Z	Fined
25-07-1941	John Percy Zugg (38), M/Z	Fined
25-07-1941	Edward Percy Geary, M/Z	Fined
25-07-1941	Francis Alice Syvret (22), M/Z	Fined
25-07-1941	John Francis Le Roux, M/Z	Fined
25-07-1941	Charles Cecil Hilliker (34), M/Z	Fined
25-07-1941	Frederick Hedley Le Riche, M/Z Trinity	
02-09-1941	Olga Linda Doris Du Feu, St. Helier	Fined
15-09-1941	Mrs Florence Whiteman, Guernsey	2 days imprisonment
21-09-1941	Trevor Horton (26), Cardiff	2 days imprisonment
28-09-1941	Jean Evelyn Etasse, St Helier	Fined
30-09-1941	John Brackenbury (41)	2 days imprisonment
30-09-1941	Amy Sylvia Arthur, St Helier	Fined
30-09-1941	Mrs Jessica Lilian Brackenbury	Fined
02-10-1941	Jean Marie Joujoux, St Peters	Fined
21-10-1941	Vera Dolejas, Vilimovec, Czechoslovakia	Fined
21-10-1941	Gisele Pelan (18) Cherboug	2 days imprisonment
26-10-1941	Walter Steele (45) Winchester	2 days imprisonment

01-11-1941	Madeleine Victoria Gould (née Laffoley)	2 days imprisonment
04-11-1941	Morgan O'Brien (45), Eire	4 days imprisonment
21-11-1941	Florence Margaret Marriott, Grouville	4 days imprisonment
21-11-1941	Doris Helen Marie Esnouf (20)	Fined
21-11-1941	Jean Marie Joujoux, St. Peters	2 days imprisonment
03-12-1941	Walter George Wason (21), Wales	Fined
11-12-1941	Eleanor Irene Wheeler (39)(née Noel)	Fined
11-12-1941	Edward Philip Du Feu (17)	Fined
22-12-1941	Mary Cotter, (25), Cork	2 days imprisonment
22-12-1941	Annie Walsh, (22), Cork	2 days imprisonment

At the time Madeleine Victoria Gould was being sentenced by the Royal Court, for breaking the German Curfew Order, her husband was serving in the British Forces.

11-01-1942	Joyce Abrahams (17), St Helier	Fined
11-01-1942	Mabel Mary Minchington (18), St John	Fined
30-01-1942	Shirley Margaret Gosling (née Bedfert)	Fined
07-03-1942	Charlotte Duffin Rutland (58)	2 days imprisonment
12-03-1942	Hannah Gibson (née Sullivan), Eire	4 days imprisonment
16-03-1942	John Peter Tostevin (71), St Helier	2 days imprisonment
18-03-1942	Evelyn Jane Drelaud (21)	Fined
08-04-1942	Lilly Hilda Acourt (21), St Helier	Fined
08-04-1942	John Gowan (34), Cork, Eire	8 days imprisonment
08-04-1942	Patrick O'Brien (26), Cork, Eire	8 days imprisonment
12-04-1942	Rachel Winifred Lemprière (17),	Probation
13-04-1942	Coleen Marguerite Carré (21), Trinity	Fined
23-04-1942	Patrick Cashel (39), Tipperary, Eire	4 days imprisonment
01-05-1942	Clifford Donald Baudin (20), St John	Fined
10-05-1942	Philip John Rondel (19), Trinity	Fined
16-06-1942	Marcel Vincent Mercier (22), St John	Fined
20-06-1942	George Peter Videgrain (28), Grouville	7 days imprisonment
20-06-1942	Laurence George Langlois (18), St John	Fined
21-10-1942	Patrick Sweeney, (42), Cork, Eire	4 days imprisonment

Comment: Sometime in 1942 the Evening Post stopped publishing the Royal Court cases of people who had broken the German Curfew Order, we do not know why. At a good guess, it did not look good in print to read of so many of our people that were breaking the German Curfew Order and it was not a very good advert for the Royal Court, to read in the Evening Post of our Royal Court prosecuting so many of our people for breaking the German Curfew Order. In 1943, 1944, and 1945, no cases of breaking the German Curfew Order were published in the Evening Post.

My Aunty Flo, Florence Eunice Guinard, was arrested twice. She told the Attorney General what she thought of him in no uncertain terms and what she thought of and could do with his German curfew law. What a family! but British and loyal.

EVENING POST, MONDAY 23 SEPTEMBER 1940

CURFEW

IMPORTANT NOTICE

We are requested by His Majesty's Attorney-General to state that he has been asked by the German Kommandant to inform the Jersey Public;

(a) That the curfew period which is at present 11pm to 5am must be strictly observed and;

(b) that, in the cases of any breaches in the future, the Island Kommandant will have no option but to prosecute.

Der Feldkommandant
gez. Knackfuss Oberst

EVENING POST, SATURDAY 10 OCTOBER 1942

NOTICE

CONCERNING CURFEW HOUR

The Curfew Hour for the civil population within the Channel Islands will be altered from 9 o'clock pm to 6.30 am. The Curfew Hour for all Public Houses will be 8.30pm. This comes into force on 11 October 1942.

Der Feldkommandant
gez. Knackfuss Oberst

EVENING POST, MONDAY 29 MARCH 1943

NOTICE

CONCERNING CURFEW HOUR

From 29 March 1943 the curfew hour for the civil population in Jersey will be altered from; 10 o'clock pm to 6.30am

The curfew hours for all Public Houses will be 9.30pm

Der Feldkommandant
gez. Knackfuss Oberst

EVENING POST, SATURDAY 28 APRIL 1943

NOTICE

CONCERNING CURFEW HOUR

Curfew for the civil population in the Channel Islands, has been fixed from;
11pm to 5am

As from 1st May 1943, in the Military Zone in Jersey the curfew shall commence at 10pm and end at 5am
The Public Houses shall close half an hour before the commencement of the curfew.

Der Feldkommandant
gez. Knackfuss Oberst

LIEUTENANT H. DOTHIE'S ESCAPE FROM FRANCE

On 1st and 2nd July 1940, the first escapees from Jersey and Guernsey left the Islands. The German harbour guards seemed not to bother or keep a look-out for people leaving the Islands. The escapees' boats slipped out of the harbours right under the noses of the German guards.

Even small fishing boats were allowed out by the Germans as the following story testifies. After his capture outside Calais in May 1940, Lieutenant W.H. Dothie managed to escape outside Boursies. He made his way across France by bicycle to Rouen, then to Rennes, then the small harbour at Bréhé where he took a small sailing fishing smack and got to one of the buoys at the Minquiers Plateau. He then made for La Corbière lighthouse. From there into St Aubins Bay where he saw three fishermen in a small dinghy pulling up crab pots. He waved to them, then shouted in English, 'I suppose there aren't any Jerries here yet?' 'Yes, they came yesterday' they replied. This was a most unwelcome shock. The fisherman indicated vigorously that he should keep away from the port of St Helier and they pointed to the West as his best route. However, he headed North and got to England in a motor boat. He was picked up by the Royal Navy patrol boat MV Aquamarine on 1st August 1940. There was a persistent rumour going round Jersey for some time after the German Occupation had started, that some fishermen employed by the Germans had seen an Englishman in a boat off Corbière in which he had escaped from France and that they had warned him that the Germans were there and he then went away. But for once it was no rumour. The Secretary of the Jersey Society in London wrote to Lieutenant Dothie stating that he had heard of his escape and was interested in the reference to Jersey in his story. W.H. Dothie's last address was; Westerham, Kent, England.

GROUVILLE HALL HOTEL AND OMMAROO HOTEL

In 1940 we were sent from our engineering works to service the Liston power plant at the Grouville Hall Hotel and check up on some of the power plug points in the corridors of the hotel.

The Germans had taken over half of the hotel for some of their officers. As we passed the dining room at about 8.30am, German officers were sitting down at the tables in one half of the room. What to me was a strange sight was in the other half of the room and sitting down to their breakfasts were the civilian residents of the hotel. Later on the civilian residents were moved out and the Germans took over the hotel.

In 1940, the Ommaroo Hotel at Havre des Pas, St Helier, was partly taken over by the Germans for some of their officers. Again like the Grouville Hall Hotel, the German officers in the dining room sat at tables in one half of the room with the civilian residents of the hotel sitting for meals in the other half (these were mostly elderly retired people). One evening, late 1940, Mr and Mrs Harold Fuller sat down to dinner. Mrs Jane Fuller was wearing a British service brooch (their son was in the R.A.F.). A German officer passed their table and noticed the brooch Mrs Fuller was wearing. He informed her that he objected to her wearing the brooch, and the well educated lady refused to remove it and told the German officers in no uncertain terms that she was proud to wear it.
At the start of the German Occupation the German officers were not against Hitler because they thought they were winning the war. Most of them were very arrogant and very bombastic.

However, the officer tried to grab the brooch from Mrs Fuller. She pushed him away and again he tried and by this time Mrs Fuller was getting very upset at this treatment. Her husband got hold of the officer and pushed him with some force. The officer fell over two chairs and onto the floor. The German Military Police arrived and arrested the Fullers. They were taken to the German military prison in St Helier. Within two weeks they both had to face a German military court. Mrs Fuller was fined 120 reichmarks. Mr Fuller was sentenced to 12 months' imprisonment. A week later he was deported under armed escort to France. They were both on the lists to being deported to Germany in 1942 but they were not deported owing to being ill and too old to travel.

AIR RAID PRECAUTIONS

The Jersey ARP (Air Raid Precautions) wanted volunteers to act as dispatch riders. We thought it was going to be fun riding motor bikes. So John Dingle, Victor Webb, David Dawson and myself went along to the St Helier headquarters of the Air Raid Precautions at the Town Arsenal to volunteer our services After we had signed up, we soon found out that it was not motor bikes but our own bicycles we would be using. The reason for bicycles was that, after an air raid, young lads like us could ride and lift our bikes over rubble to take messages from one place to another. They issued us with helmets and armbands and started to train and instruct us on the use of the stirrup pump. They also trained us how to recognise different gases, how to use our gas masks etc. It was fun while it lasted.

We also had to pass on any new information on any new German fortifications getting constructed. This information was given to Mr Dawson (David's father) verbally and was passed on to higher-up people. We think that is why the Germans now and again closed down the ARP network. The Germans were very suspicious of the ARP although they could never prove anything against them. In the main Air Raid

Precautions room at the Town Arsenal there was a large map that covered one wall. On this map were locations of the different depots and parish ARP centres. The map had different coloured pins for homes. Certain ARP wardens would use these pin markers as a very good map reference for any new German bunkers etc. We have never discovered what became of all the old ARP records, lists of names of wardens etc . These old records would be of such great value to researchers of our Occupation history.

GERMAN BROTHELS IN JERSEY

German Brothel at Havre des Pas, Jersey

I was fifteen and a half years old in 1942, and learning a trade at the Axis Supplies Engineering Works in Hilgrove Street, St Helier. One morning, the boss, Mr P. P. Day, called me into his office. The Germans had brought him an order from the German headquarters in Jersey. It was over-stamped with a States of Jersey stamp. It was an order to supply electric light bulbs to the German forces brothel at the Victor Hugo Hotel at Grève d'Azette. Mr Day stated that the brothel was run by a Monsieur and Madame Blatié, and being that I could speak French I was to take 20 light bulbs from our store in La Motte Street and deliver them to the brothel. I was to collect cash for the bulbs from Monsieur Bernard and Madame Marie Blatié who ran the brothel for

PARTICULARS
(NAHERE ANGABEN)

The holder of this Card MIÈRE Joseph Arthur
(Inhaber dieser Karte ist)

Residing at 25 Midvale Road, St Helier
(Wohnhaft)

Born on the 22·11·1926
(Geboren am)

27 - 7 - 1926.

My first ID card, aged fifteen years old.

the German forces. I was to charge half a German mark (one shilling and a half penny) for each bulb, a total 10 German marks. So off I went.

I arrived at the place, parked the firm's bike outside, then made my way to the main door of the hotel. There was already a queue of about ten German soldiers waiting for the brothel to open. I knocked at the main door but there was no reply. The first soldier in the queue told me by words and hand signs that I was to get in the queue because he was first in line, so was going to have first choice of the girls. He being so thick headed I did not argue with him, so I went to the end of the queue. By this time the queue was getting longer with about 20 German servicemen. They started to take the mickey out of me with rude remarks such as 'would I last at so young an age' etc, etc. However the main door partly opened and a tall Frenchman with a flat nose, broken at some time or other, polo necked sweater, and flared trousers, made a sign that I was to follow him into the hotel.

He took me to a door on the right side of the entrance hall, and into a very large room/hall (which I found out later was the reception hall where the troops met their choice of brothel girl). The room was full of women, about 12 to 14 of them and they were all wearing a sort of dress that looked like lace curtain material. These dresses were real see-through and held at the neck with a shoelace sort of tie. They also wore arab style slippers. As Monsieur Blatié was asking me how much was a half mark in French francs, the women moved close to us, and they soon joined in the conversation about German marks and French francs.

By this time I was getting hot under the collar and started to feel my face go red. One young woman even leaned on my shoulder and asked if I was French or English. All the women seemed to speak at once and I was getting more embarrassed, having never seen so many half dressed women in my young life. Then the main door opened and in came the German servicemen, picking out their choice of women like goods in a supermarket. Monsieur Blatié took me into a side room, placed a wad of German marks in my hand and told me he would pay me on delivery. I left the brothel by a side door, found my bike and I rode to a side lane and started to count the German mark notes.

Monsieur Blatié had over-paid me by 30 marks and my boss, Mr Day, was so pleased he gave me a 5 Mark tip (10.8pence or at today's rate 53pence). My wage per week was only two and a half marks.

The next morning at about 9am, I took 20 more light bulbs to the German brothel but it was closed as it was the girls' day off. I found a side door and went into a large kitchen. A young woman was ironing a dress Her name was Louise, and she told me that Monsieur Blatié would be back from town soon, and she asked me if I would like breakfast while waiting for Monsieur and Madame's return. I sat down at a big table with two other brothel women and Louise gave me a big bowl of real coffee and some real French bread and good butter. She told me she came from the South of France and she had a brother my age. While at the table four other brothel girls came in for breakfast. They all had a chat with me, all in French. Whilst eating, eight young women passed through the kitchen with two older women. They were going for a walk. I told Louise that the two older women looked a bit past it and she said the two older ones were "femmes brûlées" - burnt out. I could not make out what she meant so she explained that femmes brûlées was French brothel slang for women who were worn out after working for years in the trade.

Louise said that Monsieur Blatié kept them on because they knew the work and were very useful in the brothel doing lots of jobs you could not get an outsider to do, such as escorting the girls when they went for a walk - like the eight women who had passed through the kitchen with the two older women. Monsieur Blatié returned and paid me the correct number of marks for the light bulbs.

After an incident later on at my work in which I knocked down the foreman who was a big bully, I was sacked from my job and taken to the police court. After that the States Labour Department sent me to work as a hairdresser at First Tower and the Germans had opened a brothel nearby. Yes you are right, the brothel girls used to come to the hairdressers every two weeks to have a trim and set. My boss, Mr Washington, could not speak French, so I had the job of asking the brothel girls what hair style they wanted, etc.

Many years later, someone asked me if I knew that the Germans had brothels in Jersey but I just smiled. That person must still be wondering why I thought it such a funny question. Did I know? What, after having had breakfast in one! Even at this young time in my life I had a very nice young girl friend who was a good girl in every way. She was a farmer's daughter and she was, like me, very shy. So I thought to myself I hope she never finds out that I have been in a brothel, even though I was only making a delivery and not a customer. She was a bit religious, and that would have ended our romance fast.

RAID ON O.T. VEGETABLE STORE, HILGROVE STREET

Eddie Le Corré

Next door to the Axis Engineering Works in Hilgrove Street (where I was learning engineering) was Le Sueur's Coal Store. If you look into the old coal store in La Motte Street (now used for parking) this top coal store has a sloping floor, and the floor could be lifted up in sections to allow coal trucks to tip loads of coal down into the lower store in Hilgrove Street. At this time in 1941 the German Organisation Todt used the lower store in Hilgrove Street to store a variety of vegetables.

Eddie Le Corré also worked at the Axis Works with me and he was a very good boxer but also a very good friend in times of trouble. One day Eddie and I got over our works forge roof and with the advice of one of the foremen, Mr W. Garnier, we cut away the holding bolts that held the corrugated iron sheets which formed the outside walls of the top coal store (up to this date they are still in place). However, we got into the top store which was empty. We then lifted up two of the large heavy wooden floor sections and with a well secured rope we descended into the dark lower store. The smell of the vegetables was very strong, and with our torches we found the store full of high stacks of all kinds of vegetables. As fast as we could we filled up two sandbag sacks and got them to the rope. We got up on top again and pulled the rope up with the sacks. We replaced the wooden floor sections then got out of the top store onto our false roof, replaced the corrugated iron sheets and secured the sheets with new bolts. These bolts were special bolts we had made to give us easy access on our next raid.

One day we were down in the lower store filling up small sacks with more vegetables when we heard a vehicle pull up outside the lower store in Hilgrove Street. We were at the back and at a very dark end of the lower store. We had no time to make for the rope so we dived behind a large heap of potatoes. The big roller doors were lifting up and two O.T. men came into the store. They and two other men started to unload big boxes from a truck outside. They placed the boxes just in the entrance of the store then left the store and after pulling down the roller doors we heard them drive off. 'My word,' Eddie said, 'that was close.' If the OT men had looked deeper in the store and looked up they would have seen our rope and caught us red handed. After this we kept away from the store for two weeks. Mind you we all missed the free vegetables. Every time I pass the coal store in La Motte Street, I think of Eddie and our raid on the German store.

RAID ON BLAKE'S MEAT STORE, HILGROVE STREET

One night, when it seemed that every anti-aircraft gun on the Island had fired at passing Allied planes, the falling steel fragments of shrapnel had broken panes of glass in our Axis Works glass roof. Three of us apprentices were ordered to take long planks of wood and replace the broken glass on the roof. There were three of us, Eddie Le Corré, Jimmy Jordan and myself. On the West side of the works was Blake's the butchers meat store. As we replaced the broken glass we looked into the meat store through a large window that was at the back of the meat store. There was only the window frame, no glass. Looking into the store we saw hanging up on hooks about twenty half carcasses of pigs. We placed one of the wooden planks from our works roof onto the open windowsill. Eddie and I got across and into the meat store. We unhooked two sides of pigs (they were young pigs) and passed them out to Jimmy and another lad who had come up from the works. We took the two sides of pork to our works store. We cut them up into fair portions so all the works staff could have a share of the pork. And did it taste good!

Two days later Mr Monamy who was employed by Blake's the butcher approached me and accused me of stealing the two sides of pigs. He informed me that he was going to get the police onto me unless I returned the two sides of pork. I informed him that we did not mind paying for the pork at the controlled price, and as for him getting the police that was up to him but the police would be very interested as to how he had so much pork in this store. I told him that anyone could see it was black market meat. Poor little man. He went off with words all of a mumble

But this was not the end of the matter as the funny outcome was that a few weeks later our works had the contract to make steel bars to be fixed on the meat store windows. So that was the end of our Sunday joint.

JOY RIDE IN A GERMAN 3-WHEELED TRUCK

One day a German parked his small three wheeled truck outside our Axis works in Hilgrove Street. The small truck was manufactured by a British/German factory in Germany (Standard Motors). The German had left the keys in the truck and had gone into our works.

My pal Eddie Le Corré called out to me 'Come on Joe, let's go for a spin around the block before he returns!' So we got into the truck and off we went with Eddie driving the truck. We both did not possess a driving licence, but when you are only 15 years old you do not see the danger. It was great fun, so we thought, until on the way back the engine stalled outside West's Cinema. It would not start. I suggested we make a run for it. Eddie said 'let's try once more.' He was right and off we went. We had just parked back at work, got out and we had just stood outside the truck when the German returned. He gave us a look, got in the truck and drove off.

Our works foreman was a bully. He used to hit the young apprentices in the face, sometimes a fist in the back, or kick you up the behind very hard. One day I was passing the works yard when he hit me very hard on the back. I was carrying a metal bucket at the time so I hit him with it, and the blow laid him down, he was out cold. In no time I was sacked from the Axis Works, and two days later found myself in the police court charged with assault on the works foreman. Eddie gave me great help by being my witness. But no luck. I did not stand a chance and was given 18 months probation.

So now I had a police record and the bully foreman got away with assaulting me. I went to see the States of Jersey for help to find a job. The Jersey States Labour Department did help young people to learn a trade. But all they could offer me at that time was hairdressing. I did not want to be a hairdresser but it was better than working for the Germans, so I started at Washington's at First Tower.

A SAD NO-GO ROMANCE IN WAR TIME OCCUPIED JERSEY

In June 1943, I was walking up Midvale Road, St Helier, to my home (same road) when outside Portland House, the Organisation Todt headquarters in Jersey, a lovely looking young lady called me over and in good English said 'Could you please help me.' It was to help her lift a wooden box into the boot of a car. She looked so nice so I said yes. I thought she was one of the foreign workers for the O.T. After a little chat, she thanked me for my help and with a handshake we parted.

Two days later I was passing the OT headquarters when the same young lady came out from Portland House, saw me and once more thanked me for my help. We had a long chat, and being young, I did like pretty girls that were nice to talk to, I knew she was flirting with me. She was was so lovely that I went along with the flirting. She asked me if I had a girlfriend or partner (I did have two girls that I went out with now and again but nothing steady). I informed her that I did not have a girlfriend. She told me that she had two tickets for a show at the Forum (it was run by the Germans) and would I like to accompany her there the next evening. Her friend was working so could not get the time off.

I did ask her about the later hour that they came out of the Forum, there being the curfew, etc. She told me not to worry - she could get me a special pass. She wrote down my full name and address etc and my ID card number. We met in Midvale Road and walked down to the Forum. What surprised me was that she placed her arm on my arm and off we went. She looked so lovely in a two piece suit. It was not a show but a German film. After the film was over we walked back at a late hour. I was taking her back to the billet at the top of Queens Road. But at the top of Midvale Road she gave me a light kiss and told me that I could not go to her billet because the time on my late night pass was up.

Two days later we went for a long walk in the Grand Vaux valley. We sat on a seat in a little garden open to the public (the little garden is still there). Again, a long chat and like other young people we kissed. I was starting to fall in love with her. She was such a nice girl. She told me that she had seen me pass many times in Midvale Road and found me to be a very good looking man and she loved my black curly hair. I was very flattered by these very kind remarks. She told me to call her Erica. I was big for my age but was only seventeen and was very taken up by this lovely girl. She seemed a woman of the world and was twenty five years old.

Mind you, I was starting to wonder if she was German. Her name rang warning bells in my head but being in love one gets a little careless about race. But I did not have to wonder very long if she was German, after finding her billet. Her quarters were in a big house on the right hand side up Queens Road. She had requested me to meet her there. Erica opened the door and greeted me with a warm and lovely smile. I was really taken aback because she had just come off duty and was wearing a white uniform of a German Red Cross sister. I thought to myself that I must end this relationship very fast, otherwise I could end up as a male Jerry bag and that would never do. We went into a big room where there were two other Red Cross sisters. Erica introduced me to them. They both smiled at me and said something to Erica in German. She beamed and told me what they had said. 'They think you are a very good looking young man and the best of luck to the both of you.' Again I was very flattered by these nice and kind remarks. Later after we all had drinks and cake, there were handshakes and the two sisters left.

Erica then told me that her full name was Erica Maria Inga von Kielmannseg. She also stated that she had an uncle who was high up in the German Army. We then had some more drinks and a cosy chat. She then kissed me and I could not help myself but to kiss her back. I did think that it was going to be very hard to part with her. Erica put the radio on to nice dance music. I told her that I was not a great dancer. She told me that she would in time teach me to dance. We started to dance and she got very passionate, We swayed with the music and sat down to have another drink.

I then saw my chance and told her I was very sorry we could not carry on our friendship any longer. I was not very happy to end this romance with this lovely girl. I stated that she was a German service woman and I was a very British person and that my family and friends would not understand being under the present war and the times, and with very deep regret we would have to part.

Erica started to cry and asked me was it another woman that I had in mind? She told me that she had fallen in love with me the first time she saw me and spoke to me. I told her that I did not want to part with her but as things were I had no choice and I told her that I was also in love with her. She got very upset and tried so hard to get me to change my mind. We sat up well after the curfew hour holding hands and kissing goodbye. It was such an agonising time having to part.

It hurt me badly for a very long time after we had parted. However, she phoned me a week later, saying that she had some news for me and wanted to say goodbye once more for the last time. We went for a walk over Tower Hill Road and found a seat in St Andrews Park. Again we kissed and cuddled fondly. Erica informed me that she was getting posted back to Germany. One of the sisters had reported her to her head sister. Erica told me that the head sister informed her that she (Erica) was not allowed to have a relationship with any local man or anyone who was not German and that was why Erica was getting posted back to Germany (just as well because things were getting to hot up between us). She told me she was broken hearted about our parting and she would write to keep contact until after the war ended when we could be together once more with no bar to our love. But I never received any letters or news from her.

I still have a lovely photo she gave me when we parted. War can make things so sad for people who fall in love. After the war, I was stationed in the army in Germany and tried to trace her but as her home was in the Russian zone, I had no luck finding her.

In the late 1980's a German friend checking-up German records for me came across by chance a report of 1945 about a German hospital train which was bombed by the Russians outside Berlin. Many were killed and many were badly injured. Among the casualty list were many German doctors and Red Cross sisters. One of the names listed was Sister Von Kielmannseg, but no first name, just that she was born in Silesia, Germany 1918. She had lost both her legs, an eye, and her face was very badly burnt.

Could this have been Erica? I do hope and pray that it is not. Erica was a lovely warm person, very kind and loving, who I can only describe as "my one time sweet enemy."

I am a very happily married man who loves his wife to bits. But for old times sake and to respect war history, I would like to know if Erica lived after wars end. If the above is Erica what a sad end to such a young life. I remember telling her that she being German and I British made it a sad no-go romance for both of us.

HOSTAGES IN JERSEY 1942
CONFISCATION OF WIRELESS SETS

On the 3rd June 1942, the Germans ordered the confiscation of all wireless sets in Jersey. The Jersey Superior Council protested against the confiscation of the population's wireless sets. The Bailiff of Jersey then attempted to get the order withdrawn. The Bailiff was informed by the Feldkommandantur that the order came from the German General Staff of the Supreme Command of the German forces and could not be interfered with by the local Kommandant.

The Bailiff of Jersey refused to sign the order for confiscating radio sets. Pamphlets were circulating around the Island, calling for the Jersey population to refuse to hand them in. In Guernsey the Bailiff of that Island had signed the order

On 17th June 1942 the Germans issued a notice that, following further acts of sabotage of telephonic communications and distributions of leaflets inciting Jersey people to disobey German orders, the Germans would take hostages and hold them until the perpetrators of the acts of sabotage against the German Occupation forces were apprehended or gave themselves up. On the same day the German Secret Field Police arrested the following ten men, and held them in the German prison in St. Helier, Jersey.

Frank Tregear

Tony Huelin

George Le Cocq

Phil Le Cornu

W.H.Kennett

Harry Ferguson

Advocate Giffard

Doctor Mattas

Colonel Welbourne

Henry Vallois

The Germans also arrested Connétable Crill and Arthur Verrin. These two were released on 18 June 1942.

24 June 1942, three more hostages arrested; George Smith, Frank Smith and Alfred Marett.

25 June 1942, George Smith (who knew the authors of the anti-German leaflets) left the German prison and, accompanied by the German police, called at the Food Control Office.

The German police then arrested Herbert Gallichan and his brother George (both were the authors of the leaflets).

Herbert Gallichan

George Gallichan

26 June 1942, the Germans arrested Mr Collins who had printed the leaflets. They also arrested James McDermott who had helped to distribute the leaflets.

26 June 1942, Germans released Frank Smith and Alfred Marett.

The Germans gave until 30 June 1942, for the perpetrators of the acts of sabotage to come forward or they would take twenty more hostages. On 29 June 1942, the Germans released the ten hostages. Also on this date the Germans arrested seven more hostages.

A. J. Verni   C. Gaskin
R. R. Nicolle   **D.C. Grove**
R Williams   W. Vardon
R. Reeves

On 16 July 1942, the German Military Court sentenced Herbert Gallican to five years imprisonment (concentration camp) and his brother George Gallichan to one years imprisonment (Dijon prison, France).

On 10th July 1942, the Germans released the first seven hostages.

George Gallichan returned to Jersey, and died in the 1980's. Herbert Gallichan survived the war, and returned to Jersey. He died in America in the 1990's.

Remember that the hostages were held under the death penalty.

The man who pointed them out did not want to denounce them but found that if the two brothers did not give themselves up many innocent people would suffer. He informed the two brothers that they must give themselves up to the Germans within 24 hours or he would have to disclose who they were.

Conscience is a very strange thing when it comes to a sense of right and wrong, or its moral obligations to one's fellow man.

A.J.Verni   Reg Nicolle   D.C. Grove

DEPORTATION OF UK PEOPLE TO GERMANY 1942-1943

On 15 September 1941, the Bailiff of Jersey was ordered by the German Field Kommandant to provide a list of men over 15 years old and the number of English nationals living in Jersey.

The Island authorities replied that the total population was 41,101, and that they had no idea how many English nationals there were. Later the Kommandant ordered the States of Jersey to provide a list of UK people between the ages of 15 and 56 years, and 56 and 68 years. On 28 October 1941 the Germans asked that all United Kingdom women and children should be added to the lists. These lists were compiled and given to the Kommandant by the Bailiff of Jersey on 3 November 1941. On 10th November 1941 the Guernsey Bailiff supplied lists of UK born Islanders living in Guernsey.

The figures for Jersey were:

men 18 to 45	1305
men 46 to 60	700
men over 60	728
women over 18	2391
boys under 18	213
girls under 18	189
Total	5526

The figures for Guernsey were:

men 18 to 45	432
men 46 to 60	359
men over 60	444
women over 18	1525
children 5-18	70
Total	2,830

By order of the German Kommandant the States of Jersey compiled a list of people who had been sentenced by the Royal and Police courts for various offences since 1928. The lists were supplied to the Germans on 23 January 1942.

On 15 September 1942, the Bailiff of Jersey, the Attorney General and the 12 parish Connétables were summoned by the German Kommandant, Colonel Knackfuss, to discuss the deportation from Jersey to Germany of the UK born Channel Islanders living in Jersey. He, the German Kommandant, wanted deportation notices to be served by the 12 parish Connétables that night, and for 1,200 people to be on their way to Germany the following day, 16 September 1942.

The Bailiff of Jersey was appalled that he had not received any previous warning. He protested strongly at this order and he wanted an interview to discuss the matter. He was informed that there was no time for such preliminary interviews, that they had their orders to carry out and it was no use discussing the matter any further. The order came from the Führer himself and no one had the power to vary it in any way. The order would be carried out to the letter whatsoever the Bailiff might say or do. The Bailiff stated that in view of what was proposed he and the other members of the Island Government who wished to do so would be entitled to resign, and he, the Bailiff, must have time to consider whether that step was not the proper one to be adopted by him and the members of the Island Government, and how this would reflect upon the 12 Connétables.

Kommandant Knackfuss replied that it was clearly in the interest of the people of Jersey that the Bailiff and his Government should remain in office. The Bailiff said that whether that was so or not, he could not consent to the Connétables being asked to select people for evacuation. If the order had to be carried out by the Feldkommandantur, the selection of persons to be evacuated must be made by the German Military Authorities, and the Connétables role must be limited to showing cause why the person selected should not be evacuated.

Colonel Knackfuss agreed with the Bailiff on this, and authorised him to inform the Connétables. It was then agreed that the notices should be given by members of the German forces, the Connétables only being required to supply a guide for finding the addresses. At College House the 12 parish Connétables were there to point out people from their parish who were known to be disabled or too old or ill to travel.

Many of the United Kingdom deportees harboured a dim view of the apparent co-operation of the parish Connétables who had been ordered by the Germans to be present at the selection of the UK people to be deported to Germany. Many of the UK deportees did not take kindly to the true fact that not all the deportation notices were served by German servicemen. Many of the notices were served at the deportees door by local uniformed and honorary policemen, and Parish Officials. Sometimes accompanied by a German soldier. The Germans could not have found the addresses of so many people in so short a time without the help of the Jersey police forces. You have only to ask the deportees who still live in Jersey who knocked at their door on the evening of 15 September 1942.

On their return to Jersey in 1945-1946 many of the deportees wrote letters to the Evening Post. They asked why local police and parish officers served them the deportation notices. Some of the local police like my cousin George or my Uncle René refused to serve the notices on their own people. They both were informed that the order came from the Jersey Attorney General's office. To refuse to carry out the police order they could be dismissed from the force. My cousin and uncle still refused to do the German's dirty work. They were both sent home on sick leave. Fred and Jenny Thomas who lived at our house in Midvale Road were two of the English people deported to Germany in 1942. It was I who answered the door to Centenier Pirouet who called late one evening in September to serve the deportation notice on Fred and Jenny Thomas. The Centenier was on his own. Fred Thomas went mad, he wanted to hit the Centenier right there. Jenny and I had to hold Fred back. He was calling the Centenier all the names under the sun. Fred had been a good soldier in his young days and very British to the bone. He told the Centenier he did not mind a German soldier serving him the notice. After all, the soldier was only doing his duty, but your own people doing the Germans' dirty work. This Fred could not forgive, he felt it was a betrayal.

Fred Thomas

Jenny Thomas

Jenny died some years ago, and she asked me if I ever wrote a book would I not forget her and Fred and to write the truth of who served them the deportation notices. And, my dear Jenny, I have kept my word because I loved you both, and we were all upset to see you deported. When they both returned to Jersey in 1945, Fred told me that as they went aboard the German ship they could hear the singing from South Hill. He said to Jenny, I bet Joe and his family are on that demonstration! And good old Fred was right. One English born family (I have their name),the mother asked the German officer who was at the St Helier Town Hall, do they have to go because one of her own two children was mentally handicapped. The officer told her that it was up to the Connétable of St Helier if the family had to go or not. The mother spoke to the Connétable and he informed her that she and her two children could stay in Jersey, but her husband would have to go to Germany on the next boat. A few days later he was deported.

One evening Frank Le Pennec (my best friend) and I were passing the Hotel Normandie when we saw a big man and his wife and two little children coming out of a small house alongside the Normandie Hotel. They had two suitcases with them.

They told us they were being deported and were walking to the Weighbridge. So Frank and I each took a suitcase and the man and wife carried each child. Later, after demonstrating at the Weighbridge, we were walking along when we again met the little family who were on their way back home. For some reason or other they were not deported that evening. Frank and I again gave them a hand with the suitcases.

After the long walk back to their home we had a shock because coming out of the house were the next door neighbours with rolled up carpets and furniture, etc. The neighbours were looting the small house. The big man and his wife just broke down, sat on their suitcases and cried. So much for friends and neighbours, and there were many people whose homes were looted by so called friends and neighbours. How low some people could stoop to loot a friend's home!

If the deportees' claim for compensation was ever entertained by the German and British governments, a full enquiry would have to take place. This should have been done years ago, a lot of things would have come to light. One cannot find any parish files on the role the Connétables played in the deporting of the UK people. I wrote to the Connétable of St Helier, Bob Le Brocq, about these files. He informed me by phone that alot of old time files were dumped to make room for other more up-to-date documents.

Deportation Order 15 September 1942

Feldkommandantur 515,   Jersey, den 15 September 1942

Mr Frederic Thomas and Mrs Jenny Thomas, 25 Midvale Road, St. Helier.

In pursuance of a higher command, British subjects are to be evacuated and brought to Germany.

You have to appear therefore on 16-9-1942, not later than 4pm at the Garage, Weighbridge, St Helier with children of minor age. You have to take with you all papers proving your identity. It is necessary to outfit yourself with warm clothes, strong boots and provision for two days, meal dishes, drinking bowl and if possible with a blanket. Your luggage must not be heavier than you can carry and must bear a label with your full address.

It is further left to you to place ready for each person a ruck packed with clothes to be sent after, labelled with full address. It is also left to you to take with you an amount of money not exceeding RM 10. in German notes for each person or Reich credit notes. All valuables (jewels) must be deposited as far as possible with the banks. Keys of houses are to be handed over to the Constables. Should you fail to obey this order, punishment by the Court Martial will be effected.

Sometimes you could see and read the bad spelling in this German Deportation Order. The Germans often made mistakes when translating their orders from German into English.

Letters to the EP, May 1945

TWO QUESTIONS

Dear Sir,

Now that the excitement of Liberation has somewhat abated and we may once more again speak freely through the press, the undersigned would appreciate an answer to the following questions.

(1)   Who was responsible for drawing up the lists of English residents who were deported to Germany?

(2)   Was it necessary for local officials to co-operate so wholeheartedly with the enemy in this respect?

The Germans would have been considerably hindered in the execution of their duty had the local help not been forthcoming.

We hope the above questions will not receive the protective mantle of Mr Morrison's legislative whitewashing.

Yours faithfully

C. B. Dunn
42 New Street
St Helier
May 28 1945

Letters to the EP, May 1945

TO WHOM THE RESPONSIBILITY

Sir,

I thank Mr Dunn for his letter. The questions he raises were generally discussed on the boat which left Jersey on that memorable evening of September 16 1942, as they were later on in the camps of Biberach and Laufen. The Jersey policeman and the German officer called at my house at 10.30 on the previous evening. I have the same sense of sorrow for the man or men responsible for this act of betrayal as I have for him or they who issued orders for the arrest of young Russians, for they bring to my mind the tale of Judas and his subsequent shame.

Yours faithfully

A. L. Chapman
Prospect House
St Martins
May 30 1945

On 9 June 1964 Her Majesty's Government and the Federal Republic of Germany signed an agreement, Article 1 of which is as follows:

1. The Federal Republic of Germany shall pay to the United Kingdom of Great Britain and Northern Ireland (hereinafter referred to as "The United Kingdom") the sum of one million pounds Sterling for the benefit of United Kingdom nationals who were victims of National Socialist measures of persecution and who, as a result of such measures, suffered loss of liberty or damage to their health, or in the case of those who died in consequence of such measures, for the benefit of their dependents.

2. The distribution of this sum shall be left to the discretion of Her Majesty's Government in the United Kingdom.

In the exercise of the discretion reserved in Article 1(2) of that Agreement Her Majesty's Government are now inviting applications for registration for United Kingdom nationals who were victims of National Socialist persecution or, if they have died, for their dependents.

3. For the purposes of this registration the terms "United Kingdom National,", "National Socialist persecution" and "dependents" have the meanings assigned to them in paragraphs 4 to 10 of these Notes and only persons who satisfy these requirements are eligible to apply for registration. Acceptance of an application does not constitute a right to participate in the distribution. No distribution can take place until adequate opportunity to register has been given to all those who may be eligible. Until the exact number of these is known, it is impossible to calculate how much can be paid to each. Registration will therefore close on July 3 1965, and no applications can be accepted after that date. Payments, irrespective of their size, are not intended to be a form of economic assistance but as a token recognition of the sufferings undergone by United Kingdom nationals as a result of Nazi persecution.

4.   For the purposes of this registration: "United Kingdom National' means:-

(a)   a person who on June 9 1964, had (or would but for his prior death have had) the status described in paragraph 5 and at the time of persecution had the status described in paragraph 6; or (b) a person, who fulfils the conditions set out in paragraph 7.

5.   Status on June 9, 1964

(a)   A citizen of the United Kingdom and Colonies; or
(b)   A citizen of Southern Rhodesia; or
(c)   A British subject without citizenship; or
(d)   A British subject by virtue of Section 2(1) or (2) of the British Nationality Act 1948; or
(e)   A British protected person within the meaning of the British Nationality Act 1948.

6.   Status at the time of persecution

(a)   A person who at the time of persecution was a British subject under the British Nationality and Status of Aliens Acts 1914 to 1943;
(b)   A woman who had been a British subject before the time of persecution but had ceased to be such on marriage; or
(c)   A person whose father was a British subject at the date of his birth, and who would have been a British subject at the time of persecution if his birth had been registered at a British Consulate; or
(d)   a person who was a British protected person at the time of persecution.

7.   Naturalisation

The term "United Kingdom National" also includes a person who, after the time of persecution but before 1st October 1953, became a person naturalised in the United Kingdom and Colonies within the meaning of the British Nationality Act 1948 or a citizen of the United Kingdom and Colonies by registration under that Act.

8.   No application can be accepted in respect of any United Kingdom national who is or if deceased was also a national of any other country unless at least one of the following conditions is satisfied, that is to say that such United Kingdom national:-

(a)   Was on June 9, 1964, or if he died before that date, at the date of his death was ordinarily resident in the United Kingdom or in any territory of the international relations of which Her Majesty's Government in the United Kingdom was responsible;

(b)   That he has, or if deceased, had been in Crown service under Her Majesty's Government in the United Kingdom;

(c)   That he is, or if deceased, was regularly included in a consular register of British residents, or is, or if deceased, was the holder of a British passport issued by Her Majesty's Government in the United Kingdom or the Government of any colony, protectorate, United Kingdom mandated territory or United Kingdom trust territory, and evidence is produced to the satisfaction of the Secretary of State that he maintains or, if deceased, maintained close connections with the United Kingdom or any such colony, protectorate or territory as aforesaid.

9.   For the purposes of this registration: National Socialist persecution means the infliction by members of the National Socialist Party or their agents for reasons for race, religion, nationality, political views or political opposition to National Socialism of treatment involving detention in Germany or in any territory occupied by Germany in a concentration camp, or in an institution where the conditions were comparable with those in a concentration camp. Hardships suffered in a normal civil prison, civilian internment camp or prisoner of war camp do not constitute Nazi persecution nor does treatment contrary to the Geneva conventions and the rules of war, even though resulting in permanent injury or death. Applications for registration should not be made in respect of such hardships or treatment. In applying for registration in respect of detention in a concentration camp or comparable institution details should be given of the duration of such detention and whether as a consequence of treatment received during it the victim suffered death or permanent disability. The nature of such treatment should be stated.

10.   For the purposes of this registration: "United Kingdom National" means either
(i)   a surviving spouse or, failing such spouse,
(ii)   any surviving legitimate children or, failing such children,
(iii)   surviving parent or parents or, failing such parent,
(iv)   any surviving brothers or sisters of the whole blood.

Applications cannot be accepted from any relations nor from any of the above groups if there is a surviving member of any preceding group.

11.   No application for registration can be accepted in respect of loss of property or of any form of monetary or economic loss.

12.   No application for registration can be accepted in respect of any person who had made a declaration of renunciation of citizenship of the United Kingdom and Colonies under Section 19 of the British Nationality Act 1948 or who had been deprived of such citizenship under Section 20 of that Act.

13. No application for registration can be accepted in respect of any person if compensation in respect of the imprisonment, death or disablement of that person had been paid, or is or was payable, out of other monies provided by the Government of the Federal Republic of Germany.

OFFICE Of CHIEF OF COUNSEL
FOR WAR CRIMES
APO 696 A   U.S. ARMY

Staff Evidence Analysis, Ministries Division.

By: M. A. Garnier
Date: 30 October 1947

Document Number: NG-3349

Title and/or general nature: Letters from WOERMANN and ALBRECHT to the German Embassy in Paris, and from SCHLEIER to the Military Commander in France about the arrest of British subjects as reprisal for the transfer of 300 Germans from Iran to the British.

Form of Document: Typescript

Stamps and other endorsements:

A)   None
B)   Initialled by MOSTITZ
C)   Initialled by MOSTITZ
D)   Stamped "secret", initialled by MOSTITZ.

Date:

A)   7 September 1941
B)   14 September 1941
C)   14 September 1941
D)   17 September 1941

Source: Botschaft Paris, Paket 22

Pol II Dr. 1 D Internierte
1941-1942; original at MoNair
Barracks, Berlin, FO-SD Mission, Building Z
OCG-BBT 2986

Persons of Organisations Implicated:

WOERMANN
ALBRECHT
MOSTITZ
SCHLEIER
Von STUELPNAGEL
ERNST, Dr.

TO BE FILED UNDER THESE REFERENCE HEADINGS:

NG - Foreign Office
NOKW -OKH

STAFF EVIDENCE ANALYSIS, Ministries Division NG-3349

SUMMARY:

A) In his telegram, WOERMANN asks the German Embassy in Paris to contact the Military Commander in Paris about the British subjects to be arrested and to keep RIBBENTROP informed.

B) Telegram from ALBRECHT to the German Embassy in Paris asking them to contact the Military Commander in France about the arrest of 5,000 British subjects and their transfer from the Channel Islands as a reprisal for the transfer of Germans from Iran to the British.

C) In his letter to the Military Commander in France, SCHLEIER forwards the request of the Foreign Office concerning the arrest of 5,000 British subjects.

D) Letter from SCHLEIER to the Military Commander in France on the same subject.

In 1942 and 1943, the Germans deported 2,190 UK born Channel Islanders to internment camps in Germany.

Biberach internment camp
Dorsten internment camp
Laufen internment camp
Liebanau internment camp
Wurzach internment camp

PATRIOTIC DEMONSTRATION, 6 SEPTEMBER 1942

PATRIOTIC DEMONSTRATIONS, ST. HELIER, JERSEY, SEPTEMBER 1942.
THE NAMES OF SOME OF THE FIVE THOUSAND PLUS LOYAL JERSEY PEOPLE WHO TOOK PART IN THE SEPTEMBER 1942 DEMONSTRATIONS AGAINST THE GERMANS DEPORTING BY FORCE THE ENGLISH BORN CHANNEL ISLANDERS TO CAMPS IN GERMANY.

NAME	DEMONSTRATION	ARRESTED AT DEMONSTRATION
BARBIER, EMILE	THE WEIGHBRIDGE	ARRESTED SEPTEMBER 1942
BARTLETT, DAVID	SOUTH HILL	
BISSON, JOHN	THE WEIGHBRIDGE	
CORFIELD, KENNETH	THE WEIGHBRIDGE	ARRESTED SEPTEMBER 1942
CURWOOD, JOHN	THE WEIGHBRIDGE	
CURWOOD, PETER	THE WEIGHBRIDGE	
DU FEU, THOMAS	CONWAY STREET	ARRESTED SEPTEMBER 1942
DURELL, LENARD	THE WEIGHBRIDGE	ARRESTED SEPTEMBER 1942
GIBAUT, ELDON	THE WEIGHBRIDGE	ARRESTED SEPTEMBER 1942
HANNAFORD, RAYMOND	THE WEIGHBRIDGE	ARRESTED SEPTEMBER 1942
HARRIS, RONALD	THE WEIGHBRIDGE	ARRESTED SEPTEMBER 1942
HILL, MAURICE	THE WEIGHBRIDGE	ARRESTED SEPTEMBER 1942
KENT, JOE	CONWAY STREET	ARRESTED SEPTEMBER 1942
KENT, RONALD	CONWAY STREET	ARRESTED SEPTEMBER 1942
KILLER, FRANK	THE WEIGHBRIDGE	ARRESTED SEPTEMBER 1942
LE CLOCHE, HUGH	THE WEIGHBRIDGE	ARRESTED SEPTEMBER 1942
LE COCQ, KEVIN	SOUTH HILL	ARRESTED SEPTEMBER 1942
LE CORNU, MARTIN	THE WEIGHBRIDGE	
LE CUIROT, DENNIS	THE WEIGHBRIDGE	ARRESTED SEPTEMBER 1942
LE PENNEC, FRANK	SOUTH HILL	ARRESTED SEPTEMBER 1942
LE PENNEC, GEORGE	SOUTH HILL	
LIRON, DOUGLAS	THE WEIGHBRIDGE	ARRESTED SEPTEMBER 1942
LUCE, FRANK	THE WEIGHBRIDGE	
MATHEW KENNETH	CONWAY STREET	ARRESTED SEPTEMBER 1942
MIÈRE, JOE	SOUTH HILL	ARRESTED SEPTEMBER 1942
MIÈRE, MARGUÉRITÈ	SOUTH HILL	
TURNER, BELZA	THE WEIGHBRIDGE	

WHEN READING THIS IF YOU OR YOUR FAMILY TOOK PART IN THE SEPTEMBER 1942 DEMONSTRATIONS OR WERE ARRESTED BY THE GERMANS. COULD YOU PLEASE GET IN TOUCH WITH **JOE MIÈRE** TEL: **(01534) 727592** WE WOULD LIKE TO RECORD YOUR STORY FOR OUR OCCUPATION HISTORY. THANK YOU.

Early evening of 16 September 1942, four of our group, Frank Le Pennec, George Le Pennec, my sister Marguérite Mière and myself were standing among a crowd of about 100 people, mostly very young Jersey people. We were standing by the high wall that overlooks the harbour road and the left side of the South Pier. Behind us were the old military buildings and grass field.

We were all looking across the harbour to the German transport ship berthed at the Albert Pier. There was no shouting or singing from the deportees who were boarding the ship. Around us there were only comments and remarks about the Germans and the deportations going on. My sister Marguérite, with the tears running down her cheeks, started to sing "There'll always be an England." She was accompanied by George Le Pennec who had a lovely deep singing voice. We all joined in, about a hundred of us singing at the top of our voices. Many more people had joined the crowd, so in the end there must have been nearly 200 local people around us. Then, as we were singing, across the harbour came the many voices singing from the deportees on the ship. It seemed that all of us had lumps in our throats. This was followed by "Jersey Jersey," then "God save the King," the deportees' voices blending with our voices.

We were just warming up and starting to sing again when we spotted fully armed German soldiers coming up the steps from Pier Road. They were out of wind after the very long steps. We four headed up Mount Bingham and over the big gate at Rope Walk (now the Cheshire Homes) but an old chap came along and started to shout at us, he thought we were after his apples and pears. After trading insults with the old sod, we retreated to the South Hill Gymnasium, saw no Germans around so went back down the hill to the same wall. But we had hardly got past the old military building when the German soldiers seemed to come from nowhere.

They started to shout in German at us. One pointed us out to the others and about seven or eight Germans surrounded us. The crowd of people tried to get between us and the soldiers, with the soldiers shouting and making a grab for us. Marguérite and George with the help of the crowd managed to slip away, but Frank and I were grabbed by soldiers each side of us.

A big staff car with a German officer sitting in front pulled up. We were both shoved roughly into the back seat with a guard squashed on each side of us. They drove down Pier Road to the Pomme d'Or Hotel. We were marched inside and placed on forms in the old glass roofed winter gardens. There were already other Jersey lads seated there, all of them under armed guards.

Later we were taken one by one upstairs to a small room where sitting there was the German officer who had sat in the front of the car. With him were two big ugly German military policemen. My heart sank because the look these German police gave us left us in no doubt that we were in for a rough time. But the officer, speaking in good English, was firm but correct. He wanted to know what resistance group we belonged to, who was the leader etc, who had organised the protest, age, name, address. We stated that we were only passing when the soldiers had grabbed us. The officer wrote it all down.

Later that evening, it must have been well after the curfew hour, Frank and I were taken with four other Jersey lads to the prison in Gloucester Street. It was the St Helier police van that transported us to the prison, the driver being a local policeman, with one German policeman with us in the van, another German policeman with the driver. At the prison and after the German police had rung the prison side door bell, a Jersey prison warder let the group in, then up the long path to the next guard lodge door, then across a small yard to the German military side of the prison. After having details taken in the guard room (pre-war matrons quarters) we were both placed in cell no 2 of C block. This block was used mostly by German servicemen.

We both had been in this German prison before, but only a short stay. Strange thing is, in 1944, 1945, I was placed in this same No 2 cell, and Frank in cell No 1. However, the next morning about 7am the German guard brought us coffee (mud) and black rye bread and what looked like a dab of marg. No wash or shave and about 8am the guard took us to the guard room. There once again was the same officer with the same two ugly German military policemen. Their officer stated that we had told him a pack of lies, and we had been in trouble with the German police before, and had been arrested for insulting a German officer. But he was letting us go with a final warning. If we got into trouble with the German forces or even the local police we would be arrested and deported to a prison in France or Germany.

The officer then stated 'We know how you feel about your people being deported but we have our orders to carry out, and we will not tolerate any interference in our military orders. Do you both understand?' We both nodded in assent. The officer then spoke in German to the two military policemen. We were then taken to the main side gate where a Jersey prison warder unlocked the door. But as we were passing into the street one of the Germans gave Frank a hard clout across the face, and as I passed the door the other brute gave me a hard kick up the backside and I landed on the pavement of Gloucester Street.

We think they let us and the other lads go because they were trying to play down the deporting of the United Kingdom people to Germany. And they thought that our patriotic demonstration the evening before was a one off. How wrong they were. A few days later we were back singing at the Weighbridge but we had learned a good lesson. We moved away very fast when any German soldiers came along to arrest people.

A few days later the Germans arrested 16 demonstrators. One of the main demonstrators was Emile Barbier who was sentenced to 5 years imprisonment. He was deported to France, then Germany. Emile survived the brutal prison camps and returned to Jersey in 1945. Of the others, six of them were given prison sentences in the German prison in Jersey. Nine of the rest who had been arrested in September 1942 and held in custody in the German prison in St Helier were released on 12 October. (See inset)

On 18 September 1942 another patriotic demonstration took place at the Weighbridge, Bond Street, Kensington Place, Hill Street and Broad Street. These demonstrations were on a larger scale than the 16 September demonstrations at South Hill. Fights broke out between Jersey youths and armed German soldiers. One lad knocked out a German officer, others played football with a German helmet. 16 youths were arrested that evening and taken to the German prison.

As time went on, every deportation was followed by a demonstration, and of course more young Jersey people were arrested. By March 1943 over 2,000 UK born Channel

**Gericht
der Feldkommandantur 515**
Str.L.376/42

St.Helier/Jersey, 12.Okt.1942

An das <u>engl.Staatsgefängnis</u>
St.Helier/Jersey, Gloucester Street.

      Es wird hiermit angeordnet, daß die nachstehend aufgeführten Personen sofort aus der Haft zu entlassen sind:

1.) Kenneth James C o r f i e l d ,
2.) Kenneth Alfred M a t h e w ,
3.) Ronald John H a r r i s ,
4.) Kevin John Le C o c q ,
5.) Hugh de Beauvoir La C l o c h e ,
6.) Douglas Charles L i r o n ,
7.) David Alfred B a r t l e t t ,
8.) Raymond H a n n a f o r d .
9.) Eldon Stanley G i b a u t .
      Um Entlassungsbescheinigung mit genauer Angabe der Uhrzeit der Entlassung wird ersucht.

                                 Peqer

                         Kriegsgerichtsrat.

Islanders had been deported by force to camps in Germany. Among this number were over 60 Jersey and Guernsey men, some born in the Channel Islands. Some had been in trouble with the Germans, others had been before the Royal Court and police courts in the Islands.

The Germans ordered the States of Jersey and Guernsey to supply a list of people who had been before the courts and sentenced by those courts since 1928. It seems that these lists were supplied without any objections raised by our local authorities. The names included some of the five thousand plus loyal Jersey people who took part in the September 1942 demonstrations against the Germans deporting the UK born Channel Islanders.

Emile Barbier   David Bartlett   Kenneth Corfield

Peter Curwood   Eldon Gibaut   Raymond Hannaford

Ronald Harris   Maurice Hill   Joe Kent

Ronald Kent

Frank Killer

Hugh Le Cloche

Frank Le Pennec

Kevin Le Cocq

George Le Pennec

Frank Luce

Kenneth Mathew

Belza Turner

Marguerite Mière

Joe Mière

MR K. BELL - AIRCRAFT IN LOFT 1941

Mr. K. Bell

There was an airfield at L'Erée, Guernsey, prior to the war. The Guernsey Aero Club gave instructional courses in flying and gliding. The school was in the charge of Mr C. Noel, Assistant Controller of the Airport. The airfield at L'Erée contained a hangar to house the plane and glider used for instruction. One night, during an exceptional storm, the hangar was blown down and the plane damaged. Some time afterwards the plane was purchased by Mr H. Le Parmentier and placed in the top loft of Motor House, St Julian's Avenue, to be rebuilt at leisure. At the time of the evacuation in 1940 it was in full state of repair except for a canvas as cover over the rudder.

The Motor House employees were evacuated on block to England in 1940. Two weeks later Mr K. Bell was put in charge. The door of the loft was locked and the key was handed over to an employee of Motor House Ltd, who claimed that he had the custody of the plane for Mr Le Parmentier. So Mr Bell did not consider it under his charge as it was not his property.

In March 1941, a German order was issued regarding the removal of all flammable matter from the top stories of houses and business buildings, and in order to comply with the German order Mr Bell knew he must try to move the machine, wood and books from the top loft of Motor House. Mr Bell also knew that if the Germans found the plane they would inflict a severe penalty.

After a few days consideration Mr Bell decided to declare the machine. Mr Bell thought it better not to report the existence of the machine to any local official, and therefore he declared it in person at Grange Lodge. The Germans ordered him to meet them at 10am the same morning, which was a Saturday. The head German officer together with the head of the Feldgendarmerie arrived to question Mr Bell. The machine unfortunately and unknown to Mr Bell, had been put in full working order and freshly oiled. Mr Bell had told the Germans that he had not seen the machine for many weeks, but the Germans pointed out that the fresh oil was evidence, and very good evidence, that the machine had received attention during the last few days. Mr Bell was therefore placed under an armed guard and a sentry was placed at the door of the room when the German officials left the premises. They returned about half an hour later with the German Air Force chief and the German Secret Field Police photographer who took photos from all angles. After a lengthy discussion among themselves they left the building, but first demanded the key of the garages, closed the doors and placed an armed guard outside the premises.

Mr Bell was taken to Fort George and placed in an improvised prison on the second floor of the original R.E. offices. The windows of the prison were barred and the room was permanently blacked out. The furniture was a bed which the guard told Mr Bell had just been vacated by a foreign female prisoner, one chair and a half burnt table. Mr Bell remained in solitary confinement for nine days. During that time he did not see daylight, nor did he have any physical exercise. On Sunday, the day after Bell had been placed in the prison, he was interviewed by the local Luftwaffe chief who suggested that he should name any States official who knew of the existence of the machine, in which case he would be immediately released.

When Mr Bell asked what would happen to him in the event of answering in the negative, the Luftwaffe chief shrugged his shoulders and said: 'You will have to remain here.' The Luftwaffe chief asked if Mr Le Parmentier had a brother and sister living in the Island but Mr Bell did not offer this information. He was left alone for ten days, then one morning a German Secret Field Police officer came and asked if he was all right. This officer appeared to be greatly surprised to find that he was not getting an hour of daily exercise.

Mr Bell did not wash or shave from Saturday till Thursday, when his toilet requirements were brought to him by the guard. He was then imprisoned on the ground floor of the same building where the heat and dust caused him great inconvenience for three days. Then he was moved to the old detention room which was attached to the guard room just inside the main entrance to Fort George. Here he remained for a further eight days.

The nine days of solitary confinement were the most difficult period for Mr Bell. He had no reading matter and he found the time passed very slowly. But on the last day a good samaritan passed by and managed to smuggle in a few books. He was very grateful to Major Langlois, for that was his benefactor. Mr Bell was subsequently found not guilty of whatever charges that had been preferred against him, without having been able to answer any charge. He was told that he could go home, and immediately he was taken home in a car by a plain clothes German Secret Field Policeman.

(This story was told by Mr K. Bell to the Guernsey Evening Press, June 1946.)
Source; Guernsey Evening Press, Wednesday 20th June 1946. ref 11678

S. S. NORMAND AND CREW, JUNE 1941

In June 1941 the captain and crew of the S. S. Normand who were sailing under the Jersey Flag to bring essential supplies to the Channel Islands told the States of Jersey and the German Authorities that they would not sail the ship if it carried German servicemen or ammunition or any German war material.

The German Feldkommandant, Colonel Schumacher, noted the protest. He informed the Hafenkommandanten of Granville of the protest and attitude of the Captain and crew of the S. S. Normand. He also stated that the S. S. Normand and the S. S. Spinl came under the Harbour Command in Granville, France.

A list was drawn up for the signature of crewmen wishing to remain on duty until an agreement was reached between the captain and crew and the German authorities re the crew refusing to sail with German servicemen and war material on board the ship.

In August 1941, the captain and crew once again refused to sail with German ammunition and guns on board. Some of the crew walked off the ship, others waited until the Jersey Labour Department could guarantee them employment on land.

Later on, the ships bringing supplies to the Channel Islands for the civilian population were taken over by the German Kriegsmarine Command in Granville, France.

```
Feldkommandantur 515                        Jersey,den 24.Juni 1941.
  - Mil.Verw.Gr. -
Az.: Wi 21 - 1.
   Ld.


        An den
              Kapitän Lerbalestier

        des  Dampfer "Normand".


              Ich habe davon Kenntnis genommen, dass Sie und Ihre
        Mannschaft es nach Ihren Gesetzen nicht verantworten können,
        den Dampfer "Normand" zu fahren,wenn dieses Schiff weiterhin
        unter Geleitschutz deutscher Kriegsschiffe zum Transport grös-
        serer deutscher Truppeneinheiten eingesetzt und zu diesem
        Zweck besonders bewaffnet wird.
              Wie Ihnen bereits bekannt ist, sind die beiden Schiffe
        "Normand" und "Spinel" dem Hafenkommandanten von Granville
        unterstellt worden. Ich habe mich daher mit dem Hafenkomman-
        danten von Granville fernmündlich in Verbindung gesetzt und
        ihm von Ihrer Stellungnahme Kenntnis gegeben.

                      Der Feldkommandant

                          [signature]
                      Oberst.
```

TRANSLATION

Field Command 515
Az. Wi 21-1

24th June 1941

To Captain Larbalestier,

    S.S. Normand.

    . I have noted that you and your crew, in accordance with your laws, cannot be responsible for sailing the S.Sip Normand if this ship continues under convoy protection of German warships, to be used for the transport of large numbers of German troop units and is especially armed for this purpose.

    As you already know, the S.S. Normand and S.S. Spinel come under the Harbour Command in Granville. I have, therefore, got into touch with the Harbour Commander in Granville by telephone and informed him of your attitude.

                The FieldCommander,

                   Schumacher, Colonel.

List of S.S. Normand Crew.

NAME.	RANK.	SIGNATURE OF MEN WISHING TO REMAIN ON.
E. LARBALESTIER.	MASTER. X	-
S. LE RICHE.	1ST MATE.	-
I. COOM.	2ND MATE.	-
J. MACFARLANE.	1ST ENGINEER.	-
J. WALTON.	2ND ENGINEER.	-
J. LARBALESTIER.	3RD ENGINEER.	
J. REIDY.	CARPENTER.	J. W. Reidy
A. BENOIT.	DONKEYMAN.	A. Benoit
F. LE SAUX.	BOSUN. X	F. H. Saux
C. GAVEY.	A.B	C. Gaity
J. SMITH.	A.B	J. Smith
H. BARRET.	A.B.	H. Barrett
E. GRANDIN.	O.S. X	
W. BATTRICK.	Q.M. X	H. Battrick
S. CLAY.	FIREMAN.	S. Clay
T. RILEY.	FIREMAN.	Riley
J. BARNET.	FIREMAN.	J. Barnet
J. DUFFIELD.	FIREMAN.	Duffield
J. HANLEY.	FIREMAN.	Hanley
T. QUIRKE.	FIREMAN.	Thomas Quirke
A. LE LUAN.	STEWARD X	
G. GARBUTT.	COOK.	Garbutt

RAID ON GERMAN OFFICERS QUARTERS, GLOSTER TERRACE

I n the following story some of the seven people in the raiding party are still alive and still living in Jersey.

Some of the big houses in Gloster Terrace were taken over by the German Army and used as officers quarters. The Terrace was always patrolled by an armed sentry. We intended to raid one of the houses to look for weapons, etc, so we started to case the place, one or two of us at a time. We timed the sentry's movements and at about 10am he would leave his post and go towards the basement of the lower end house, either for a hot drink or to relieve himself or for a quiet smoke. We never found out which.

We also timed the sentry and noticed that he started his sentry duty from the Queens Road end of the Terrace and made his way down slowly to the lower end near the old Government House (now the Hotel Savoy). We also noticed that at week-ends the German officers quarters were always fully occupied, with comings and goings. But most weekdays you could tell that no officers or their batmen were in residence because there were no staff cars parked in the Terrace, and no comings and goings, so things were fairly safe but you were never sure.

A good time for a raid was 10am and noon. So one weekday morning in 1943, Frank Le Pennec, John Dingle, Victor Webb, David Dawson, Ken Williams and I went into the Terrace and up the steps and through the big open front door and into the big entrance hall.

We went up the staircase to the first landing. One of the lads kept watch from a window that faced the front of the house. We already had my sister Marguérite watching from the road opposite the house. If the sentry looked as if he was returning she was to approach him and ask him if he knew if captain so and so was in his quarters, or could she leave a message, etc. At first Marguérite did not want to act this part. She said: 'People will think I am a jerry-bag.' No way would she take this part. But we promised her that she could have first pick of any arms we found in the house and she could be on the next raid that we planned. So after this, she went along with our plan to delay the sentry if he suddenly turned towards the house we had gone into. She was a very brave girl, and very beautiful with auburn hair and startling blue eyes.

Back to the main raiding party. We went into bedrooms and found machine pistols hanging on walls, also hand-guns and 9mm ammunition in little cardboard boxes. We were ready to leave when our lookout warned us that a German officer and a civilian were crossing from Curwoods Garage that was opposite and they were heading towards the house we were in. What to do, no time to sit down and think things over. So we went into a bathroom that had a window that overlooked a flat roof. We opened the window and placed all the weapons and ammunition on the flat roof.

Our lookout told us that the German officer and the civilian had started to mount the steps from the Terrace to the open front door. I told the lads there is only one way and Frank agreed with me, bluff our way out.

As the five of us trooped down the main staircase we had nearly reached the bottom when in came the officer and civilian whom I recognised as Mr Curwood who owned Curwoods Garage which was opposite Gloster Terrace. Mr Curwood recognised me but did not let on. He knew my father and my family. He said: 'What are you lads doing here?' I replied: 'We are a work party.' He then said: 'These are Army officers quarters. Go up Queen's Road to a big house on the right, then up a long drive and you will find the Air Force officers quarters.

We thanked him for his help, and walked out, down the steps then went up the Terrace, then up Queens Road. Part of the way up on the right hand side there is a lane that comes out in Ralegh Avenue. When we arrived at this lane we split up our group, John and Victor going to their homes, Ken to his home in Upper Midvale Road, David, Frank and myself heading for Midvale Road. Marguérite had seen us leave the Terrace, so she made her way home to Midvale Road, taking a roundabout route.

There is an interesting end to this Gloster Terrace story. A German officer on holiday with his family in Jersey, paid a visit to the German Military Underground Hospital. He was Major Wolperding. He and his family invited my Marie and I for a drink at the guest house where they were staying in Rouge Bouillon. At that date I did not want to socialise with an ex-German officer or soldier. But when he informed me that he was staying in the same house in Gloster Terrace where he had been billeted in 1944-1945 (now a guest house), I realised it was the same house that we had raided in 1943.

After this interesting news I could not resist his kind invitation. It was strange to be sitting there and drinking in that same house, drinking and remembering our narrow escape in those far off days. The ex-German officer did not remember any report about weapons being found on a flat roof. I introduced Major Wolperding to Michael Ginns from the Occupation Society. Michael got photographs and the full history of this ex-German Occupation officer, and I can tell you it is very interesting.

RAID ON STORE - 27 MIDVALE ROAD

The German OT had taken over the house next door to us, number 27 Midvale Road. Some low type of French women who collaborated with the Germans used the top floors for sleeping quarters. The other big rooms were used for storage. The basement rooms were used as kitchen, mess hall and laundry. One November morning when all the Germans and French women had left number 27 to work at other places in the Island, four of our group, David Dawson, Eddie Le Corré, Ken Williams and I got into the back garden. We broke a pane of glass and entered the house.

After looking around, we made our way upstairs and found in the big front room high piles of men's cotton underwear, long johns, vests. etc. In the big back room there were high piles of French army shirts and royal blue French boiler suits. We took as many pieces of underwear as we could carry. Eddie Le Corré took four boiler suits that were his size. In the basement was a large old table, used as a dining table.

I went back to my father's garage to fetch a hand saw. We then cut the legs of the table, (we thought it a great joke at the time). David Dawson who lived opposite took the table legs home for firewood, not a very smart thing to do but as he said next day to us, the wood made a fine fire.

However, we left number 27 by the back door, then home. The next morning Eddie called at my home so we could cycle to work together (we both worked at the same place). I could not believe my eyes, when I saw that Eddie was wearing one of the boiler suits he had taken only the day before. 'What's wrong, Joe?' he said. I told him I didn't think it was a good idea for him to wear one of the suits so soon after the raid. 'Don't fuss, Joe. Come on, we will be late for work,' - and off we went.

To many States of Jersey people and local police we were stealing, to them stealing was stealing but we never looked at it that way. Anything that could be done against the Germans we did, in our own limited way. We did not take the goods to sell, which we could have done and got a good price. We gave all the underwear to old people we knew, and as winter was starting they really appreciated the gifts. We did not tell them where the goods came from and did not leave our names. Of interest is the fact that the underwear was not German or French but captured British army stocks from France.

I gave four pairs of the long underpants and two vests to my uncle, P.C. René Le Huquet. Two days later he came to see me. 'You little sod,' he cried. 'You did not tell me the underwear you gave me had been pinched from the Germans. I nearly had a heart attack - and don't you even dare to smile.' Uncle René then stated the following:

'I was standing in the duty sergeant's room with other policemen awaiting daily orders when this German officer came in to the room to report that a robbery had taken place at one of the OT stores in Midvale Road. German goods had been stolen, etc. The German officer's English was not very good. He tried to explain what goods had been taken. What sounded like "undermention" had been taken. None of us knew what he meant. He then asked one of the policemen next to me to lift his trouser leg up. This policeman was wearing long underpants and one could see they were old and worn. The German Officer pointed to the long underpants, then it clicked. 'Long underpants,' said the duty sergeant. 'Ja, Ja,' said the German officer. I was in a real sweat. If the German had asked me to lift my trouser leg up he would have seen the brand new long pants and I would have been in trouble, arrested for receiving stolen goods. I would have been imprisoned not only by the police court but by the Germans and lost my job. You young devil, Joe, they will catch you one day and they will hurt you badly.' he said. My Uncle René was right, they did get me years later and hurt me badly.

But this was not the end of the OT Midvale Road raid story. A few days later I arrived home one evening only just before the curfew hour. What looked in the dark to be two German officers were putting questions to my mother at the front door. As I was going into the basement door my mother called to me. 'These two gentlemen are asking about a robbery they state took place next door.' I went up the steps to the front door to talk to them, thinking to myself, we have been found out.

However, the two Germans were very correct and polite. They asked me if I had heard any noise late at night, or seen anyone leaving number 27 with big bundles. I told them that one night I thought I heard glass getting broken, but thought it was only some one throwing a bottle against a wall or onto the road. They asked me from what direction did the sound come from. I said it was from the back of the houses. They then informed me that they were investigating a robbery of their goods that were in transit in Jersey for their unit in Alderney. They then told me that they would like to speak to me again the next day. I was to report to them at noon at the OT headquarters at Portland House in Midvale Road. They both then thanked me and my mother and with a good night, they went down the road.

I thought to myself, something is not right, they were too correct and too polite. I thought, they are just playing with me and somehow just waiting to catch me out. I again thought I must keep calm and try to bluff it out, come what may the next day. I did not sleep very well that night.

The next day I reported at noon to the two Germans at the OT headquarters. When they arrived I could see that they were not officers. Both were very tall, one blond, the other with dark hair. Their uniforms were very well tailored, and very well cut.

Both were wearing high officer boots. I did not recognise the collar badges, or the cap badges which were a skull in silver. It was only later that I found out that they were S.S. men from the camps on Alderney. They took me around to the back garden of number 27 and asked if the sound of broken glass came from this area. I stated that it seemed to come from this garden. One of the Germans said: 'You are right because there is a pane of glass broken by the door.' Then they asked if I had given any thought to what they had asked me the night before about if I had seen anyone leaving number 27 with big bundles. I then thought about those French women who were always reporting to the Germans about local people who lived in the road. These French women hated the British and were always well in with the troops in the German camps. I told the two Germans that the French women were always leaving number 27 with big bundles. The two Germans told me that they had already checked up on the French women, and the bundles were laundry for the OT. One of the Germans made notes in a small notebook. The two Germans then took me back to the OT headquarters in Midvale Road. They told me to stand in front and facing a big window, and not to move.

Some time later, three OT men came to the window and had a good look at me. They went away and other OT men and women took their place. About three lots of people came to the window. I think I was on an identity parade. After about three minutes the two Germans came out. 'You are free to go.' Then both shook my hand, and the blond one said: 'You have been a great service to the Reich we thank you.' Then they both gave me a Hitler salute, then went back inside. I was ready to run but I walked away slowly. Inside I was very shaken, it seemed that I was ready to faint.

A good friend of ours, Clare Gordon, was passing at this time and saw the two Germans shake my hand. 'I did not know you were friendly with that lot, Joe.' said Clare with a big grin. I could not tell her what was going on, too much of a risk. After the war I did tell her the whole story. I nearly did not turn up at the OT headquarters but if I had not, the two S.S. Germans would have suspected me and would have arrested me and all my family.

That night I told Eddie, Ken and David what had taken place. They were very pleased that I had not involved them, otherwise they all thought it was very funny and a good laugh. But I can tell you I did not feel like laughing at the time. It really shook me for weeks. And those S.S. men - so polite and correct towards me. It's hard to believe that they could murder people. It just goes to show how you can be taken in by looks. After the war when we knew all about the S.S., I then realised how luck was on my side.

WORKING AT WASHINGTON'S AT FIRST TOWER

Mr. Len Washington

At the start of my work at Washington's at First Tower a lot of Germans came for a haircut. I had never cut hair before so these Germans left our shop with funny haircuts. As a matter of fact, they looked as if the moths had got at their hair. After that we never saw many Germans in our shop. One German said to me 'English haircuts no good I will never come here again and I will tell my friends how badly you cut hair.' It was just the job - no Germans in our shop.

I did learn the trade very fast and many of my friends came to us for haircuts. Later on our shop was always full. My boss was very pleased.

In no time I received three certificates for hairdressing but I still did not want to spend my young life in this trade. Another thing about working at Washington's was that we had our fair share of "Jerry-bags" in the ladies side of our shop. But bit by bit the girls (there were 6 girls working in our shop) and I put the Jerry-bags off from coming. One day I was talking with a pal about the Jerry-bags when a voice from the ladies side of the shop said to my boss, 'That young man of yours had better watch himself because my boyfriend is a German officer.' I called out over the cubicle partition that divided the gents and ladies departments, 'Wait till the war ends, I will remember you and our loyal people will sort you out.' The Jerry-bag left the shop very fast and told my boss that she would never come again. 'And through your young man you have lost my custom.'

My boss, poor old Mr Washington, did not know what to do for the best. He did not know whether to sack me or what. I was on the mat in front of him, I told him it was up to him if he sacked me. I also said that by getting rid of the German soldiers and Jerry-bags we would have more loyal Jersey people. And I was right. When Jersey people found out that we did not want or need Germans or collaborators our shop was always full with good loyal Jersey people. Even my boss saw this and thanked me by giving me a good pay rise.

On one fine and warm August morning in 1942 we were working at Washington's Hairdressing Salon at First Tower, (the salon/shop is still there). As it was such a warm day we had the door open. We heard a commotion coming from Victoria Avenue. Some of us went outside onto the pavement to see what was going on. Passing along the Avenue we saw groups of about fifty people in each batch. They were shuffling along and in a terrible state, many dressed in rags and most of them with no footwear. These groups were getting herded along by OT guards who were armed with long wooden staffs and pick handles. These brutal guards did not hesitate to lay into these poor people.

We found out later that they were slave labour brought over from Russia but mainly from the Ukraine. As one group went past a very young slave girl dropped her little bundle of odds and ends on the road. As she ran back to retrieve it, stooping to pick it up, a big brute of an OT guard struck her on the head with his long wooden club. The poor girl screamed with pain as the blood ran down through the grime that covered her face. I am no hero but I was filled with anger at this brutal treatment of this young girl, and without thinking of the consequences I started to move forward to try and stop the brutal guard from striking the girl again. As I stepped out I was held back by my boss, Mr Washington, with three other staff and pulled back into the salon with the boss remarking, 'You young fool. You will get us all arrested.' Dear old Mrs Garnier, our salon cleaning lady who had witnessed the brutal guard's actions towards the young girl, with the tears running down her face, cried out: 'Oh my God, where are you?' But it seemed that God had taken the day off.

In the meantime the young slave girl had run to catch up with the shuffling batch of slaves. Even after all these years I still get upset thinking of what we had witnessed. I could not stop thinking about that poor slave girl. We did find out where the German OT guards had taken these poor people. It was to a camp opposite La Moye School on the Route Orange, St Brelade.

A few days later half of our boxing club members rode out to this slave camp. On the way we stopped and asked a Jersey farmer if he would sell us some of his apples which we wanted to give with the other odds and ends of food we had collected for the poor slaves. The farmer told us to clear off. He would not sell or give anything for the slaves. So while four of us kept him busy trading insults in Norman French, Kenny Williams, Eddie Le Corré and two other pals jumped over the orchard hedge and filled a small sandbag full of apples, not windfalls but picked off the trees.

When the farmer saw what was happening he shouted for his wife (she was as ugly as he was) to phone for the police. Kenny wanted to fight the farmer, but the boys persuaded him that it was time to go. We then made our way to the slave camp on the Route Orange. There did not seem to be any guards about so we started to chat (sign language) to the Russians who were beyond a high wire fence.

We threw the small parcels of food etc over the fence. Most of these poor people were very young, but in a terrible condition. They fought like wild animals over the parcels of food, and before you knew it, it seemed like hundreds of the poor slaves were pressing against the wire fence, hands held out, using the international code of gestures for eating and smoking.

And I found once again the little slave girl among the many that came to the high fence. Her head was covered by a dirty old towel. She did not understand my English, but she seemed to know that I was asking if she was OK, pointing to her head. She spoke the first Russian I had ever heard. She said "Nitchevo" which means in English "Never mind, it's OK". She had beautiful green eyes. One of the slaves pointed to my bike and said "Velomachine." We were getting on well with these Russians, when all of a sudden the slaves went quiet and disappeared into their wooden huts. We turned around and saw the reason why they had moved away so fast; crossing the road from their police van were three big Feldgendarmerie, (military police). The three approached us shouting in German. With their helmets and dog collar chain breast plates, they looked an ugly bunch. One spoke to us in English, took down our names and checked our ID cards, etc. We were informed that we were not allowed to give food or any other goods to the prisoners. The English speaking one stated 'It is forbidden. You understand?' He went on to say that we would be let off this time, but if ever we were caught again we would be in serious trouble. So, with other warnings, we rode back to town. We did go again and again to visit the Russians, but posted lookouts. We had learned a lot from our first visit.

One day, it was a Sunday, I rode past the camp very slowly and once more saw my little Russian Rose, that's the name I had for the little Russian slave girl. She saw me and called out something in Russian to me. That was the last time I saw our little Russian Rose. We all prayed and hoped that the young Russian girl at wars end would return to her family and home.

Many of our Jersey people and U.K. residents at the start of the German Occupation did not or would not believe the stories and rumours that were brought to the Island by forced labourers or the crews of ships carrying Jersey people who had after serving their sentences in German or French prisons and camps returned to Jersey. They informed us that the Germans were arresting Jews and French and Polish people and deporting them to their deaths in concentration camps in Germany. It was only when the Germans brought over to Jersey the Russian and Ukrainian slaves to work at building fortifications that their eyes were opened and then they saw the brutal side of the enemy.

We were very young patriots but we knew that if the Germans won the war we would all be slaves.

SLAVE WORKERS BROUGHT TO JERSEY

Having been a prisoner and shared a cell with recaptured Russians and Ukrainians, and being an eye witness of the German treatment of the slave workers that were brought to Jersey, it was only right that I should record some of the facts and history of these victims. And please remember that there were many good policemen, uniformed and honorary and others who helped these slaves at great risk to themselves and their families. But I hate to admit it there were some only too ready to obey and carry out German orders. During the dark Occupation years you did not want to know what race or religion a person belonged to as long as you all faced the same common enemy-Nazi Germany. We were all brothers and sisters together in our struggle against inhuman treatment. I often look upon the war and the Occupation of these Islands as a test, a very cruel test one has to admit when the strong stood up to be counted and defended the weak.

Michael

One Russian "Michael" who was locked up with us in the German prison in Gloucester Street had escaped from a work party in France. He broke into a farm house and stole a woman's dress and underwear, etc, Thus in disguise, he took a short cut through a very quiet village. Michael knew he had made a bad judgement when three drunk Germans came out of a house, saw him and thought they would have some fun with this late night woman traveller. They grabbed him and threw him onto a patch of grass. As they started to undress him they soon realised when the padding fell out of his bra and his private parts were exposed that here was no woman. They were so furious that they beat him up till he was unconscious. Michael woke up next day in a French prison cell.

One week later he was on a ship, bound for Jersey. He again escaped from the camp at St Ouen's. A few days later he was working on a farm north of the Island for a farmer who had given him shelter and food, until one day the local police arrived and arrested him. They handed him over to the OT in Midvale Road. After being beaten up once more he was imprisoned with us in the German prison in Gloucester Street.

We asked him how was he caught. He told us he took too many risks. He would leave the farm at night to visit a neighbouring farm to make love to the farmer's wife.

She was about 30 years old and her husband over 70. He found out about his wife's infidelity because she always went to the stable late at night, so one evening her husband followed her and caught her with Michael making love. The husband reported the Russian to the local police. Michael told us that the woman was no beauty, but very sex starved.

Michael returned to Russia in 1945, we only had news of him once, but no news of him since. Like a lot of Russians who were ex-prisoners returning to Russia, he could have ended up in some Siberian work camp.

Pyotry Bokatenko, a young slave worker from a Ukrainian village, made five escapes from German camps in Jersey. He was flung into a stone prison cell and flogged with whips then left for days tied to an outside wooden pole. He escaped again and was given

Lucy Schwob

refuge in St Brelade by Lucy Schwob and her sister Suzanne Malherbe at their home "La Rocquaise", St Brelade's Bay. Pyotry told us that the two sisters fed and looked after him very well, but he had to smile because although the two sisters were not snobs he had to eat in the kitchen not the dining room.

Suzanne Malherbe

He also had to do his share of the housework, like cleaning and seeing to the fireplace. He slept in the out-house but there was a good reason for this. If the Germans on a search raid arrived at the main house he could slip out very fast and make his escape over the sea wall which was at the end of the garden. And this is how Pyotry made his escape from "La Rocquaise" when one day in 1944 the German Secret Field Police arrived and arrested the two sisters. They were sentenced to death by a German military court. For a time they were in the next cell to mine in the German military prison in Gloucester Street. We became friends and I will always remember them. They survived the war. In the late 1950s Lucy died, then in the 1970s Suzanne died. Their remains are buried in St Brelade's cemetery by St Brelade's Bay within sight of their old home. On the headstone is the star of David with the words "and I see a new world."

Pyotry was then given refuge by Mike Le Cornu and his sister Alice at their home in St Ouen's. Pyotry survived the war and served in the Russian Army. Mike Le Cornu and his sister Alice now live in England, and they keep in touch with Pyotry who lives in the Ukraine.

Many slave workers left their camps at night to steal food and other goods from houses and farms. Some of these escaped slave workers killed people who were trying to stop them stealing their food. One or two of these desperate men were also killed by local people who were protecting their homes or farms from being raided. Sometimes the local uniformed and honorary police forces had some legal justification for rounding up and arresting these escaped slave workers. It was the duty of the local police to protect the local population from these escaped prisoners who were terrorising the local people in some parts of the Island. That is what made it bad for the rest of the slave workers who escaped from the camps and only wanted to find some place to have shelter and food. They had to sometimes suffer arrest and imprisonment because of the actions of the bad and villainous among them. Russian slave workers imprisoned with us in the German prison in St Helier often told us that after some person or other had informed the local police that escaped slave workers were being given shelter by a farmer and his family, the local police arrived and arrested the escaped slave workers. The local police then handed them over to the German police. We also had farmers in the German prison who had been imprisoned for helping these slave workers. These farmers told us that within an hour of the fugitive being arrested on their premises the German military police arrived and arrested and imprisoned the farmer himself who had given shelter to the slave workers. One old farmer, Mr Le Cornu, told us that when he was arrested he told the German police that they had no proof that he or his family had given shelter to a Russian. The German military police informed him that the local police had reported him to them and had given them the address of the farm where they had arrested the escaped Russian. We had never heard anyone swear so much in Jersey French as that old farmer, Mr Le Cornu. We did learn some new Jersey French words from the good old chap.

The Organization Todt had their headquarters in Jersey at what is now called the Portland Hotel in Midvale Road. They also occupied the house next door, number 19. Midvale road. Here they had converted the back basement rooms into holding cells. Any escaped slave workers who were captured were brought to this address by the German or local police. We lived at number 25, and on many nights, looking out from our top windows, we had seen the local police van (called the Black Maria) pull up outside number 19 and unload recaptured slave workers, and handing them over to the OT who kicked and hit them with long batons all the way down the basement steps of the house. You did not have to wait long before dreadful screams came from number 19 as the brutal OT beat up the recaptured men or women in the basement.

My father complained to Dr Shone who was at one time one of the Red Cross representatives in Jersey. Dr Shone's house, Royde House at 21 Midvale Road, was between our house and number 19. Dr Shone did complain to the Germans and to the Bailiff about the treatment of these recaptured slave workers. About a week later Dr Shone informed my father that he had been told by the Germans to mind his own business. Dr Shone went again to see the Bailiff, and told him that he would not let the matter rest. The Bailiff advised Dr Shone to have a word with the Attorney General. The Attorney General, Duret Aubin, told him that nothing could be done. The Germans had total control over their prisoners.

Dr Shone told my father that he did not like the Attorney General's unkind attitude towards the slave workers. Duret Aubin told Dr Shone that all the Russians and all the other slave and forced labourers the Germans had brought over to Jersey were a bunch of savage heathens and criminals. Many of us were not surprised by Aubin's attitude after all he thought us political prisoners who had been arrested and imprisoned by the Germans were a bunch of criminals because, after we had been tried by the German military court, the Germans sent the Attorney General a copy of our court documents which stated our offence, sentence, etc. The Attorney General then instructed the Connétable of St Helier to register our names in the Police Register Book. To our minds this was treating loyal Jersey people as criminals. You can read this in the Law Office files at the Jersey Archives Service. I have tried many times to try and find the St Helier police register books of 1940-1945. I wrote to the Connétable of St Helier in 1999 about them. He informed me by phone that, to make room for other documents a lot of these old books and records were destroyed many years ago in the 1960s. But I still have not given up, I am sure that they are stored somewhere in Jersey. They would be so interesting to read. We were informed after the war ended that there were no German Court documents in Jersey but a few years ago I found out that the Law Officers did have our German Military Court documents, I have not only seen them but I have got copies of my German Military Court documents, courtesy of the Bailiff of Jersey, the Attorney General and the Jersey Archive Service. I will state that the Bailiff of Jersey, Sir Philip Bailhache has always been very kind and always helpful in my requests for information.

One evening in 1942 I had to collect something or other from our garage which was at the end of our long garden in Midvale Road. When I went in I saw in the light of my torch what looked like a person huddled up in the far corner. I immediately returned to the house to fetch my father. We both entered the garage and saw a young man crouching in there. Father told me to go back to the house, try to find some food and bring a jug of water. On my return, Father told me not to approach the poor chap but leave the food and water on the work bench.

Father then unlocked the big garage doors and pointed with his torch. The young man understood that this was to make it easy for him to get away because he nodded to us. By now we knew that he was an escaped Russian slave worker from the basement of number 19 Midvale Road. The young man's face was covered in grime and what looked like dried blood.

He also had no footwear or any coat or even a shirt, he had only trousers and a torn old vest. We left an old pair of sandals and an old jacket. We closed the garden garage door and went back to the house. The next morning the Russian had gone, so was one of my shirts from the garden clothes line. We also noticed his foot marks where he had walked from the garden wall to the garage. Father cleansed any trace or marks left by the young escapee in case the Germans came searching for the prisoner. Father was right. We had barely sat down to breakfast when the door bell rang. It was the OT searching for their escaped prisoner. They searched all over the house, garden and garage. They stated that the escaped prisoner must have passed through our garden, they asked 'did we hear or see anyone?'

After they had gone we prayed and hoped the young Russian got away to a safe farm. The Germans did carry out secret burials of unknown slave workers at the Strangers Cemetery at West Mount, St Helier. Mr P.C. Pallot the Superintendent of the St Helier Cemeteries, made a report on the 13th July, 1942 to C.J. Cuming, Connétable of St Helier.

Dear Sir,

I beg to report that Friday morning 10th July, I received an order from Messrs J B Le Quesne and Son, Funeral Directors, submitted to them by the Burial Department of the Organisation Todt to dig out two graves for the burial of two Frenchmen in the French Section (as worked out on their plan) in the Strangers Cemetery at West Mount. I therefore sounded in that section of the cemetery to ascertain the most convenient position to dig out these two graves. After determining the two positions I consulted the OBL Gefolgschaftstelle of the Oganisation Todt, and agreed with the Chief of this department to dig in these two positions. Saturday morning I have instructions to my grave digger to proceed with the digging of these graves. After digging about two feet he came across a coffin which to all appearances had recently been interred and out of alignment with the marking stone. I gave instructions to stop digging there and proceed with the next grave and to my surprise another new coffin was found. I immediately stopped any further digging and proceeded to OBL Gefolgschaftstelle and interviewed the chief of the department, reporting my discovery, and he came to the cemetery and together we decided on two new positions to dig out the graves as required. At the same time I had these places sounded and in sounding I found that another body had been buried near and I therefore reported this fact to him. I then compared my entries in the books with the burials marked on the plan of the Strangers Cemetery which this Department had made and given me a duplicate, but I cannot trace any records of any burials other than these marked on the plan and entered in my books. I have therefore interviewed Messrs H.I.S. Déslandes, and Messrs J.B. Le Quesne and Sons, Funeral Directors, who have been the only two Undertakers who have been interested in the burial of any member of the OT who have died in Jersey and comparing their records with mine these prove to be identical except for the Algerians, which record was compared with the OBL Gefolgschaftstelle and proved correct. I can further state that in the course of my inquiries it has come to my knowledge that we have not been responsible for every burial performed, as a German Unit has opened graves and interred bodies themselves. Prior to the use of the Strangers Cemetery by the German Forces and OT the last burial was in 1934.

I have the honour to be, Sir, Your obedient servant,

Signed;   P.C. Pallot

Young Russian Slave worker shot in Old Street, St. Helier, 1943

One early evening in September 1943, my pal, Frank Le Pennec, and I were passing the St Helier Town Hall when a young man dressed in rags and bare footed ran past us towards Old Street. He was followed by two German military policemen, with a grey van following behind. As he started to run up Old Street the German military police called out to the man to halt but he kept running. Then all of a sudden, two shots rang out.

We had followed up behind the van and as we got near we saw the young man lying on the roadway. The two German military police were picking up the shot man and were half carrying and half dragging him towards the grey van. We could see he had been shot, the front of his shirt was covered in blood. The two Germans saw us staring at what was going on. They started to shout at us to clear off. We did not need another warning we could just about understand German and the look on their faces told us that they did not want us around as witnesses to the shooting of the young man.

Later on we found out that the man who had been shot was a Russian slave worker who had escaped from his German escort. Before they drove off we did hear the driver of the grey van ask the two German military police something in German, one of the German military police told him "Todt" dead.

We reported to the duty policeman at the Town Hall what we had witnessed. He told us to go home and forget what we had seen. He also stated that there was nothing they, the local police, could do. The Germans were a law onto themselves.

The shooting of the slave worker was like watching a film. Every time I pass Old Street I think of that poor young Russian. Goodness knows how many of these poor people were killed in this way and buried in unknown graves.

My pal, Frank Le Pennec, was cutting down trees for the States of Jersey Labour Department in St Peter's Valley. One day he was working by one of the entrances to the German tunnels. Frank spoke to the French OT Supervisor about the young Russian we had witnessed being shot. Frank told him we would like to know his name and history. Frank was on good talking terms with the French Supervisor. As a matter of fact, the supervisor used to let Frank and his workmates have a bowl of hot soup that was being cooked on the site. The Frenchman told Frank that he would try and find out.

However, a week went by before the French Supervisor informed Frank that the dead young man was a Russian slave worker who had escaped from a camp in St Ouen's. The Germans had been searching for him for over two weeks. The German Feldgendarmerie had stopped him in Conway Street and had asked for his papers. He immediately took to his heels and made a run for it, with the German police in pursuit along Broad Street to the Town Hall and Old Street. The young Russian was 18 years old, and his name was Mikael Korintsky. We have many times searched in the records but have never found any trace of his grave in Jersey. Another Russian slave worker with the same Christian name Mikael shared the same cell with me in the German prison in Jersey. When one day I told him the story of the shot young Russian, Mikael Korintsky he told me he had known him and they had been prisoners in the same camps in France and Jersey. This Mikael Korinstsky came from the Ukraine and had made two attempts to escape in France. When he was shot in 1943 this had been his third and tragically last attempt to escape.

Another Russian soldier who escaped from a camp in Jersey was also a Mikhael Mikhael Krokhim taken prisoner in the Ukraine in September 1941. Twice he escaped from camps in Jersey. His second bid to escape succeeded and he was given refuge by Mrs Augusta Metcalfe and her sister Miss C. Donitrieva and their family. They taught him English in six months. Norman Le Brocq and Les Huelin provided Mikhael with false documents so that he was able to walk around the town. Even Doctor McKinstry provided him with spectacles to disguise his appearance. Mikhail Krokhim is not yet retired, he is working as a Factory Engineer. The last we heard from him he was living with is his sons Victor and Geennadi, and his grandchildren at Chimkent Kazakhstan.

And another Russian, Feodor Burilly (Bill) escaped from a German slave camp in Jersey and was given shelter by Mrs Louise Gould and her brother Harold Le Druillenec. Louise and Harold were arrested by the German Secret Field Police and imprisoned in the German prison in Jersey. Both sister and brother were sent to German concentration camps. Louise Gould was murdered at the notorious Ravensbruck concentration camp in Germany in 1945. Her brother Harold was found barely alive at Belsen concentration camp in Germany by the Allied Liberating Army. Harold died in his beloved Jersey 1985 a very brave and loyal Jerseyman. Feodor Burilly (Bill) was a pilot in the Russian Air Force, he was shot down over Smolensk in 1941. Taken prisoner by the Germans, he escaped and was recaptured and transported to Jersey as slave labour in 1942.

So many people helped these escaped slave workers Bob Le Sueur, Roseelle Colivet, Berthe Pitolet, Florence Hacquoil, Oscar Le Breuilly, Bernard Brée, Mrs Louisa Gould, sister and brother in law, Ivy and Arthur Forster, René Le Motte, Mr and Mrs Désverges,

Stuart Williams, Dorothy Huelin, René Franoux, Michael Froud and many more people helped the starving slaves, hiding them, and sharing their small rations of food. The courage of these people will never be forgotten by the Russian people or by us political prisoners. We all have a duty to pass on to our own grandchildren the truth of the German Occupation, and keep the memory of these brave people fresh in our minds.

One could go on and on writing about these poor slave workers in Jersey, 1942-1945. One Russian that did not return to Russia was George Kozloff. His story is too long for this modest book. Like many stories of the German Occupation it needs a book on its own. George Kozloff was a slave worker in Jersey, 1941-1945. At wars end he did not wish to return to Russia, so he jumped the train taking him home and started a new life in East Germany. It was a difficult decision because it meant that he would never see his parents again. After the war George became a physical education instructor. The last we heard or saw of George was in 1995, in the south of England, and he was still keeping fit.

Mr. Joe Miere
The German Military
Underground Hospital Museum
St. Lowrence
Jersey
Channel Islands

OFFICE OF THE MILITARY ATTACHÉS
OF THE U.S.S.R. IN GREAT BRITAIN
————
16 KENSINGTON PALACE GARDENS
LONDON, W.8
TELEPHONE: 01-229 6451

4-th August 1989

Dear Mr. J. Mière,

Excuse my bothering you but I have to apply to you
because to my mind you are the only person in UK who
can help me.

The matter is that USSR Ministry of Defence is going
to publish "The Book of Memory" devoted to my compatriots
who died during World War II including those who were
killed and buried on the territory of Channel Islands.

As far as I remember at your Museum you have got the
full list of the Soviet citizens who took part in the
construction of the German military underground hospital.

That is why will you be so kind to supply me with the
list of the names of my compatriots who lost their lives
and were buried in Jersey and Alderney during the Second
World War.

If you have any additional information on the subject
I am interested in, please let me know.

Best wishes and regards.

Sincerely yours,

Y. Yelyutin
Lt.Col. Y. Yelyutin
Assistant Military Attache

Mr. Joe Miere
The German Military
Underground Hospital Museum
St. Lowrence
Jersey
Channel Islands

OFFICE OF THE MILITARY ATTACHÈS
OF THE U.S.S.R. IN GREAT BRITAIN
————
16 KENSINGTON PALACE GARDENS
LONDON, W.8
TELEPHONE: 01-229 6451

9-th August 1989

Dear Mr. Joe Miere,

Thank you very much for your letter and information about my
compatriots who were buried in Jersey during the Second World
War I received last Wednesday. It is very kind of you.

Unfortunately I do not know French and that is why it will be
very difficult for me to contact the people in France you mentione
in your letter and to explain to them my problem.

Excuse my wasting your time but if you have an opportunity to
get the information about my compatriots who were buried in
Jersey, Alderney and Guernsey during World War II and whose
remains were transfered later from the Channel Islands to France,
please send this information to me.

I know you are very busy but I really need your help.

Many thanks again.

My best wishes to you and your family.

Yours sincerely,

Y. Yelyutin
Lt.Col. Y. Yelyutin
Assistant Military Attache

HENRY PETER TURPIN

Twenty nine year old Jerseyman, Henry Peter Turpin, was shot and killed at about 11pm on the evening of Saturday, the first day of February 1941, on La Grande Route des Mielles (Five Mile Road) St Ouen's, Jersey. He was in the military zone outside his home La Mielle Bungalow on the Five Mile Road. Having left the home of Mr Bougeard, 50 yards away, when he was challenged by a German army patrol to halt. He started to run and he ignored the German patrol warning to halt. After a second warning to halt the patrol fired the rifle bullet which struck his left shoulder, killing him. His son who was only seven years old remembers seeing his dead father the next morning, lying on his back in front of the garage of Westward House Bungalow. Henry Peter Turpin and his young son, Henry Turpin Jnr lived at his grandmothers home, La Mielle Bungalow. Young Henry Turpin Jnr's mother and sister left Jersey in 1940. Henry Turpin Jnr paid a visit to Jersey in February 2002 from his home in New Jersey USA. He contacted me to collect more information on his father's death. We were able with the very kind help of the Deputy Viscount Peter de Gruchy to get the full story for Henry Turpin Jnr family records in America.

In October 1940 a full publication in the Evening Post showing the areas of the Military Zone around the Island, warning people living in the Zone to be within the confines of their homes before 8pm, and to stay there till 7.30am the next morning. Also people who lived or worked in the Military Zone had to carry a green identification card which was issued by the Connétable of the Parish they lived or worked in. I worked at First Tower in the Military Zone. Besides your identity card you had to carry a green extra identity card. This extra Military Zone identity card came into force on the first of November 1940.

Mr Henry Turpin
221 York Towne Drive
Little Egg Harbour
New Jersey
USA
08087

21st August 2002

To whom it may concern

Re: Inquest report for Mr Henry Turpin Snr

I Henry Turpin of the above address hereby request a copy of the inquest of my father Mr Henry Turpin Snr for my personal use. I hereby give permission to Mr Joe Mière to pass onto me a copy of the said inquest.

Yours faithfully

Henry Turpin

JEWS IN THE CHANNEL ISLANDS

Marianne Grunfeld

Augusta Spitz

Thérèse Steiner

THE THERESE STEINER STORY

In 1938 when the Nazis invaded Austria, Thérèse Steiner was living in Vienna. Realising that Jews like themselves were in great danger, her mother and father urged their daughter to flee to England. Thérèse, then 22, arrived in London alone. She found work as a nanny with the family Potts. When war broke out in 1939, the Potts family moved to the small Channel Island of Sark and Thérèse went with them, As the Germans swept into France the Potts family and Thérèse moved to Guernsey.

In Guernsey the Potts and Thérèse planned to move to the safety of England. But Thérèse encountered Chief Inspector William Sculpher, head of the Guernsey police force. He informed Thérèse that as she was Austrian and an enemy alien, she had to stay in Guernsey. Thérèse pleaded with him, she explained that as she was Jewish and a refugee she was in danger from the Nazis, but Sculpher refused her plea. He sent her to work as a nurse in the Guernsey Castel Hospital. She became friends with another nurse named Barbara.

Before long the Germans occupied Guernsey. Thérèse was a gifted pianist. She was issued with a identity card and was very upset because stamped in large letters across the card was "Juden" in red ink. The Guernsey Bailiff, Victor Carey, was asked by the Germans for a list with names and addresses of all Jews living in Guernsey. Carey asked his police chief, Sculpher, to compile the list. All details were sent to the German Feldkommandant. The Guernsey Bailiff wrote on 2 May 1941 to the Kommandant;

Dear Sir, I have the honour to acknowledge your letter regarding measures against the Jews. The instructions contained therein are receiving attention. I will report to you further in due course.
   I have the honour to be, Sir, Your obedient servant,
   Victor Carey, Bailiff of Guernsey
(This says it all!)

Thérèse's friend, Barbara, remembers how Thérèse appeared one day very worried and upset. She told Barbara that she had received notification that she was to be deported from Guernsey. One morning Barbara walked with her and two other Jewish women, Augusta Spitz and Marianne Grunfeld, down to the harbour. The boat was sailing to St Malo in France from St Peter Port. Thérèse and her two Jewish friends were placed into wagons and transported to another part of France. Five months later, Thérèse arrived in Auschwitz concentration camp where she met her death in the gas chambers.

Many documents and records are still locked away in both Jersey and Guernsey. They are not available to the public. They are kept in the locked files for another 40-50 years.

As a true and loyal Jerseyman, I honour the name of the three Jewish ladies who met their deaths in German concentration camps. If some people don't like me writing the truth of how the three Jewish ladies were betrayed and handed over to the Germans - well they can check up the facts, and come and talk to me about it in front of the TV and newspaper reporters. All out in the open as it should have been in 1945-1946.

JEWS TO REGISTER

The Bailiffs of Jersey and Guernsey received two Orders from the Germans relating to measures to be taken for the registration of Jews who were living in the Channel Islands.

The first Order against the Jews was registered in the Royal Court of Jersey on 21 October 1940, and in Guernsey on 23 October 1940. Jews in Jersey were required to register at the Chief Aliens Office. The Bailiff of Jersey entrusted the registration of the Jews to the Chief Aliens Officer and it took place on Wednesday, 23 and Thursday, 24 October 1940 at Number 6 Hill Street, St. Helier. Twelve Jews were registered at this office in Jersey.

In Guernsey the Jews had to register at the office of William Schulpher, the Guernsey Inspector of Police. Four Jews registered. The Guernsey Bailiff passed all the information relating to the Jews on 29 October, 1940, to the Feldkommandantur.

Not one member in the Royal Court of Jersey opposed these disgusting anti-Jewish laws, but in Guernsey one member openly and categorically refused his assent and stated his grave objections to the Guernsey Royal Court about passing this German anti Jewish Law. The gentleman was Jurat Sir Abraham Laine. The Germans never arrested him. What a shining light he must have been to the loyal Guernsey people in those dark days.

The second Order relating to measures against the Jews was registered in the Royal Courts of Jersey 16 November, 1940 and in Guernsey on the 27 November 1940.

The Third Order relating to measures against the Jews was registered in the Royal Courts of Jersey on 31 May 1941 and in Guernsey on 17 June 1941. There was a Fourth Order relating to the Jews. The Fifth Order relating to measures against the Jews was registered in the Royal Court of Jersey 1 November 1941, and in Guernsey on 28 October 1941.

The Sixth Order relating to measures against the Jews was registered in the Royal Court of Jersey on 7 March 1942, and in Guernsey on 21 March 1942.

The Seventh Order relating to measures the Jews was registered in the Royal Court of Jersey on 9 May 1942, and Guernsey on 30 June 1042. It required that Jews must at all times in public wear a yellow star with the word Jew in Black. The Eighth Order was not registered in the Royal Court of Jersey, as the Bailiff advised the Germans that this Order should not be registered or put into execution in Jersey. The Germans agreed that they would take no further action at present.

The Ninth Order relating to measures against the Jews was registered in the Royal Court of Jersey on 15 August 1942, and in Guernsey on 21 August 1942.

As we have seen Thérèse Steiner, Augusta Spitz, and Marianne Grunfeld were deported from Guernsey to France, leading to their deaths at Auschwitz-Birkenau concentration camp. On 17 June 1941 the Bailiff of Guernsey informed the Feldkommandant that he had the honour of ensuring that further measures against the Jews had been registered.

Not many years ago a register of Jews living in occupied Western Europe was found at the Ministry of War Veterans in Paris. The Ministry had persistently denied possession of these Jewish master files, even two weeks before they were handed over to the French Government authorities. The documents are a very damning confirmation of the extent to which the occupied authorities in France co-operated with Nazis. Many organisations have sought these documents since 1944. One report in these files states "Danneker" head of the Gestapo section dealing with Jews in France and occupied Western Europe, including the occupied Channel Islands, paid tribute to the good work of all concerned, the police and civilian authorities, in making a model list of the Jews.

It would be interesting to see how many Channel Island Jewish files there are among these documents. The files are still held by the French Examining Magistrate in Paris which deal with Nazi collaboration charges against some of the French wartime Vichy officials. At the Liberation in May 1945 of the Channel Islands, British Military Intelligence officers, Major Cotton, Major Haddock, Captain Richards, Captain Kent, Captain Dempsey and Lieutenants Godard and Poole, went through a stack of Jersey and Guernsey German Kommandantur files and documents. After 1945 many of the files went missing when sent to London. The missing documents turned up at the "Yad Vashem" Central Archives of the Holocaust Museum in Isreal. Much of the original correspondence between the Bailiffs of the Channel Islands and the German Kommandantur is in these files. Many historians and a few writers have seen and read them.

The Guernsey Attorney General, the late Ambrose Sherwill, has left an account of the Guernsey Royal Court discussions of the first Anti-Jewish measures registered on 23 October 1940. He wrote later that the Order had disgusted him but he felt there was no point in opposing it. Nevertheless, he still felt ashamed that he had not done something by way of protest to the Germans.

The German Officer responsible for the persecution of the Jews living in these Islands was Dr Casper. His orders came from the SS and Gestapo, based in Paris. One letter from Dr Casper to SS headquarters, dated 17 June, 1942 (now in MI 19 files) gives the number of Jews living in the Channel Islands and recommends that they be sent to a concentration camp "not to return." From the way that Dr Casper states his case anyone would think that he was kind and helpful to the Jews. Yes, helpful to get them to a concentration camp and murder them. This so called officer made me sick with his lies.

However, if any researcher into the history of the German Occupation of these Islands needs to read up on the subject of the Channel Island Jews, I can recommend the following two books. Firstly , "The Jews in the Channel Islands during the German Occupation 1940-1945" by Frederick Cohen, published in 1998. His research is exemplary, first class and well documented. He has dug deep into closed and open archives.

The second book I would recommend is "The Jews in the Channel Islands and the Rule of Law" by David Fraser, published by Sussex Academic Press. David is a Lecturer in the Faculty of Law at the University of Sydney. He has certainly gone deeply into the subject and has had access to the Jersey Law Officer's files. I wish our local historians had had the same. It sometimes occurs to me that the authorities concerned do not consider that we Jerseymen are bright enough to research and write our own Occupation history.

In May 1981, a well known local historian friend of mine came to my home to seek advice and any information I could give him on whether there were Jews in Jersey during the Occupation. He chose not take my advise and informed me that he was going to write a letter for publication in the Jersey Evening Post and he would say that there were no Jews in the Island during that time and to think otherwise was "nonsense."

I did warn my historian friend that he was wrong and if the JEP published his letter I would have to write also to counter this pernicious opinion. On Monday, 8 June 1981, his letter appeared repeating his claim that there were no Jews in Jersey during the Occupation. On June 11 the JEP kindly published my letter refuting this historian's opinion. I referred to well documented reports in my possession and stated that I knew of five Jews living in Jersey at the time. My historian friend was very embarrassed but we remained good friends. One can look up the issues of the old JEPs for his letter, and my reply letter, of June 11th 1981.

In 1998 another local historian came to see me. He had been a fellow inmate of the Jersey German prison and was an old school friend of mine. He also wanted information on the Jews in Jersey during the Occupation. He believed that there were no Jewish slave workers brought to Jersey by the Germans and he was going to write a letter to the JEP stating it. He was so certain of his grounds that he was going to offer £100 to anyone who could supply evidence to the contrary.

Again I warned this very well known historian friend of mine that I would have to write to the JEP for them to publish the true facts and supply documented proof that the Germans did indeed bring Jewish slave workers to the Island in 1941 and that they worked at the first galleries at the German Military Underground Hospital.

On Friday 28 August 1998, the JEP published my historian friend letter, with the offer of £100. On Tuesday 1 September 1998 the JEP published my reply letter. My old school pal never wrote or spoke to me again. And I did not receive the £100.

German Orders were starting to have a very disturbing affect on the Jews still living in Jersey in 1940-1941. Doubt and anxiety made them think deeply about their future, and many wished they had taken the advice of friends and had left the Island on he last boats to leave for the safety of England. The Jews knew that, after the Royal Court of Jersey had registered the first Anti-Jewish law on behalf of the Germans in October 1940, they could not expect help from that quarter. A Jewish lady who was living in Jersey during the German Occupation years remembers the view of many of the Jews that were in Jersey at that time and stated 'The Jews were to be sacrificed to appease the Nazis.' Some people said that the few Jews in Jersey were not worth fighting for, better to appease the Germans and concentrate on protecting the local people in the verbal battles to come between the local authorities and the German Military Administration.

One Jewish couple took it on themselves to escape from Jersey and try to reach England or even France. This story had never been confirmed by other Jewish people who lived in Jersey 1940-1945. But here are the few facts that I have in my records although my research work is not complete on this Jewish couple.

By all accounts the Kleinsteins, Arthur Samuel and Marthe Helga, ran a business selling bed linen, towels, cloth, etc under a different name from their own. Their shop was in Bath Street. My family lived in Midvale Road from 1928 to the late 60s. There were a number of Jewish people living in the district but most of them left the Island before the German Occupation. The Kleinsteins rented one of the big houses around Midvale Road.

Many people rented out houses and rooms, with no records kept. These people took a very great risk to let rooms to any Jewish people because the Germans ordered every house holder to keep a list of names, nationality, place of birth, etc, pinned behind the front door of every house in Jersey. We were raided a few times and the first thing the German police looked at was the inventory behind the front door.

One night they closed off Midvale Road at both ends and everyone had to get out of bed and show their identity cards and papers to a German officer or NCO. However, to get back to the Kleinsteins, the Germans often placed a notice in the Evening Post for people they wanted or could not find. Walter de Gruchy-Le Brocq Chief reporter of the Evening Post stated that one day in March 1941 a report came into the German office at the Evening Post in Bath Street. The German Secret Field Police (Geheime Feldpolizei) were looking for a Jewish couple who had not registered with the Jersey Aliens Office in October 1940. One of the Evening post staff knew enough German to understand what he had overheard. The Germans were going to place a wanted notice in the Evening Post, asking people not to give shelter or help to a Jewish couple and to report to the Germans or local police if they knew their whereabouts.

The printing blocks were set out but before the notice could be printed a report came in stating that a boat was missing from Gorey harbour and wreckage and two bodies had been washed up on the south coast. The couple had evidently wanted to escape from Jersey and they had drowned on the South coast of Jersey. Ex-honourary police with whom I was speaking years ago did confirm the incident and could remember the year as being 1941 but not the date. The Germans took the two bodies away but left our local police in the dark - which was not so unusual for those Occupation days.

The mysteries of the German Occupation are many - but what happened to the bodies of the Kleinsteins.? Were they buried in an unknown isolated spot in Jersey? Or did the Germans bury them secretly at the Strangers Cemetery at Westmount? They had done this before, as the following evidence will bear out.

There are reports in the Parish of St Helier cemetery files from Mr Pallot, the St Helier cemetery superintendent, stating the fact that the Germans carried out at night secret burials in the Strangers Cemetery.   One report (I have copies of this) goes on to state that when the cemetery staff had been testing the ground for future burials, the rods had come in contact with coffins, sometimes one coffin on top of anther. These burials are not marked on any German or St Helier parish cemetery plans. The report goes on to state that often the locked cemetery gate had been smashed open late at night. One report ends with Mr Pallot's remark "that we are not the only ones carrying out burials in the Strangers Cemetery."

One Jewish lady married an English/Jersey bus driver the day before the Germans occupied Jersey. They rented a room from my mother in Midvale Road. It was I that took them in their wedding breakfast in bed. Years ago I saw this lady in town nearly every week but have not seen her for about two years. She was not arrested or deported to Germany - one of the lucky ones who kept her head down. Our States of Jersey (Royal Court) did pass the Anti-Jewish laws ordered by the Germans, but thank God our local States with the Bailiff as head left the Jews alone, and to their credit did not have a witch hunt against the the Island's Jewish residents.

Two other Jewish ladies that I knew very well, Lucy René Mathilde Schwob, born at Nantes, France, 25 October 1894, and her step sister Suzanne Alberte Eugenie Malherbe, Born at Nantes France 19 July 1892. Lucy was born and brought up as a Jew. Suzanne had a very old Norman name. She was not born as a Jew, but was brought up in the Jewish faith. Her father died when she was a baby. A few years later her mother married Maurice René Schwob. As very young ladies they spent many happy holidays in Jersey. Both were members of a wealthy publishing family from Nantes. Both lived in Jersey since the 1930s at La Rocquaise St Brelade's Bay. It was their home till Lucy died in 1954. They were both arrested by the German Secret Field Police 25 July 1944 and had to face a German Military Court, being sentenced to six years imprisonment and sentenced to death in November 1944 for acts against the German Forces, sabotage, and for distributing anti-Nazi news sheets. They were never downhearted, asking the German Court which sentence did they have to serve first.

As soon as he heard the news of the death sentence for these very brave ladies, the Bailiff of Jersey, Alexander Coutanche, wrote to the Kommandant asking and appealing for mercy on behalf of Lucy and Suzanne. The Bailiff's plea was successful. Both ladies were reprieved in February 1945. Lucky for them and us that the Island was cut off from France, otherwise they would have been sent to the German concentration camps.

They were for a few months in the next cell to mine. That is how we became such good friends. I am pleased that they wrote about me in the note books they left that are now at the Jersey archives. The other cell next to mine was occupied by a young German soldier who had been sentenced to death. A few cells away was his girl friend, Alice, also sentenced to death. Again the Jersey Bailiff saved her life. This was our Jersey Bailiff at his best.

Lucy died in Jersey, 8 December 1954. Suzanne moved to Beaumont, Jersey where she died on 19 February 1972. The ashes of Lucy and Suzanne are buried at St Brelade's cemetery, St Brelade's Bay. The German prison guards had great respect for these two French-Jewish ladies. Lucy and Suzanne will always be part of my life. They gave us courage and hope in those dark days. They also spoke to the young German soldier to give him hope just before the Germans took him out one morning, 27 April 1945 to be shot in the Parade Ground at Fort Regent. For a 17 year old as I was, it was death row with the next cells holding 5 people waiting for the day they also would be taken out and executed,

JEWISH REFUGEE CHILDREN SENT TO ENGLAND 1938-1939

In November 1938 came Kristallnacht (the night of broken glass) a dreadful night, when all over Germany Jewish property was attacked, the windows of Jewish shops were smashed and many Jews were arrested and imprisoned. A few weeks later, the British

Government gave their consent to refugee organisations to bring over Jewish children to England. The Germans allowed the children to leave Germany but without their parents. The route was by train to Holland then by boat to Harwich, England. Between November 1938 and August 1939 the Refugee Children Movement brought to England over 10,000 children and over 8,000 of these were Jewish children.

I wonder how many people in Jersey remember the following. The refugee children's movement with the blessing of the British government asked if the Island of Jersey authorities could they find homes/accommodation for 14 Jewish refugee children in the Island. After a lot of fuss and ballyhoo the children never came to Jersey. Some high up people who should have known better stated we did not want these foreign children in the Island, because, etc, etc.

I do remember reading in the JEP or the Jersey Morning News in 1938 or 1939 about bringing these little children to Jersey. It could have been under letters, or even in a States debate. I have never forgotten about this great shame to our Island that was brought about by some bigoted Jerseymen. And most of these children's parents were killed in German concentration camps.

My dear friend, Lucy Schwob who was Jewish, and in the next cell to mine (under sentence of death). She asked me one day if I knew about the 14 refugee children that were being sent to Jersey 1938-1939. She said it had upset her badly that they did not come. She and her sister were not married and would have taken two of the children. I told dear Lucy that I did remember and even being only 12 years old at the time it really upset me that some of our people did not want to help these little refugees. Lucy, the dear lady, took my hands and kissed me on the cheek and as she returned to her cell a tear ran down her face. I sometimes sit by the grave of the two sisters at St Brelade's. After all, friendship and life does not end at death or the grave. Lucy and her sister, Suzanne were two very brave ladies who many of the ex-political prisoners of the German prison in Jersey will never forget.

ORDERS AGAINST THE JEWS

On 12 March 1941, the Feldkommandant instructed the Bailiff of Jersey to include the registration cards of the Jews with the registration files for the Aliens, and ordered that the filing records of all Jewish persons were to be specially marked and this marking was to consist of a large red "J" in a conspicuous position. The cards were also to have a cross strip in red.

The Bailiff passed the instruction to Clifford Orange. On 17 March 1941 Orange confirmed that the cards had been marked, and enclosed a list detailing the nationalities of the 12 registered Jews. On 21 March 1941, the lists were passed on the the Germans confirming that the Feldkommandant's orders had been carried out.

YAD VASHEM   יד ושם

The Holocaust Martyrs' and Heroes' Remembrance Authority רשות הזיכרון לשואה ולגבורה

Jerusalem, 9 February 1995

Mr. Joshph Miere, Curator
The Dower House
Parkinson Drive
Millbrook
St Lawrence
Jersey
Channel - Islands
JE3 - 1JX

Dear Mr. Miere,

Thank you for your letter of 4/11/94 requesting information about the fate of The Jews in Channel-Islands. We apologize for the delay in replying.

Enclosed please find xerox-copies of the following documents: NG-3349 (the Neremberg Evidence); 09/205.

We found only a few names that were mentioned in your letter.

We hope this material will be usefull for you.

We wish you success in your project.

Sincerely yours,

Judith Kleiman
Reference Division
Archives

<u>**COPY**</u>

VAUVERT MANOR,

VAUVERT ROAL,

ST. PETER PORT.

May 5th, 1941.

A.J. Roussel Esq.,
Greffe,
Royal Court.

Sir,

I beg to acknowledge with thanks your
communication of May 2nd and wish to state that
the information given you in my letter of Dec.
2nd, 1940, is absolutely correct.

I am, Sir,

Yours faithfully,

VIOLET BLAND WOOLNOUGH

31st October 40

Pr/2/3

Sir,

<u>- Julia BRICHTA -</u>

I beg to inform you that the above named
woman has been seen. She was born on 28/11/95 at Mako, Hungary,
and states that her parents are now dead. She is at present
employed as a cook by the German Authorities at " The Thatched
House ", Rue de Putron. She states that she is of the Protestant
religion, attending Church of England. A further perusal of
her Passport will not reveal whether she is of pure aryan birth.
She was not asked the direct question.

I am,

Sir,

Your obedient servant,

W R Sculpher

Inspector.

Dr. Brosch,
Feldkommandantur,
Grange Lodge.

25. November 1940.

The Bailiff,
 Royal Court House,
  Guernsey.

Sehr geehrter Herr,

    <u>Staatsangehoerigkeit der Juden.</u>

 Ich beehre mich, Ihnen mitzuteilen, dass die in dem Bailiv
von Guernsey wohnenden Juden den folgenden Staatsangehoerigkeit
gehoeren:

 Britisch: DUQUEMIN, Elizabeth geb. Fink, Cobo Post Offic
      BROUARD, Elda geb. Bauer, 109, Victoria Road.

 Deutsch: STEINER, Theresie, Castel Hospital.
      SPITZ, Auguste, Castel Hospital.

 Czeche: WRANOWSKY, Annie, Clos de Ville, Sark.

 Es gibt keine Judische Staatsangehoerigen, die das Bailiwi
von Guernsey bewohnen.

      Hochachtungsvoll,

       W.R.Sculpher,

       Inspektor.

STATES OF GUERNSEY COMMITTEE FOR
CONTROL OF ESSENTIAL COMMODITIES.

LADIES COLLEGE,

GUERNSEY.

3. Mai 1941.

The Bailiff of Guernsey,
        Court House,
            GUERNSEY.

Sehr geehrter Herr,

    Auf Ihr Schreiben vom 2. d.M. beehre ich, Ihnen
mitzuteilen, dass die von Mrs. Middlevick zurueckgelassenen
Waren wie angewiesen verkauft worden sind.

                    Hochachtungsvoll,

                        P. DE PUTRON,

                            Custodian,
                        Business & Industry.

LAINÉ, SIR ABRAHAM JAMES, K.C.I.E. (1876–
1948). *A distinguished Guernseyman of principle
and honour — and a passive resister of the highest
order.* Born on 26 August 1876 to Rachel (*née*
Mahy), the wife of Abraham Lainé, Abraham *fils*
was educated at Elizabeth College from 1889 to
1895, whence he went up to Oxford (Pembroke),
winning a Goldsmiths' Exhibition in 1896 and
gaining honours in Moderations in 1899.

    On coming down from the University Lainé
entered the Indian Civil Service with his appointment as Assistant Magistrate and Collector in
Bengal in 1900, four years later being transferred
thence to Assam with the rank of District Commissioner. A steady climb up the ladder of ad-
vancement saw him Assistant Commissioner in
1912, Deputy Commissioner in 1915 and Second

Secretary to the Government of Assam in 1922. In the same year he became a member of Assam's Legislative Council, remaining as such until 1930 when he was promoted to the grade of Chief Secretary to the Government of Assam, made a Companion of the Order of the Indian Empire, and appointed a Member of the Assam Executive Council. This membership he retained until 1935 when he was made a Knight Commander of the Most Eminent Order of the Indian Empire and became Acting Governor of Assam. He did not, however, retain this post for very long as he retired later the same year, being by them 59 years of age.

Returning to Guernsey, Sir Abraham was elected a Jurat of the Royal Court in 1938, becoming also President of the States Ancient Monuments Committee. In the same year he was appointed President of the Essential Commodities Committee on its formation as the war clouds gathered. Two years later, as enemy occupation loomed, Sir Ambrose Sherwill (q.v.) chose him as Vice-President of the Controlling Committee and also its member responsible for food supplies. His wisdom and wide experience proved invaluable in both capacities. The Germans regarded him as a man to be reckoned with and on two notable occasions he showed that no fear of the occupying power would deter him if he felt that a vital principle was at stake.

The first of these occasions is recounted by Sir Ambrose Sherwill in his unpublished memoirs. On 23 October 1940, the Royal Court registered the German Military Administration's anti-Jewish measures, nearly all Jurats consenting thereto in the mistaken belief that no Jewish persons were left in the Bailiwick. One voice, however, spoke out in the name of humanity and decency. Sir Ambrose wrote, 'The honour of refusing to concur in its registration fell to Sir Abraham Lainé who, when called on as a Jurat to vote on the matter, openly and categorically refused his assent and stated his grave objections to such a measure. This courageous act of his should never be forgotten.'

The second occasion arose when Sir Abraham, as President of the Essential Commodities Committee, protested vehemently against the instructions emanating from the Feldkommandantur that the whores in the German Army brothels should be given extra rations, regarding such a requirement as rank injustice. Although overruled, Sir Abraham had nevertheless, once again, made a stand in the name of fair play and civilised standards of conduct. Sir Abraham's home of Le Gardinet in the Castel having been requisitioned by the Germans, he moved to 'Thistlewood', Choisi, St Peter-Port, remaining there after the Liberation. Here this Guernseyman of mettle and nobility of spirit died on 22 February 1948.

FÉDÉRATION NATIONALE DÉPORTÉS INTERNÉS RÉSISTANTS PATRIOTES

NANTERRE, le ___10 th of September 1970

SECTION DE NANTERRE
Jumelée avec la SECTION V.V.N. de RECKLINGHAUSEN
(R. F. A.)

PERMANENCE
6 bis, Rue de la Mairie,
le Dimanche de 10 h. à 12 h.

Please answer to :

Mr. Pomar Pascal
4 impasse des Abeilles
92 – NANTERRE

France

Conseil d'Administration du
"GERMAN HOSPITAL"

DAISY HILL REAL ESTATES LTD.,
1 SOMERSET PLACE,
ST. HELIER,

JERSEY C.I.

Dear Sirs,

During my stay in Jersey in August, I had an opportunity of visiting the "German Hospital".

I wish to compliment you on your way of bringing many tourists to understand what life was like in these Islands during the German occupation and what they did.

But, in the history of slavery praticed by the Nazis, there are omissions because you mention only Russians in the commentaries and the many photos on the walls of the tunnel.

Now, I am in a good position to assure you that the first deportees to work on this site were Spanish Republicans, also a group of Polish, Czecho-Slovak and Alsatian Jews arrested in the Toulouse area.

These deportees imprisoned in Fort Regent, which the Germans called "Lager Ehrembrestein" were transferred by lorry and worked from 4.00. a.m. to 7.00. p.m., so it was they who opened the first galleries.

When the Russians arrived at the end of 1942, the work had progressed well. It is true that many Russians were employed in these tunnels and in inhuman conditions, which were the same for us all, but the first victims were Spanish and Jews (French, Polish, etc...)

So, in respect to all these victims and to history, it is indispensable that Spanish and Jews should be mentioned in the comments and titles on the walls of the tunnel.

Condt.......

/Condt........

     I hope you will arrange that something is done so that history will be respected.

     I thank you very much in anticipation and would be grateful if you will let me know the result of this request.

          Very Respectfully Yours,

          P. POMAR.

Ancien Déporté Politique
Member of the Jersey International
   Anti-Nazi Committee 1942 - 1945
Ex-Interné au FORT REGENT 1941.43.
Ex-Interné au Camp n° 2 d'ALDERNEY 1943.44.

Libéré le 9 Mai,1945 à JERSEY.

A Jewish prison pal of Jimmy Pomar was Chay Ulrich, born 1921 at Colmar Alsace. Both imprisoned at Fort Regent in 1941 Jimmy stated that Chay Ukrich's grandfather was a Rabbi. (Jimmy found no trace of family in Colmar).

In 1938-39 the Germans pushed the Jews from Baden Germany across the French border. The French authorities simply incarcerated them in Gurs (Pyrenées).Eventually, the Germans gained control over these camps, and the inmates were deported to camps in Germany and Poland.

After the fall of France in 1940, the French rounded up over 100,000 so called hostile aliens, mostly Jews, and crowded them into transit camps. Some 22,000 were sent to Gurs (Pyrenées) others were sent to Watten, Vidauban (Var), Recebedou (Haute-Garonne), Rieucros (Ariège) and the rest to Toulouse.

Between 12th and 22nd November 1940, 66,000 inhabitants of Lorraine and 120,000 Alsatians were expelled by the Germans to the Free Zone of France (among them many Jewish families). This is how the Alsatian Jews came to be in the Toulouse area of France.

Liberation time in Jersey, May 1945, the slave workers had all been shipped to St Malo May-June 1944, before the Island was cut off from France. All that remained in Jersey were some Spanish, French, etc forced labour (not slaves) and the only Russians left in Jersey were those on the run, living at farms, etc.

Note: We have the States of Jersey and German lists of OT Spanish, French etc workers who were in Jersey in 1945. Their names are on the red cross lists. They all received Red Cross parcels the same as local people.

Jewish slave labour was never brought to Jersey

● **From Ward Rutherford.**

A NEWS story published in the JEP of 30 July has recently been sent to me.

A statement which cannot go unchallenged is in the penultimate paragraph: 'Apart from Jews resident in the Channel Islands at the start of the Occupation, a considerable number of Jews were transported to Jersey as slave labour, and helped in the construction of such buildings as the Underground Hospital'. While it is certainly against accepted professional journalistic usage to make assertions of this kind without sources, as they do not exist it is not surprising that they were not supplied.

The facts are, of course, that the Jews were not in general used as slave labour, except in a limited way in eastern Europe. For example, all Jews in German-occupied Poland were required to carry out forced and unpaid labour from 26 October 1939 (see, *inter alia*, Reitlinger, Gerald, The Final Solution;

Das Grosse Lexikon des Dritten Reiches, p289 *et seq*).

It might well have been better had they used Jews as slave labourers; since, terrible as the conditions they endured were, at least many thousands survived the war.

The Nazis had only one intention in regard to the Jews — their extermination. The efficient fulfilment of this required their concentration in a restricted area, not their dispersal on projects such as the building of underground hospitals in remote outposts of occupied Europe.

And concentration of the Jews of Europe was exactly what the Nazis did, moving Jewish communities from places as remote as the island of Rhodes in the Aegean to their slaughter camps in the east.

Had Jews been brought to work on German building projects, then like Jews everywhere else, they would have worn the yellow star of David. While most of us who were here during the Occupation saw very many slave workers; none of us ever saw any wearing the star of David. In any case, where had these Jews been brought from?

Lastly, since the labourers imported by the Germans were caught in the Island by the Allied invasion of France, they were still there at the Liberation. So what became of the Jewish element at that time?

So certain am I of my grounds that I am here and now prepared to offer £100 to anyone who can supply convincing evidence to support the contention that Jewish slave labour was ever brought to Jersey.

**18 Wellington Court,
Laine Close,
Brighton.**

Letters, which should be brief and to the point, are accepted for publication only on the understanding that they may be edited. They should be sent to the Editor, Jersey Evening Post, Five Oaks, St Saviour, JE4 8XQ. Fax 611622.

Jews were sent here

● From Joe Mière.

I MUST cross swords with my old school and German prison friend Ward Rutherford concerning Jewish slave labour in Jersey (JEP, 28 August).

My information comes first-hand from Pascal (Jimmy) Pomar, an ex-officer in the Spanish Republican Army, who was brought from St Malo by the Germans to Jersey in October 1941 as forced labour, and imprisoned in Lager Ehrembrestein (Fort Regent). Also Frank Font, another ex-officer in the Spanish Republican Army. They were both handed over by the Vichy French regime to the Germans.

Jimmy and Frank were both Spanish gentlemen, you could trust them with your life. In the dark days of the Occupation years Jimmy and Frank became friends with my family and myself and they both told us that some of the prisoners at Fort Regent were Jews (about 20 of them). The Germans had rounded these Jews up with the help of the Vichy French in the Toulouse area of France. Among them were Alsatian, Polish and Czecho-Slovak Jews.

They worked first at the German navy bases on the French coast, were then transported from St Malo to Jersey in 1941, and imprisoned at Fort Regent. Jimmy Pomar told us that these Jews worked on the first galleries at the German Military Underground Hospital alongside the Spanish forced labour.

By the end of 1942 these Jewish workers were replaced by the Russians, and one morning in November 1942 the small group of Jews were transported to St Malo and moved on a week later by rail to unknown parts of occupied France.

Jimmy Pomar tried many times after the war in 1945 to find out where this group of Jewish workers ended up. He thought that they ended their days in some German concentration camp.

Jimmy Pomar wrote two letters (one in English, the other French) to the director of the German Military Underground Hospital in September 1970, stating the fact that Jewish workers were brought to Jersey. These two letters were given to me by the director of the Underground Hospital, Mr E Wheeler, knowing Jimmy Pomar was a friend of mine, in case I needed them for future historical research of the German Occupation.

And how right Mr Wheeler was.

The Dower House,
La Folie Estate,
Millbrook, St Lawrence.

104

JERSEY EVENIN[G]

Occupation cover-up claim 'rubbish'

LOCAL historian Mr. Richard Mayne has described as "rubbish" some of the allegations concerning Jersey in an article on the German Occupation printed in yesterday's Observer vewspaper.

The article, by Solomon Steckoll, was based on a new book he has written about the concentration camp in Alderney.

Mr. Steckoll claims that there was a "cover-up" over many aspects of the Occupation.

In particular, he said, the fate of 22 Jews "deserves investigation". He was told that all the Jews had left the Island before the Occupation, but he claimed that he had evidence to show that there were Jews left during the Occupation and implied that the authorities, as in Guernsey, had given details of them to the Germans.

But Mr. Mayne, who has made a study of the Occupation, said this morning that this was rubbish and that there no Jews left in the Island. "He is just writing to try to cause a sensation," he said.

He also said that the article was wrong when it said that Jersey women engaged in prostitution with the Germans, although he admitted that Jersey girls obviously did go out with German soldiers.

The only prostitutes, however, were French women brought in by the Germans specifically for that purpose, Mr. Mayne said.

One of Mr. Steckoll's main allegations in his article was that there was "serious collaboration between Islanders and the German forces, and he said that this had been the subject of a cover-up.

Mr. Mayne replied that there were a large number of allegations against islanders after the war, but that a lot of them resulted from spite and jealousy and they could not be proved.

For the authorities to investigate them all would mean stirring up a hornet's nest, and would not have done any good, Mr. Mayne said.

But he admitted that if there had been detailed investigations of some of the complaints, then some people would certainly have gone to prison.

LETTERS

More about the years of Occupation

From Mr. Joe Mière.

IT WAS very interesting to read in the JEP on June 8 that Mr. R. Mayne says there were no Jews left in Jersey when the German forces arrived in the Island in 1940; we knew five Jews during the Occupation, three of British

nationality, one of French nationality, and one of South African nationality.

One left Jersey in August, 1945, for England (worked for States from 1941-45). One Jewish Lady lived at First Tower in 1943 (she was about 60). One Jewish lady married an English-man the week the Germans arrived; she is still alive, and in Jersey. (I saw her last year in town). One Jewish lady was in next cell to us in the German prison, St. Helier, in 1945. (The Germans did not know she was Jewish). She died in December 1954, Grave No 411, St. Brelade.

One Jewish gentleman was taken by the Germans to one of their concentration camps. (The Germans did not suspect that he was Jewish). He died in Jersey only a few years ago and his family still live in the Island.

So there were probably many more Jewish people in Jersey during the German Occupation we do not know about; it would

be a service to our history if anyone has information concern-ing other Jewish people who lived in Jersey from 1940-45.

As for the collaborators, the British Forces sent a batch of them to England (for their own safety) within two weeks of the Liberation of Jersey. Whatever happened to them in England would be interesting to know. There is one women and her daughter whom, we doubt, would ever show themselves again in this Island. The police saved them from being hanged; the crowd already had the rope around their necks when the police arrived and took them into protective custody.

From Mrs. Mary McCarthy.

WHY IS it that Richard Mayne is always asked by your paper for his views when some report is made about the German

Occupation? He can have his opinions, but others like myself who lived under the Occupation can have other views. What does he mean when he says (June 8) that a number of allegations were just spite and jealousy and that investigations would stir up a hornet's nest? At that time there were those who were quite open and notorious in their col-laboration. Why was it that the local banks honoured all their ill-earned German money? This was not so in other liberated countries.

My husband and I were just married. We wanted to go to England for our honeymoon but we were not allowed to leave the Island; yet those who were noto-rious left.

The war has been over for 40 years. Isn't it about time the truth were printed? Why were these blackguards allowed to en-joy their ill-gotten gains?

Château Clairval,
St. Saviour.
June 8, 1981.

86 Les Cinq Chênes,
Five Oaks,
June 8, 1981.

Jewish war file riddle

A CLAIM that a file relating to Jewish families in Jersey in the Occupation disappeared after it was given to the police has been denied.

Det-con Terry Underwood said no such file was returned to the police after the theft of wartime files from the Bailiff's Chambers two years ago.

The anonymous claim came from someone who said that he had seen the file while it was circulating among local dealers, but Det-con Underwood said that he did not remember a file of this kind among those handed in to the police.

He said: 'However, I did not have time to study the files closely. If there was a file on Jewish families, then it will be found when the files are thoroughly researched now that they are in the Island's archive.'

Det-con Underwood was aware of a file pertaining to the Krichefski family in Jersey and said that this had been put on sale locally and that a man, known only as being from southern Ireland, bought it before it could be retrieved.

■ In a letter to the editor to be published next week, Joe Mière, of St Lawrence, writes that the registration of the Jews took place on 23 and 24 October 1940 and that the lists were submitted to the German authorities on 10 November 1940.

MARIANNE GRUNFELD, AUGUSTE SPITZ AND THERESE STEINER MEMORIAL SERVICE 20 JUNE 1999

The words of Freddie Cohen, President of the Jersey Jewish congregation, rang out across the cemetery where a hundred or so mourners stood paying their respects.

'We are gathered here today to remember Marianne Grunfeld, Augusta Spitz and Thérèse Steiner who were deported from Guernsey in 1942 in the first deportation of Jews from occupied British soil to an extermination camp.

Some have said that over the last years we have placed too much stress on remembering our co-religionists who suffered during the Occupation. However, I make no apology Recognition of the fate of these Jewish ladies has been long overdue and today's dedication completes our task. If ever we needed proof of our duty in this respect, it came in a revisionist letter written only last month.

The author of this letter was Dr Wilhelm Casper, the German official who was responsible for the Nazi's Jewish policy in Jersey and Guernsey. He is now in his 90's and lives in Bonn. Dr Casper mendaciously claimed that in 1942 he had offered the Island's Jewish residents safe passage to England but Thérèse Steiner and Augusta Spitz had refused, fearing internment in Britain. Dr Casper fails to mention in his nonsensical account that his department was in fact responsible for their deportation from Guernsey, ultimately to their deaths at Auschwitz.

The true fate of Marianne, Augusta and Thérèse had remained untold for half a century. In 1980 Solomon Steckoll stumbled upon the first evidence but his findings were disparaged and as the source documents were still classified he could not prove his case. The response of one of the Island's leading historians was to publicly claim that there had been no Jewish residents in the Islands during the Occupation. It was Mr Joe Mière who publicly countered this pernicious claim. It was also Joe Mière who first ensured that the displays at the Underground Hospital included information on the Jewish slave labourers who had toiled there. When last year a vile letter was published claiming that no Jewish slave workers had been brought to Jersey it was Joe who set the record straight. I wish to take this opportunity of sincerely thanking Joe for all his efforts on our behalf.'

Freddie Cohen also made references to Marianne, Augusta and Thérèse to whom the memorial service had been dedicated. He described their experiences in the Channel Islands and their dreadful journeys locked into cattle trucks without water or sanitary facilities until they arrived at Auschwitz-Birkenau, to await death in the gas chambers. A very moving service indeed.

To the memory of

Marianne Grunfeld, born Katowice 1912.
Auguste Spitz, born Vienna 1901.
Therese Steiner, born Vienna 1916.

Jewish residents of Guernsey during the German Occupation,
Deported on 21 April 1942 to their deaths at Auschwitz-Birkenau.

Plaque at the Jewish West Mount Cemetery

MRS M. E. RICHARDSON AND ALBERT BEDANE

Mrs Mary Erica Richardson (née Algernon-Olvenich) born 7 December 1888, a Jewish lady, who with her husband lived at No 8 Overseas Flats, Dicq Road, St Saviour, Jersey. Mrs Mary Erica Richardson had not registered under the first anti-Jewish order of October 1940 as being Jewish. She was interviewed by the Germans at College House (The Feldkommandantur) and ordered for deportation from Jersey to a special camp in Germany.

She was allowed to go home and collect her jewels and valuables because she was told she was to be sent to a very nice special camp where she would be well looked after and would need her best things with her. She was escorted to her home under armed German guards to pack up her possessions. She however managed to divert the attention of her German guards and escaped to Albert Gustave Bedanes Clinic in Roseville Street where she was hidden in a secret cellar whenever the house was searched by the Germans. Albert Bedane hid Mrs Mary Richardson for over two years. She survived the remainder of the German Occupation without detection.

Immediately the Germans realised Mrs Mary Richardson was missing they instigated a search and ordered the Constable of St Helier to inform the eleven other parish Constables of her disappearance.

On 26 June 1943, Jersey's Attorney General, Charles Duret Aubin, wrote to the parish constables as follows ; I understand that you were recently informed by the Constable of St Helier, in compliance with an order of the Occupying Authorities, that a Mrs Mary Erica Richardson (née Algernon) was missing from her last registered address, 8 Overseas Flats, Dicq Road, St Saviour. I have now been requested to forward to you for your information and to assist you for the purposes of identification two copies of the photograph of Mrs Richardson which is attached to her registration papers.

Comment by Joe Mière, ex-prisoner. - see next page.

The letter written on 26 June by Jersey's Attorney General, Charles Duret Aubin, to the parish Constables of Jersey is definite proof that the parish Constables were being ordered in a roundabout way to find and report where she was living. And all this on behalf of the German authorities. If the parish Constables had found where Mrs Richardson was living they would have been forced to report back to the Attorney General, who in turn would report Mrs Richardson's whereabouts to the German authorities, as was the case in 1943 of Frederick William Page. When the Jersey Attorney General, received a St Saviour parish centenier report on Frederick Page he passed it to the German authorities resulting in Frederick Page being arrested by the German Secret Field Police and sent to a German penal prison in Germany, where he died of brutal treatment.

Mrs Mary Erica Richardson had committed no criminal act. Her only crime in the eyes of the Germans was that she was a Jew. How can anyone explain away this hunt by the local authorities for this 55 years old Jewish lady if this was not helping the German authorities and doing their dirty work for them?

Jersey Occupation Attorney General at wars end could claim the following

Extract from order for the protection of the occupying authority December 18 1942. (Registered by Act of the Royal Court dated 13 February 1943) Duties of local Law Officers (Paragraph 3)

1.   It shall be the duty of the local Law Officers to submit to the nearest German Military tribunal all information brought to their knowledge and all records and other documents relating to ....

2(a)   Offences against the German armed forces or the armed forces of an ally of Germany or against a member or an attendant thereof or against a German service or a member thereof;

(b)   Offences committed in buildings or in the places or in vessels used for the purposes of the Germans armed forces or the armed forces of an ally of Germany or of a German service;

(c)   Infractions of orders made in the occupied territory for the protecting of the German armed forces or for the purposes of the Occupation;

(d)   Offences charged against German and Italian nationals, including offences alleged to have been committed before the arrival of the German troops.

(3)   The German Military tribunal may refer the matter to the civil authorities where it considers that the matter does not merit the decision of a German Military tribunal.

The British counter intelligence M.1.19 in May 1945 was given a copy of this German Order by the Jersey Attorney General. He had to explain his actions in a written report to the British M.1.19 Officers. No further action was taken in this matter. There should have been an open public official inquiry. Three times the States of Jersey turned down any request for a full public inquiry on collaboration in Jersey, 1940-1945.

Albert Gustave Bedane

Born in France 1893. He served in the British Army 1917-1920. Masseur Physiotherapist. Hid and sheltered Francis Le Sueur who had escaped from an armed German escort. He also gave shelter to a number of escaped Russian slave workers. He also hid and gave shelter for over two years to a Jewish lady, Mrs Mary Erica Richardson. Albert Bedane hid all these people at his Clinic and home at 45 Roseville Street, St Helier, Jersey because they were wanted by the German Secret Field Police. Albert Bedane was presented with a gold watch by the Russian Government in 1965, in recognition of his efforts to save escaped Russian slave workers. On 4 January 2000, Yad Veshem announced their formal recognition of Albert Bedane as "righteous among the nations"- Israel's highest holocaust honour. Albert Gustave Bedane died in Jersey, 8 January 1980.

All the above data re Mary Richardson and Albert Bedane is extracted from the research work of Frederick Cohen who is a well respected historian, researcher and author. Before he researched work on the Jews in the Channel Islands, 1940-1945, we knew little of their Occupation history. Frederick Cohen's deep research has brought to light a part of our Occupation history that was very important but so sadly neglected by local historians.

For anyone researching this subject, I strongly recommend Frederick Cohen's book , "The Jews in the Channel Islands during the German Occupation 1940-1945."

AUSTRIAN UNTEROFFIZIER ALOIS PHILIPP KERN

Austrian soldier. Unteroffizier Alois Philipp Kern did not agree with the Nazi regime and was reported to the German Secret Field Police in Jersey. He was arrested for his anti-Nazi attitude and his criticism of the Nazi regime. He was tried by the German Military Troop Court in Jersey and was sentenced to death by the court on the 1st December 1942 and was executed by firing squad at 2pm on 17 December 1942 at La Moye Point, St Brelade, Jersey. He was buried the same day at the Strangers Cemetery at Westmount, St Helier, Jersey.

In 1980 his sister Madame Annemarie Ziegenfuss (née Kern) paid a visit to Jersey and passed on to us a photocopy of her brother's death certificate.

The death certificate was sent to his father and mother, Alois and Anna Kern on 8 March 1944. So the family had to wait over two years to learn of the fate of their soldier son.

Unteroffizier Alois Philipp Kern was born on 20 November 1917 at Klagenfurt-Karnten, Austria.

G1, G2

Sterbeurkunde

(Standesamt Wien-Döbling ------------ Nr. 176/44)

Der Unteroffizier Alois Philipp K e r n, Angestellter ---------------- -- evangelisch

wohnhaft Wien 19., Billrothstraße 47 --------- -,

ist am 17.Dezember 1942 gegen 14 Uhr ---- Minuten

in La Moye(Halbinsel Jersey) England verstorben.

Der Verstorbene war geboren am 20.November 1917

in Klagenfurt,Kärnten ------------------------

(Standesam evangelische Pfarre Klagenfurt,5/146/

Vater: Alois Kern,wohnhaft in Wien. ---------

---- -------------------------------------

Mutter: Anna Elise Kern,geborene Knoch,wohn-

haft in Wien. --------------------------------

Der Verstorbene war — nicht — verheiratet.----------------

Wien , den 8.März 1944

Der Standesbeamte
in Vertretung

Gebühr frei.

C 251, C 252 Sterbeurkunde (mit Elternangabe bezw. ohne Elternangabe).
Verlag für Standesamtswesen G. m. b. H. Berlin SW 61, Gitschiner Str. 109.
A. W. 2 Q/0293 Nachdruck verboten!

C 251 | C 252

Annemarie Ziegenfuss
Kirchmeyergasse 5, A 6
A - 1130 Wien
Tel. 02 22 / 82 31 46

Annemarie Ziegenfuss,geb. Kern,   4.Juni 1992.
Kirchmeyergasse 5, A 6
A 1130 Wien/Austria.

Mr. James E.McScowen
Curator of the German
Underground Hospital

Jersey.

Dear Curator,
      on 21th May 1992, towards midday, my friend Dr.Blanche Fischer and
I spoke with You about a hand-written sheet (apparently no longer in
existence), which was exhibited in a room when I visited the Underground
Hospital in 1980. This sheet of paper contained the names of German
military personnal who had died on Jersey. Among them, written in red
ink, were the names and dates of birth and death of those soldiers
who were "liquidated by execution or suicide". One of these entries
was of my brother "Unteroffizier" Alois Kern, geb. 20.11.1917, died on
17.12.1942. My brother, an Austrian, did not agree with the regime.

      In place of the above-mentioned hand-written sheet there is now
exhibited a typewritten register, among whose entries is included the
name of my brother, however with an incorrect date of death (17.2.1942).

      I would be most grateful if You would be so kind as to inquire
whether the original document is still in existence and, if so, whether
You could send me a photocopy of it. I enclose a photocopy of the death-
certificate relating to my brother.

      With many thanks in anticipation of Your help,

                        Yours sincerely,

                        Annemarie Ziegenfuss.

GERMAN CAR CRASH 26 AUGUST 1940

On 26 August 1940, I was cycling to work down Midvale Road about 1.30pm when a black and green Wolsey saloon car driven by a German officer passed me at a great speed. I was half way down the road when there was a loud noise like a crash. As I reached the bottom of the road I saw there the car that had passed me only moments before had crashed into a wall, the wall which made the corner of Val Plaisant and David Place. I stopped by the crashed car and saw the driver hanging half way out of the car door. Blood was running down his face from a head wound. The other officer who had ben in the other front seat seemed in a great daze, his door was open and he was partly out of the car.

I went to ride on thinking to myself "bloody Germans. Good job, that's two of the sods less." Then I thought "Germans or no Germans you cannot let them burn," because by then there was a strong smell of petrol, and smoke was coming from the smashed front of the car. The impact of the crash had opened up the bonnet and there was a good chance the car would catch fire and blow-up.

I half dragged and half carried the unconscious officer onto the pavement by the Deanery. He was a big blond man and very heavy. The other officer was already out of the car but in a state, with a cut above the eye. He did not know what was going on so I sat him down alongside the other German.

Then I ran into Dr Kennedy's house at Windsor Terrace which was close by. In the waiting room were about six children (the doctor had a large family). One of the older children called their father. He came along and I informed him briefly about the crash. He told his wife to phone for the ambulance, then grabbed his bag and we returned to the site of the crash.

Dr Kennedy attended to the badly injured officer while the other officer just sat there holding his head and moaned ceaselessly.

In the meantime an old chap had placed an old wet blanket over the smouldering car engine. The ambulance arrived and some German soldiers appeared from the direction of St Mark's Church. A small crowd had gathered to watch the goings on and a local police car pulled up, followed by more German soldiers. I cycled on to work and was told off by the works foreman for being late. I tried to explain to the foreman why I was so late for work but all he told me was 'you are giving me a load of old bull. Car crash my eye!'

About a week later Dr Kennedy paid us a visit at our house. He was a big man and he walked like John Wayne. He said to me: 'The Germans were looking for you my boy.' He saw my face drop and then said: No, you are not in trouble - but the other way round. The Germans have requested me to find you because they want to thank you in public for helping to save two German officers. I knew who you were but I wanted to know if it was all right to give them your name and address.'

I said to Dr Kennedy: 'Please do not give them my name or address because I have two brothers in the British Army trying to kill Germans while here is their young brother saving the German sods. I would die of shame.' 'Right, my boy, I did not think you wanted them to know who you were. trust me, I will not let you down. By the way, the two officers are recovering well' Then with a big smile and firm handshake, Dr Kennedy was off down the road with that John Wayne walk of his. I would love to find the German crash report. One day perhaps?

A MEETING WITH BARON MAX VON AUFSESS

This German officer was head of Civil Affairs at College House, Jersey and he comes into this story, as we shall see.

In 1941 we, Herbert (Curly) Dimond and myself, were sent from our works to the Elfine Hotel at Gorey Pier to dismantle and remove all the old power plant battery cell plates. A Mr Thomas from Gorey who worked for the Germans was there with his lorry parked outside the hotel to cart away all the old scrap metal.

The Germans were taking over the empty hotel for their troops. We started to cart away the plates from the plant room which was at the back of the Hotel through a very narrow passage (its still there) leading to the roadway. We had to wear gloves because there was still acid dripping from the plates, and we had to watch that the acid did not get onto our boots or overalls.

On one trip I was half way down the long narrow passage when a German officer started to come in the passage from the roadway. He told me to go back so that he could pass up the passageway without the plates that were still dripping acid splashing his very highly polished boots. The plates were very heavy, so I did not feel like retreating back up the passage. I told him to pass me and I did try not to let the wet plates touch his boots but my hand slipped and one of the plates did touch his boots. He went mad, and like all the so-called master race, he started to shout in English, but mostly German.

Curly came along (his mother was German so he spoke German like a native). He tried to calm the officer down who was still shouting and laying down the law to me. Curly translated what the officer was going on about. He told me that he would have me arrested the next time I caused any trouble and if his high boots were damaged I would have to pay for a new pair, and off he went.

Curly told me later after he had spoken to some other German soldiers that were hanging around the hotel, that the officer was Baron von Aufsess from College house. I was only just over 15 years old at this date and thought what a bully this Baron was, and made a note in my mind to remember his face and keep out of his way.

The next time I saw this German baron was in January 1944 we were up Westmount and in passing helped an old couple to cut a branch off a pine tree. A German staff car pulled up and out came two officers, one of them was the German Baron von Aufsess. We made a run for it up towards the old football field. As we looked back we saw the Baron was taking the old couple's identity cards away from them.

The Baron wrote his Occupation diary and published it in 1985. The diary starts in August 1944 when at this date the Germans were on the way out. I did write to him but he never had the decency to reply. I wrote again asking him to publish his diary from 1939 when the Germans were on top. Again no reply. I think he would not dare publish a diary from 1939 because, like a lot of top German officers, they were all for their beloved Führer in those days when he was winning the war. But as the end was in sight, they changed horses. You read their diaries and memoirs since the wars end and they write as if they were on our side and against Hitler. Well, if that is the case, who the hell were our people fighting against? Give me every time a German who states that he was in those days a Nazi. At least you know where you stand.

These German Occupation officers blame old Hitler, the Gestapo and the SS but there was no Gestapo or SS in Jersey in the Occupation years. It was the OT and German forces in Jersey 1940-1945 who were to blame for the brutal treatment of the slaves brought over to Jersey to work. The German officers saw the treatment dished out to the slave workers, and they just looked the other way. They did nothing to help these poor people. Matter of fact, Baron von Aufsess or any of the other German officers who write about the Occupation of Jersey never ever mention the slave labour.

To give him his due, the Bailiff of Jersey did complain to von Schmettow, the German Kommandant, about the treatment of the slave workers. But von Schmettow did nothing about it. That proves beyond doubt that he would not go against the Nazi party or his Führer.

R. A. F. PILOT

At 7.30am on 12 April 1941, Thomas W. Brouard, of Les Bordes, St Saviour, Guernsey, telephoned the Guernsey police station and informed the duty sergeant that he had a British airman at his house. 'He came here about 1am, I did not go out on account of the curfew, and phoned you as soon as I could this morning.'

23 year old Flight Sergeant Robert Taylor Glen Sterling had been on night patrol in a Hawker Hurricane when he ran out of fuel. He abandoned his plane which he believed crashed into the sea some distance from land and he parachuted down on to Lihou Island. He then made his way across the causeway and walked along the road until he found Mr Brouard's house. After receiving Mr Brouard's telephone call, Sergeant Le Lievre went to Mon Plaisir, St Jacques and collected a German Officer and two NCOs (Comment: the police did not waste any time informing the Germans, did they ?)

Together they drove to St Saviours where the Germans arrested Flight Sergeant Sterling. In the meantime PC 13 Harry Dyson had managed to arrive at the Brouard Cottage some time before the official party. Whilst he waited he arranged with Robert Sterling that he would be a link between the Constable and his wife who had been evacuated to England in 1940. As soon as he was in a POW camp, Sterling contacted Harry Dyson who wrote back. Then a letter went from Sterling to Dyson's wife in England who replied and that was passed on to Dyson. This system lasted for the rest of the Occupation. After the war both men and their families became firm friends.

FRANZEPH JOSEF LOSCH, GUERNSEY 16 JUNE 1943

The Germans did not tolerate any acts of sabotage against their Occupation forces. We do not think that many people know or remember a young Organisation Todt worker who was arrested by the German Secret Field Police in May 1943 for acts of sabotage against the German Occupation forces in Guernsey. The young OT worker, Franzeph Josef Losch, was arrested and deported to a French prison at St Malo, but within the month he was brought back to Guernsey to face a German Military court.

He was sentenced to death and was executed by firing squad at 7am on the morning of 16 June 1943 at Fort George, Guernsey.

Some people state that he and two other OT workers were transmitting messages to England and were caught red handed but so far there is no sound proof or any documents or records detailing their acts of sabotage.

JOHN DE LA HAYE SAVED USA PILOT

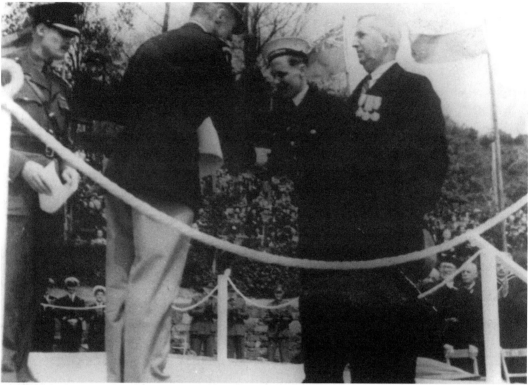

John de la Haye receiving The American Medal of Freedom from Colonel Anthony Drexel Biddle (American Army)

One Sunday afternoon in January 1945, young John de la Haye heard a plane going over his family home at St Brelade's Bay. He and other children ran out and saw that the Germans were shooting at it. They saw the plane going down and crashing on the top of Beauport. The pilot, Lt Kelly Moutray, had baled out and had landed in the sea in St Brelade's Bay. John de la Haye and a friend got hold of a paddle float that had been kept hidden by John's uncle, Pop Steel. They ran down the beach with it and John paddled out to the airman who was floating in the water. He then towed the American pilot to a rock that was getting uncovered as the tide was going down and dragged him onto it.

It was then that John saw that the pilot had bullet holes all down his leg. John then spotted the lifeboat coming out round Noirmont Point. He told the American pilot to stay where he was and wait for the lifeboat. John's float was broken so he swam from the rock to a spot facing Jesse Boot's Tomb.

The Germans came down to the rocks where he had landed and took him up the shore because it was full of mines. There they told him that he was going to prison.

John's father stopped the ambulance that John was in and said 'That's my son in there take him home.' The American pilot was taken to hospital and later transferred to France as a POW.

On 9 May 1946, John received the American medal of Freedom from Colonel Anthony Drexel Biddle of the American Army, the presentation being in the Peoples Park in St Helier, Jersey. After the war the American pilot, Lt Kelly Moutray, contacted John de la Haye and thanked him for saving his life.

John ran a pub in Plymouth for over 26 years. He returned to Jersey and ran Le Relais pub in St Ouen's Bay for a number of years. John de la Haye's medals and certificates are now on display in the Joe Mière collection at the German Military Underground Hospital museum, (now the Jersey War Tunnels), St Lawrence, Jersey.

MRS EMILY KIBBLE, MR KIBBLE, MR RENE BESSIN, GUERNSEY, 1944

A 45 year old Lancashire lady living in Guernsey outwitted the German Geheime Feldpolizei (German Secret Field Police) in 1944. She remained in hiding for over three months. Mrs Emily Kibble, living at Mount Durand, St Peter Port, Guernsey, evaded capture with the help of another Guernsey resident. She used an ingenious suicide plan to save herself from the German police.

On 30 June 1944, German Police, tipped off by an anonymous letter, searched her home. They found a radio and sentenced her husband to 9 months imprisonment. He was released in December 1944. Two days later he broke into a German food store at Granville House, Mount Durand, taking about 400 tins of foodstuffs. Unfortunately, he was caught and again arrested and sentenced by a German Military court to two years imprisonment.

The Feldgendarmarie searched the couple's home and took away all the food they had in the house. They arrested Mrs Kibble and sentenced her to three months imprisonment for receiving stolen goods. She was told to report at the prison by 5pm on 12 February, 1945.

Then she hit on a plan with a friend to defy the German police. She requested the Germans for a week's reprieve before going to prison - which was granted. The friend was Mr René Bessin of Petit Bot. Together they attempted a suicide ruse to fool the Germans.

On 19 February she was due to report to the prison but instead she went to the Southview Hotel, the home of her friend Mr René Bessin. That evening he took the clothes she had been wearing and left them on rocks near a German guardhouse between Albecq and Cobo, hoping that when the garments were found the Germans would believe she had downed.

The next morning the whole Island thought she had committed suicide, but in fact, she was hidden away at Petit Bot. She shared Mr Bessin's rations and his Red Cross parcel. She was confined to the house but could take a little exercise occasionally in the back yard. She had a narrow escape from being caught one day in May. A Guernsey girl who had previously worked at the Hotel informed the Germans that she thought she knew the whereabouts of Mrs Kibble and that she was wanted by the German Military Police.

The Hotel was searched, not by the Germans but by a Guernsey policemen. René Bessin asked him if he had a search warrant. The policeman replied 'No but I know that you are hiding the woman.' 'Are you British?' asked Mr Bessin. 'Yes, I am British' answered the policeman. 'Then act like a British person,' Mr Bessin told him 'Or get out.'

Mrs Kibble came out of hiding when Liberation Day came. She paid tribute to the spirit and help René Bessin gave her, a true friend in every way. At one time, he too suffered at the hands of the Germans. He had served in the French Army, and on discharge, returned to Guernsey. In the early days of the German Occupation, through an anonymous letter to the German police, he was arrested and sentenced to 9 months in a German penal prison in France where he had a very rough time.

(Source of information for the above, The Star, Guernsey. John Goodwin; December 1999. Frank Falla, Guernsey January 1970.)

THE DENNIS LE CUIROT ESCAPE STORY

Dennis in 1944

Dennis in the RAF

Another unusual escape from Jersey is that of Dennis Le Cuirot. His story is very much like the escape story of Colleen Querée. What is so strange is that they were both on the same ship, the SS Minotaure, that sailed from Jersey on 4 July 1944. Yet neither of them knew that the other was on board the ship, or even knew one another. I don't think that even to this date that they have ever met.

About the end of June 1944, when the United States forces were well established on the Cherbourg Peninsula a large number of French subjects who had been working in Alderney for the Germans, plus a large number of slave workers from the concentration camps on Alderney were transported to Jersey en route to France because there was a possibility of Alderney being taken by the Allied forces. And with the French workers and slaves were those in Jersey awaiting transport to France, Dennis Le Cuirot got friendly with some of them. He ascertained that there was little or no check on their numbers or descriptions, and he decided that here was his chance to escape from Jersey to France.

He told his mother that the Germans had ordered him to report to College house on the evening of 3 July 1944. He said to her: 'They have got me at last.' He collected some small articles together with some money and went off. (After the war in a letter to his mother he explained that he had told her this so she would not know that he was trying to escape from Jersey and so she would not get into trouble with the German Police.

Carrying his small suitcase, Dennis calmly walked aboard the SS Minotaure right under the noses of the German harbour guards. And that evening, 4 July 1944, the ship carrying 500 men and women set sail for Granville, France. On the way the ship changed course, and in the early hours of the next day it was off the Island of Chausey when flares were seen. The flares were put up by a force of British MTBs as an order for the convoy to stop. The Germans refused to stop and tried to make a run for it. Then a fight started and in a short while the seven escort vessels were sunk by the MTBs and a torpedo hit the bow of the ship causing shell damage.

As the ship appeared likely to sink, Dennis took a dive overboard and was in the water for a quarter of an hour. By then, the ship being still afloat, Dennis decided to get back on board. After some time she started off again and was eventually towed into St Malo. Of the 500 people on board only 100 women and 75 men landed from the ship. They were all taken to a barracks in St Servan and kept under guard.

On 6 July 1944, Dennis with two Frenchmen decided to try and escape from the barracks. They climbed the barracks wall and got clear away. They heard that the Americans were near St Lo so the three decided to make their way there. On the way Dennis left the talking when they stopped to the two Frenchmen, as his English accent might have given them away. After three days the three escapees reached St Lo.

At St Lo, Dennis joined the United States 3rd Army as an interpreter. Between 1 and 13 August 1944 Dennis was back in Granville. He was then flown to England, where he learned that he would not be returning to the American Army. He applied for work through the labour exchange and was directed to the Ever Ready Company where he worked for a short time. He then joined the RAF.

The week Dennis escaped from Jersey, there were some rumours going around that he had been drowned for the news that the German convoy had been attacked soon got around although the Germans tried to keep the facts dark. And Dennis's mother, Mrs Le Cuirot was naturally very worried. She actually went to Silivertide, the notorious German Secret Police Headquarters (called in Jersey the Gestapo) and accused them of taking her son away to his death. But they denied all knowledge of his whereabouts, a denial which she did not believe but which, as it turned out, was quite genuine. The German Secret Field Police were as puzzled as she was as to his whereabouts. Hence the hue and cry. His photograph and his description were posted up at the St Helier police station by order of the German Police.

Dennis Le Cuirot now lives in Burton on Trent, England. His sister still lives in Jersey. We often stop and have a chat in town when we meet.

COLLEEN QUEREE - ESCAPE FROM JERSEY

The brave escapees from Jersey 1940-1945 have been well documented, and their stories of escape or attempted escape have been published in several books and by the JEP and other British newspapers. So there is no need for me to go over the same old ground but one of the most unusual escapes was that of Colleen Margaret Querée.

She was born on 1 April 1921, Trinity. In 1943 she left Jersey to work for the Germans in Alderney. In June 1944 she left Alderney to return to Jersey and lived at number one Parade Square, Cannon Street, St Helier. After having made friends with a couple of French girls, she made up her mind to escape from Jersey and get to France. One of the French girls, a Mademoiselle Jackie Andrea lent Colleen a French passport. It had belonged to Jackie's deceased sister. So with the dead French girl's passport she tried to board the German ship the SS Minotaure which was taking foreign workers to France. But it was not so easy as she thought to board the ship.

Colleen had great difficulty in passing the German harbour police who at first would not let her board another ship. But after a while she was able to convince them that she was French. The Germans were still doubtful but with the help of Jackie Andrea she was allowed to pass. On reaching the SS Minotaure she was asked for her Marsch Befehl (Marching order) and naturally she did not have one. But after a short argument she was allowed to board the ship.

So on the evening of 4 July 1944 the ship left Jersey at 10 pm. The weather was fair and the sea not too rough. The ship sailed with 500 men and women on board and the ship was escorted by seven other German vessels, bound for Granville, France. On the way the course was changed and in the early hours of the next day the ship with her seven escorting craft was off the Island of Chausey when flares were seen.

The people on the ship could not make out what they were but as we have already learned they had come from a force of British MTBs as an order for the German convoy to stop. The British MTBs circled around the German ships for quite a while. But they refused to stop and tried to make a run for it. The German escorts closed in on the SS Minotaure, apparently to protect her. Then the battle started - the Germans opened fire and the British MTBs responded. In a quarter of an hour four German escort vessels were sunk. A torpedo hit the SS Minotaur's bows and a hit aft of the ship. Another torpedo hit the ship causing 29 men and women to lose their lives. Several men and boys jumped overboard and most were left to drown. Help arrived from St Malo and she was towed into the harbour. When the British MTBs attacked the SS Minotaure the French girls who had helped Colleen to board the ship were ready to give her up to the Germans, because some of their friends had been killed by the attack by the British. They called Colleen a dirty tommy, and a filthy swine.

Before the attack the French had been quite friendly with her, and she had worked amongst them in Alderney. Her two French friends reported her to the Germans and they were chiefly responsible for her arrest. After arriving at St Malo, Colleen and all the other people still on board the ship were marched from the harbour to the soldier's home where everyone was sorted out and sent to different camps, until they could be returned to their own homes.

Colleen was sent to an OT camp at St Servan. After she was given some food and a drink, she was escorted by the German Military Police to Dinard. There she was cross-examined and as she had no ID papers whatsoever they shut her up in a room for four days. Each morning she was cross-examined then taken back and locked up in the empty room. One of the things she witnessed was the trial of a young Polish girl for espionage. The young Polish girl's trial lasted only a matter of four minutes, and then the poor girl was led away to face her death.

Colleen thought her time had also come. The next day she was taken by the Feldgendarmerie to the prison in Rennes. She was there for 21 days. And after the German Military had got in touch with Jersey they found out who she really was. On 21 July she was escorted back to Jersey. The German military police were at the harbour in St Helier and arrested her for espionage.

She was taken to the German harbour police's head-quarters. There she was identified by a German sailor who knew her. It was the sailor who saved her from imprisonment. From that day on she had to report to the German harbour office before and after she returned from work. Colleen's address in July 1945 was number 18 Gloucester Street, St Helier. I would like to know - did Margaret Querée get to England after all or did she run off with her German sailor friend ?

Platzkommandantur 1 St. Helier
xFeldkommandanturx515
Az. wi 17 allg. /Rth.
- Mil. Verw. Gr. -

O.U., den 6. Juli 1944

Betr.: Rationskarten.
Bezug: - . -

An das
Aliens-Office
hier

Es ist bekannt geworden, dass die Colleen Margaret QUEREE, geb.
1.4.21. nach ihrer Rückkehr aus Alderney wohnhaft: 50 Kensington Place,
die Insel verlassen hat. Die Rationskarten sind einzuziehen.

Für den Platzkommandanten:

M.V.Rat.

It has become known that Colleen Margaret QUEREE, born 1st April 1921,
after her return from Alderney, resident 50 Kensington Place, has left
the Island. The ration books are to be withdrawn.

DEAD BUT WOULD NOT LIE DOWN

On the evening of 4 June 1944, I arrived home at 25 Midvale Road, locked the door and entered the lower hall. I was about to climb the stairs when I was seized with a great pain on the right side. It was the same pain I had had for weeks but this pain seemed to burn and grew rapidly worse. I must have passed out because I did not remember anything more until my father found me laying at the bottom of the stairs at about 7am the next morning . He phoned for the ambulance and it arrived at the same time as our family doctor.

The doctor stated that I had an acute inflammation of the appendix and was to be operated on as soon as possible. Otherwise the appendix could burst open, and I could die. Mother would not let them take me to the General Hospital. She told the ambulance men to take me to the Limes Nursing Home in Green Street and she would phone them that we were on our way.

By the time we got there I was in a bad state. Dr Graham, a local GP and an ex-army surgeon, was called to the Limes. The Germans had taken over part of the nursing home for their officers. They had also taken over the lift in the east wing, so I had to be carried on a mattress to the operating theatre.

I did remember waking up and it seemed that I was floating on air. It was of course the kind nuns carrying me down to the operating theatre. But with their lovely smiling faces and the flowers alongside a statue of the Virgin Mary, and some one playing the organ in the little chapel, for one moment I thought I had died and was about to enter Heaven . Silly boy.

I did not remember anything until the early morning of 6 June 1944 (D Day) Something woke me up, I looked around the room and saw the old night nurse alongside my bed had fallen asleep on her chair. There were loud bangs and it seems that every German gun on the Island had fired. The Germans had opened fire on the huge American Air Force armada that was passing over the Island. These American aircraft were carrying American paratroopers and after passing over the French coast dropped them over Normandy.

My family later told me that on that morning Father Maré from St Thomas's Church came to the Limes and gave me the blessing and last rites of the church for a person that was at the point of death. Even the family undertaker had already been summoned. The doctors informed my father that they had done their best but I had died on the operating table. My mother and my two sisters were crying because they had lost their Joe.

As they approached the Limes main gate the two doctors were trying to comfort them with kind words. Then Sister Marie Louise rushed out and called the two doctors to one side. She informed them that as they were washing my body and preparing me for the undertaker's coffin my face twitched and my eyes opened.

The doctors quickly returned to my bedside and somehow got me breathing again. The family doctor told my father not to tell my mother that I was still alive, because, as he said, they sometimes come around for a very short time, then pass away. But I did recover. I was very weak and in great pain. But as the days went by I got stronger.

People were very kind. They brought me flowers, tinned food, sugar and even champagne. I did not know that I had so many good friends. They all came to visit me. My girl friend was one of the first to visit. She was so upset. Sister Marie Louise had to comfort her. She was a nice and good girl but like me she was very shy. The other boys and girls came to visit me and tease me.

Later I was taken home by ambulance but Joe was not going to be carried into his home, oh no! As I walked slowly up our front steps, half way up I slipped and, with weakness fell down the steps. Silly young fool. The fall opened up my operation stitches so the ambulance had to take me back to the Limes. Sister Marie Louise gave me a good old telling off. She was a wonderful nurse and a fine lady.

There was a reason why I lived, and when I look at my dear lovely Marie, our three children and our seven grand children, then I know why God spared me. What a lucky guy I am to have such a loving family and such a loving wife.

The Lighthouse Memorial on the New North Quay, St Helier to the 22 that never returned.

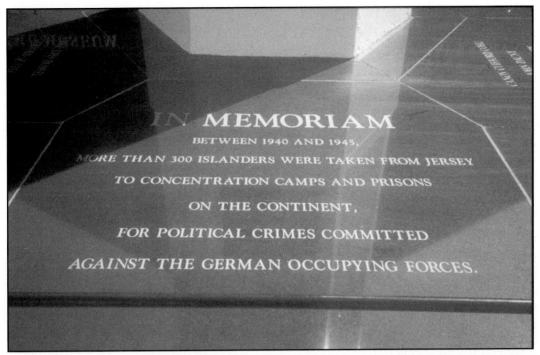

The total of Channel Islanders taken from all the Islands now stands at 621 due to new information found and dedicated research.

The total number of people from Jersey who never returned now stands at twenty two.

THE 22 THAT DID NOT RETURN

CANON CLIFFORD COHU

Arrested by the German Military police for spreading the BBC war news, March 1943. Sentenced to 18 months imprisonment. Deported to a German penal prison in France. Transferred to Naumburg-Saale, Germany, then to the concentration camp at Spergau where after brutal treatment he died in February 1945.

WALTER ALLAN STANLEY DAUNY

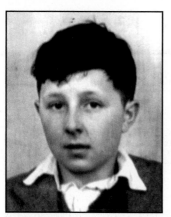

Seventeen year old Jersey youth arrested by the German police, 5 January 1944, for sabotage. Deported to St Lo, France, February 1944. Transferred to Villeneuve St Georges till 4 October 1944. He disappeared after the Germans withdrew from France. It is presumed he went missing in a German concentration camp in 1945. No trace since.

ARTHUR DIMMERY

Arrested by the GSFP for spreading the BBC war news. He was one of the eighteen people arrested in what was known as the St Saviour's Wireless Case. The trial took place at the Committee Room of the States of Jersey building, Royal Square. Arthur Dimmery was sentenced to three months imprisonment, 9 April 1943. He was deported to Fort d'Hauteville, France. Transferred to Neuengamme concentration camp, outside Hamburg. Arthur Dimmery was for unknown reasons transferred to Laufen internment camp in Germany. He died there on 4 April 1944, and is buried at Salzach Municipal Cemetery.

GEORGE JAMES FOX

Arrested by the German Military Police June 1943. Charged with serious military larceny. Sentenced to two years imprisonment. Deported to Fort d'Hauteville, France, 13 July 1943. Then to Saabrucken prison, then Frankfurt Preungesheim on 6 January 1944. In July 1944 he was transferred to the German penal prison at Naumburg-an-Saale. On 11 March 1945 George Fox died, the brutal treatment, and the appaling conditions and neglect in the prison, took their toll. George left behind in Jersey four children. He is buried in the British cemetery in Heerstrasse, Berlin.

MAURICE JAY GOULD AND PETER HASSALL

On 3 May 1997, a service was held at St Luke's Church and a short ceremony was held at the grave side in the war cemetery at the Howard Davis Park. At last Maurice's' last wish to Peter was "bring me back home". Peter's fifty year struggle to bring his old friends remains back to Jersey came true.

Peter often told me that there are many of our loyal people that are buried in foreign soil that should be bought home to Jersey to lay alongside Maurice's grave in our war cemetery . And I for one agree with Peter. Peter Hassall died, December 1998 in Canada. Peter's son Andrew who is a police officer in the Toronto police service keeps in touch.

Old school friends, Peter Hassall and me at the German Underground Hospital on 9th May 1997.

18 years old Maurice Gould, Peter Hassall and Dennis Audrain attempted to escape from Jersey to England by boat, Sunday 3 May 1942. A large wave threw the small boat against a rock and the boat capsized. Maurice and Peter tried to save their friend, Dennis, who could not swim and drowned. When Maurice and Peter reached the shore they were both arrested by the German Harbour Police who were waiting for them. The German Police had been informed that the three young men were going to attempt an escape that day.

Peter, an old friend of mine, told me that he knew who the person was who informed on them. That person was sitting in one of the German police cars when they were arrested. Maurice and Peter were taken to the German Harbour Police HQ at the Pomme d'Or Hotel. Next day they were imprisoned in the German prison in Gloucester Street.

The German Harbour Police had found their small suitcase when it was washed ashore. Inside it were maps and photographs of German fortifications in the Island. Maurice and Peter were both transported to Paris. They found themselves bundled into the Gestapo headquarters in the Rue des Saussais where they suffered brutal interrogations. Later they were imprisoned at Fresnes prison, just outside Paris. On 12 June 1942 they were sent to Trier, then to an SS special camp at Hinzert. Here the brutal treatment nearly killed Maurice.

On 24 July they were transferred to Wittlich penal prison in Germany. The brutal treatment at the SS camp at Hinzert took its toll and Maurice died on 1 October, 1943 in Peter's arms. His remains were buried in the cemetery at Wittlich but in 1972 they were moved and buried alongside Waffen SS men in a war cemetery in Germany.

Wittlich, den 2. Oktober 1943

Der Schlosserlehrling Moritz Gould, evangelisch,

wohnhaft unbekannt

ist am 1. Oktober 1943 um 10 Uhr 30 Minuten

in Wittlich Hindenburgstraße 32 verstorben.

D.. Verstorbene war geboren am 31 Mai 1924

in Leicester, England.

(Standesamt _____ Nr. _____)

Vater: Unbekannt.

Mutter: Unbekannt.

D.. Verstorbene war — nicht — verheiratet.

Eingetragen auf mündliche — schriftliche — Anzeige des Regierungs-
medizinalrates Doktor der Medizin de Saint-Paul
D.. Anzeigende in Wittlich

Vorgelesen, genehmigt und unterschrieben

Maurice's death certificate. Note lack of information regarding
cause of death, residence and parents. Truly a Night and Fog
document.

Der Standesbeamte

In Vertretung:

Ablichtung aus dem Sterbebuch (Sterberegister) des Standesamts
Wittlich-Stadt. Die Übereinstimmung mit dem Eintrag wird hiermit
beglaubigt. Die Ablichtung enthält - keinen - ——— Randvermerk(e).

Wittlich, den _____

Der Standesbeamte

135

Serious efforts were made to find a final resting place for Maurice in Jersey. Help came from the Jersey branch of the Royal British Legion whose chairman was Gerald Bisson. He played the major part of the operation to bring Maurice's remains back to Jersey. The States of Jersey voted funds.

LOUISA GOULD

Arrested by the German Secret Field Police 25 May 1944. Charged with failure to surrender a wireless receiving apparatus and giving assistance to an escaped Russian POW. She sheltered him for 20 months. Her brother, Harold Le Druillenec, her sister, Mrs Ivy Foster, her maid, Alice Gavey, Elenea Le Feuvre and Dora Hacquoil were all arrested with Louisa Gould. Her brother, Harold, was later sent to Neuengamme, Wilhelmshaven, Bergen and Belson concentration camps.

On 29 June 1944, Louisa Gould was deported with 18 other Jersey prisoners to Rennes prison in France. Louisa Gould was then sent on to Ravensbruck concentration camp, north of Berlin. She perished in a gas chamber at Ravensbruck concentration camp in February 1945. Her brother, Harold asked me that if ever I wrote about his sister, 'Please state, Joe, that she was murdered' and he was right, it was murder. There is a commemorative plaque that was unveiled in 1995 at La Fontaine, Millais, St Ouen's.

Harrold Le Druillenec

Mrs Ivy Foster

PETER BRUCE JOHNSON

Peter Bruce Johnson, an Australian deaf mute, was arrested by the German Secret Field Police for acts of sabotage. Deported to the prison at St Lo, France in 1944 and last seen at the Dora Mittelbau concentration camp in the Harz mountains. This was a very brutal German camp. There has been no trace of him since. People who have never heard of Peter Bruce Johnson were starting to doubt that he ever existed at all. Then an old friend of ours, Geoffrey Delauney, came forward and stated that Peter Bruce Johnson had been in the St Lo prison with him and other Jerseymen.

Peter Johnson had no family in Jersey but he had lived in Pier Road in St Helier. I knew Peter Johnson when he worked at Le Sueur's coal store in Hilgrove Street. One morning he came into our engineering works which was next door. He had caught his hand in the saw machine he was using to cut up logs. The saw blade took his left thumb right off. The poor chap could not even cry out. Our foreman tied a rag around Peter's hand and an ambulance took him to hospital.

So far we have never found any German documents with his name on. Even the Australian authorities have not got any documents relating to a Peter Bruce Johnson. One day we might be allowed to look at the old hospital records of the Occupation years - that is if they still exist. I never give up hope in trying to trace our local Occupation people. They must never be forgotten.

JAMES HOUILLEBECQ

Arrested by the German Secret Field Police and charged with being in possession of stolen German arms and ammunition. The entire family were arrested and imprisoned. He was deported August 1944, to Fresnes prison in France. James (Ginger) was then transferred to Neuengamme concentration camp outside Hamburg. After brutal treatment he died on 29 January 1945 at the camp. James was only 17 years old and was an old school pal of mine, so was his sister, Nancy, with whom I still keep in touch.

FRANK LE VILLIO

Arrested by the German Military Police June 1944 and charged with serious military larcery. Sentenced to three months imprisonment by the German troop court. Deported to Fresnes prison France. Then Belfort, then sent to Neuengamme concentration camp in Germany. Frank ended up in Belson concentration camp. Following his repatriation to England he was treated for TB. As time went on his health deteriorated beyond recovery. On 26 September 1946 he died in the hospital at Nottingham, England at the age of 21. Frank was brought up at Sacré Coeur orphanage in Jersey. As a young lad, Frank was always up to tricks, but he was kind and very generous and a good sport. He looked for but never received any parental love or guidance. His dear mother died when he was very young. His sisters always loved him and are still alive and living in Jersey and France.

WILLIAM MARSH

Arrested by the German Feldgendarmerie February 1944. He was charged with insulting the German forces, disturbing the working peace and disseminating anti-German information. He was sentenced to one year and three months imprisonment. He was deported to Frankfurt where he arrived 18 April 1944. Then on to the penal prison at Karlsruhe, Germany. He was transferred to Naumburg-am-Saale penal prison where he died of ill treatment 12 March 1945, aged 24.

EDWARD PETER MUELS

Edward Peter Muels born in St Helier, Jersey, 2 July 1912. The German Military Police on 2 January 1944 were searching the eastern parishes for a German soldier who had shot an under-officer called Alfred Koenig. The soldier managed to escape. He went to an inn at La Rocque and asked for a set of clothes which was refused by the innkeeper. The German Military Police were very angry with the licensee of the inn for not reporting the matter to them. The soldier was subsequently found. He was Gefreiter David Hoost. He was arrested and imprisoned in the German prison in Gloucester Street, St Helier.

When arrested the soldier was wearing a shirt and other clothes given to him by a Jersey family living at Sea Breeze, La Rocque, Grouville. According to Mrs Muels, the German soldier used to call at their house now and again and they gave him food. One day he called and told the Muels that he had shot his officer. The soldier asked for food and clothing and said he was going to commit suicide. The Muels refused to give him clothes at first as they did not want to get involved. But in the end they gave him some old overalls and a jacket which the family used for fishing. The soldier then went off. The family noted that the soldier still had his revolver with him.

That night the Germans searched the Muels house. They knew somehow that the said soldier used to visit the family. They found nothing so they left but they returned later because they had traced the clothes the soldier was wearing to the Muels family. The German Military Police arrested Mr Edward Peter Muels and he was imprisoned in the German prison in Gloucester Street. He was then sent before a German Military court and sentenced to a term of imprisonment.

On 2 June 1944, Edward Peter Muels and 20 other political prisoners were taken by lorries from the prison to St Helier harbour, and placed on board a German ship bound for St Malo. At St Malo prisoners were taken for a meal, then to a penal prison for the night. The next morning they were put on a train bound for a German concentration camp. There are two versions of how Edward Peter Muels died. First; the German prison train taking the prisoners to Germany was bombed by the RAF and many of the prisoners were injured or killed. Among the killed was Edward Muels.

Second; a Monsieur Florin of "Arosa" Canton of Grisons, Switzerland, who had been a fellow prisoner with Edward Muels stated in 1947 that he had heard after his release from the camp that Edward Peter Muels had died at the Liegenhelm concentration camp which was near Kassel in Germany. The Lagerführer at this camp was Otto Barnewad of the SS.

Edward Peter Muels had a son, David Muels. The Jersey Evening Post received an e-mail from him which is on the following pages and are still in touch. He lives in the North of England. David is a Jehova's Witness. We hope he can throw some light on the history of his father's death.

We have also kindly received information from a Mrs Ferguson from Spain. She is a niece of Edward Peter Muels. Also from Mrs René Morlay, of Jersey. Also information from Mrs Morlay's sister, Dorothy Burton and from Maureen Runacres of Jersey. Mrs René Morlay kindly sent us the following interesting information. She wrote; "This is what I remember about the German soldier who came to our house. He asked my father, Stanley Perchard, for help. He said he had been listening to the English radio and was in trouble. He was dressed in civilian clothes."

"My father told him he could not do anything because he had a wife and five children and had to think of the impossible situation it would put him in. I think it was about a week later when a Gestapo man came and asked for my father. He was on Gorey pier helping to do something to a boat. I was told to go and get him, which I did. While I was doing that he questioned my mother. I duly came back with my father. He then questioned him and told him that the soldier had said he had been listening to the English radio."

"The Gestapo man told us that he had shot his officer. He then asked my father to go out to the car to identify the soldier who had come to our home. The Gestapo man spoke to him in German. The only word my father could understand was radio. The soldier answered in German yes. My father was very upset to see the state the soldier was in . The German soldier spoke perfect English. At the time my father was working at Plat Rocque (I think that was the place). The Germans were billeted there. My father told us many times there was soldier there who was very much against the war and Hitler. He said if he was not careful he would get into trouble. This was this soldier. I feel now how sad it all was and hope we never face a situation like that again."

The German soldier who had shot a German under-officer faced a German Military court. He was sentenced to death. The soldier Gefreiter David Hoost, was shot by firing square on the morning of 27 April 1944. He was buried in grave G6 in the German military section at the Strangers Cemetery, Westmount, St Helier, Jersey.

The German under-officer who had been shot by Gefreiter David Hoost, was Alfred Koenig, born 26 February 1906. He was buried in the German military cemetery at St Brelade's Jersey, grave no 131. His unit was HKB 470.

To the Editor of
"The Jersey Evening Post"
Channel Islands
29th April 2003

Dear Sir.

It was with great surprise and humbleness that I received yesterday from England cuttings of the 'Jersey Evening Post' issues of January 15th 25th 28th & February 10th 2003
relating to the Plaque commemorating those who died in the 'Holocaust' from Jersey.

One of the two mentioned in your report was Edward Peter Muels, this man was my father, I am now 66 years old, and was very moved by the picture of him, in your issue of the 10th of February 2003. This is how I remember my father, being 7 years old when I last saw him alive. However I remember very vividly as if it were yesterday the events that lead up to his imprisonment, so for a few moments would you bear with me as I relate to you how the events unfolded.................

.................Oh! how I have often remembered the happy times I had with my father in those months before his imprisonment, two events that have stuck in my mind, was, a warm evening playing on the common opposite our home in 'Sea Breeze' La Rocque, a childs game of hide and seek around the 'sea weed stacks, and on another warm evening fishing off the slip road just above the common for mackerel, I can remember the sea being so full of fish the the 'Whiting' at the edge of the water were so thick that you had to wade through, pushing the fish away as you walked, these two little occasions of being with my father have been with me all through my life.

Now how did we come to meet the young German 'Gefreiter David Hoost' (I only new him as David) well, it was one Sunday he came to our house as we had a bicycle pump and his tyres were flat and needed air in, I recall on this hot Sunday afternoon outside the side entrance to 'Sea

Breeze' a conversation started between himself and my father & mother, he told them that he had just come from being 18 months on the Russian front with no leave, then he made this interesting comment, "How I wish I had enough faith to be like my Uncle, Aunt and cousins, they are all Jehovah's Witnesses" (many at that time were already in the concentration camps in Germany, as recent recorded history is making known) Little did David know that at that moment of time, we too were studying the Bible with Jehovah's Witnesses, my parents tried to comfort him, with the little Bible knowledge they had already learned, each week thereafter he would come to see us, and my parents would share with him their new found faith, all this was taking place in the fall of 1943.

On New Year Eve 1943 David had been promised leave to see his fiancee who was a school teacher, somehow his leave was canceled and it made him very depressed. He came to see us on that Saturday night between 4-5 pm my parents tried to cheer him up, however he left as he was due on sentry duty at 6pm.

A little after 7pm that evening there was a knock on the door, on opening, standing there was David, his hands covered in blood, he said he thought he had killed his commandant (you see it was the order of the day that only with a special pass word could any German reenter the barracks, bearing in mind there were no lights of any kind permitted, all was total darkness, this person in the dark did not have the right password, and was drunk. Hence as a sentry on duty, this young soldier had no option but to obey orders and shoot.) he panicked and came to us asking for clothes. He threatened to kill himself (he was armed) so sooner then have him kill himself in our back yard my mother had some old clothes in the outside shed that she used for fishing so these were given him, and he went on his way.

I remember very vividly that night as I was in bed when the Gestapo came to our house and searched it from top to bottom. A short while afterwards David was captured, he was terrible beaten, and in a very weaken state told that it was my father & mother that gave him the clothes, however when offered his military uniform to put on again and be returned to the Russian front, he refused and said he would never fight again, so they then executed him

Not long after this my father was arrested, and sentenced by a military court to 18 months hard labour, on the first three Saturdays of his sentence, my mother and I were able to see him in the Jersey prison, however on the forth Saturday when we got there was told that he had the evening before been sent to Germany to a concentration camp.

From then on we heard nothing, in 1945 the war ended, many were returning home, I used to go on a Saturday to St Helier to see if my father was on any of the boats returning from Germany, but no, 1946, 1947 still no news, then finally in the early part of 1948 we heard through the Austrian embassy of a man that was supposed to have been with my father in the concentration camp in Germany. We invited him over to Jersey to see us, and he stated that my father had died in the camp three week before it had been liberated (a little different from your account) We have a death certificate, sent to us by the Red Cross, but gives very little details.

Now as I bring this account to a conclusion I would like to just mention that I too am one of Jehovah's Witnesses, and have been ever since that time in 1943 when my parents were first introduced to the faith, but I do not wish to use this account as a means to preach, but, our faith does indeed have a bearing on the events as they unfold, and cannot be omitted from the account.

My mother Olive Dorothy Muels (Now Dartnell) is still alive, in her 90th year, living with her husband in the north of England. I too shall be returning to England in the near future, and I will indeed wish to be able to come to Jersey again and see the 'plaque' in memory of outstanding men, in doing what they thought was best for their fellow man, of whatever race.

Now on behalf of my wife here in Hong Kong, my first wife died 5 years ago after 41 years of marriage, just under a year ago I remarried, its been a pleasure to be able to show these tributes to my present wife about my father, and my three daughters in England by my first wife are looking forward with interest to reading your accounts, and a copy of the e-mail I am sending you.

As a family man myself, I am so grateful to be able to look back at some sad but many happy times I had throughout my life, my fathers experience being no exception, but am so grateful at the example that my mother has always set before me, and what a tower of strength she was in bringing me up as a single parent, not an easy task in the last year of the war and the post war years. But she too has enjoyed happiness what with her strong faith, a new husband, she married again in 1961 and though 90 this year, along with her husband, my step-father, has enjoyed a full and rewarding life.

My I thank you in advance for the reading of this account, and you have my permission if you so wish to publish this account <u>in full</u>.

May I remain Yours Sincerely

> DAVID EDWARD MUELS
> Tuesday 11:45am 22 April 2003
> 3rd Floor 2 San Fat Street
> Shek Wu Hui
> Sheung Shui N.T.
> Hong Kong
> TEL: Home 2672 6948
> Mobile 6124 5629

On a personal note, Where ever did you get the picture of my Father printed in the 10th February 2003 issue of your paper?, its one I have never seen before.

A : The photo came from the Jersey Archives.

JOHN WHITLEY NICOLLE

Arrested by the German Secret Field Police 5 March 1943 for spreading the BBC war news. He was one of eighteen people arrested in what was known as the St Saviour's Wireless Case. The trial took place of the eighteen people on 9 April 1943 behind closed doors at the Committee Room of the States of Jersey building in the Royal Square St Helier. John Whitley Nicolle was sentenced to three years imprisonment. He was deported to Fort d'Hauteville France. Then to Saarbrucken. On 27 December 1943 he was transported to Zweibrucken. On 17 April 1944 he was sent to Bochum. On 21 April 1944 he was once again moved to the penal prison at Dortmund. John Nicolle died at this vile prison from starvation and overwork, plus the very brutal treatment he received.

ADVOCATE LEONCE L'HERMITTE OGIER AND SON, RICHARD.

Arrested with his son, Richard, by the German Secret Field Police 12 February 1943. When the Ogier family home was searched, the German police found a map with the German fortifications in Jersey marked out. The German police also found a box camera. Father and son were both interrogated and imprisoned. In March 1943 both were deported to Paris for interrogation at the Gestapo headquarters and later taken to the prison at Fresnes. Richard Ogier who was suffering from a brain tumour was admitted to St Anne's hospital in Paris. He remained there till his repatriation to London in November 1944. Advocate Ogier was sentenced to six months imprisonment in May 1943. But he was immediately pardoned and sent back to Jersey. When he arrived on 24 May 1943, a large crowd turned out to welcome him home. As they saw it, he had become an icon for the loyal Jersey people.

The Germans were irritated by the display of popular reaction for a man they had arrested and imprisoned. On the 10 July 1943, the German Secret Field Police arrested Advocate Ogier once more, and the same day they deported him to Biberach internment camp in Germany. He was at the time seriously ill with cancer. On his arrival at Biberach 15 July 1943, he was admitted to the camp hospital. He collapsed through loss of blood and was taken to the hospital at Ulm. He died on 1 August 1943.

Two relatives were present at his death bed. His ashes were returned by the Astes family and placed to rest at St Saviour's cemetery. Kenneth Ogier, Advocate Ogier's elder son who after the war lived in Paris, always kept in touch with my family, until he died in September 1996. For the full story of the Ogier family please read the book *"The Ultimate Sacrifice"* by Paul Sanders.

FREDERICK WILLIAM PAGE

Arrested for a wireless offence the Jersey Attorney General reported Page to the German authorities who sentenced him to 21 months imprisonment and deported him to Fort d'Hauteville, France, 18 September, 1943. He was transferred to the German penal prison at Naumburg-am-Saale where he died at 6am on 5 January 1945.

Mrs Page.

This is about the arrest of Frederick William Page in Jersey, 1943 by the German Feldgendarmerie, after they had received a report from the Jersey Attorney General C.W. Duret Aubin. The report compiled by Centenier Garden of the Jersey Honorary Police.

I am not anti the States, or even ever personally knew our States members during the German Occupation. They had a very hard time trying to act as a buffer between the Germans and the Jersey population. But sometimes, like the following (taken from the German Occupation Law Office files) they did not always think straight, or did not realise their actions would sometimes end in tragedy. If we like it or not, there were some very dirty parts of the German Occupation that most people would like to forget.

But I believe one should research and record the bad parts, as well as the good parts of the German Occupation of Jersey 1940-1945. To respect our Island history, the truth should be recorded and the bad parts should not be brushed under the mat. Because if they are left out for some unknown reason, they turn up somewhere and at sometime and some place.

If the truth had been spoken just after the war in 1945 it would have been all out in the open, and people involved in the bad parts of the German Occupation would have had the chance to defend their actions. But strange as it seems, many records could have been destroyed by persons involved in what we see as disloyal actions. The fact that most of these records were not destroyed, shows how legalised (dyed in the wool) some of our people were.

Some of our officials carried out the law to the letter, be it British or German law. A law breaker (to their way of thinking) was a law breaker. As my old Guernsey friend, Frank Falla, stated in his book "The Silent War," it was right to give that impression to the Nazis but it should not have been applied officially to our own people.

In the locked records at the Jersey Archives Service there are the office files of the German Occupation Laws, 1940-1945. In these file are details of the arrest and German Military Court trial of Frederick William Page, born in Portsmouth, 20 November 1900, who lived at Coriade, Tower Road, St Helier. He was married and worked as a labourer. A St Saviour Centenier named Harry C. Garden who lived at La Rue Patier, St Saviour, found out that Frederick and four other men, James Davey, Issac Davey, Owen Dore and George Sty were listening to the BBC news and were in possession of three wireless sets which were forbidden by the German authorities at James Davey's home at Le Coin Bungalow at Route des Près, St Saviours. The Centenier did not know if he should report these illegal radios to the German authorities so he asked the Jersey Attorney General, C.W. Duret Aubin's advice. The Attorney General told the Centenier that he could not be his conscience but if the Centenier made out a report he, the Attorney General, would pass the report on to the German authorities.

In due time His Majesty's Jersey Attorney General passed over to the German authorities the Centenier's report. As a result of this report the German Feldgendarmerie one morning at 6am arrested the five men in June 1943. The five men were taken to the Felgendarmerie headquarters at Tudor House, Bagatelle Road, to be interrogated.On 19 July 1943 Frederick and the four other men faced charges at a German Military Court for a wireless offence. The charge being failing to surrender wireless sets.

Frederick was sentenced to 21 months imprisonment, and James Davey to 18 months imprisonment, the offence having been committed at Le Con Bungalow, Rue des Prés, St Saviours. The other three men charged were fined 100-150 Reichmarks for having listened to wireless broadcasts in company with others.

Clarence James Davey	Owen Dore	George Sty

Str.L.Nr.115/43

Einstellschein I

~~Der Gerichteherr und Befehlshaber der Feldkommandantur 515~~

1. Bestrafter Clarence James D a v e y
   (Vor-u.Zuname, Rufnamen unterstreichen)

2. Geburtstag 23.9. 1910

3. Dienstgrad

4. Truppenteil usw. St.Saviour's/Jersey, Route des Pres "Le Coin
   Wohnort: Bungalow

5. Bürgerlicher Beruf Stukkateur

6. Tag des Diensteintrittes

7. Verheiratet ja

8. Vorstrafen keine

9. Zu vollziehende Strafe
   a) von welchem Gericht und wann verhängt:
      Gericht der Feldkommandantur 515 - 19.Juli 1943
   b) Strafart: Gefängnis
   c) Strafdauer: 1 Jahr 9 Monate
   d) Strafgrund Nichtablieferung von Rundfunkgerät
   e) Strafzeit
      Beginn: 5. August 1943
      Ende: 4. Mai 1945

Beglaubigte Abschrift der Urteilsformel der Strafverfügung
mit Bescheinigung der Vollstreckbarkeit liegt bei.

                    Gericht der
                    Feldkommandantur 515

        O.U.,den 31.Juli 1943

                              Kriegsgerichtsrat.

Extract   from   Order   for   the   protection   of   the   Occupying   Authority.

December 18th,   1942.

(Registered   by   Act   of   the   Royal   Court,   dated   13th February   1943.)

Duties   of   local   Law   Officers.

Paragraph   3.

1)   It   shall   be   the   duty of the   local   Law   Officers   to   submit   to   the   nearest   German   Military   tribunal   all   information   brought   to   their   knowledge   and   all   records   and   other   documents   relating   to   --

a)   Offences   against   the   German   armed   forces   or   the   armed   forces   of   an   ally   of   Germany   or   against   a   member   or   an   attendant   thereof   or   against   a   German   service   or   a   member   thereof ;

b)   Offences   committed   in   buildings   or   other   places   or   in   vessels   used   for   the   purposes   of   the   German   armed   forces   or   the   armed   forces   of   an   ally   of   Germany   or   of   a   German   service ;

c)   Infractions   of   orders   made   in   the   occupied   territory   for   the   for   the   protecting   of   the   German   armed   forces   or   for   the   purposes   of   the   occupation ;

d)   Offences   charged   against   German   and   Italian   Nationals,   including   offences   alleged   to   have   been   committed   before   the   arrival   of   the   German   Troops,

2)   The   German   Military   tribunal   may   refer   the   matter   to   the   civil   authorities   where   it   considers   that   the   matter   does   not   merit   the   decision   of   a   German   military   tribunal.

Left: Clarence James Davey's German Military Court documents.

St Saviour's   2nd   June   1943.

Sir,

I have the honour to inform you that whilst investigating a robbery which had been committed at " Brookhall " Route des Prés, in this Parish, I found it necessary to search a house known as " Le Coin Bungalow " Route des Prés, occupied by a man named Clarence James Davey. This search proved of no value to me and I continued my interrogation of persons concerned. During this period it came to my knowledge that the man Davey had a wireless set at his residence and in consequence, accompanied by Police Constable Kezourrec, I again visited " Le Coin Bungalow " where Mrs Davey pointed out a loose panel which gives access to roof - space in which she informed me were three Wireless sets. The roof - space in question was not searched on the first occasion as there is not fitted with any recognized trap or other means of entrance.   On entering the roof - space I found the following wireless sets ;   One   " Pilot " console model

                            One   " Marconi " table model

                            One   table set (make unknown)

I also found a quantity of spare wireless parts.   I sequestrated all these effects and placed them in safe custody at the Parish Hall. From information supplied by Mrs Davey I ascertained that the set of unknown make is the property of her husband, the above mentioned Clarence James Davey, and that the " Pilot" and " Marconi " models are the property of a man named Frederick Page, whose exact address is not known, but who is believed to be residing at First Tower, in the Parish of St Helier.

All of which I have the honour to report.

                        (Signed) Harry C. Garden.

C.W. Duret Aubin Esq.   Centenier.

   Attorney   General.

On the 2nd June, 1943, I received from Centenier Garden a police report of which a copy is attached hereto and marked " A ".

On the 3rd June 1943, I forwarded the report in question to the Military Court of Field Command 515 in compliance with the legal obligation imposed upon me by paragraph 3 of the order of December 10th, 1942, for the protection of the Occupying Authority by which was registered by the Royal Court of Jersey on February 13th, 1943, and thus became the law of the Island. A copy of the relevant paragraph of the Order in question is attached hereto and marked 'B'. This Order confirmed in a statutory form a written Order which had been given to me by the Occupying Authority very soon after the Occupation.

Some days before I received the report in question from Centenier Garden, he called upon me and told me that he was gravely disturbed in his own mind as to what action he should take in consequence of the discovery by him during the course of a police investigation of the possession, contrary to a German Order by a civilian; of one or more sets of wireless receiving apparatus. Centenier Garden informed me that the police investigation which he had been making emerged from a neighbours quarrel, and that he was afraid that his discovery of the wireless sets in question was known to and being generally talked about by several people who were hostile to one another and that, therefore, there was a grave risk that knowledge of the police discovery of the wireless sets question would soon reach the ears of the German Police. In these circumstances, he was in doubt, he told me, where his duty lay; whether to report the facts, as was his legal obligation, and thus expose a civilian to prosecution or to conceal the facts and thus run the risk, in the event of the Germans discovering the facts, of the police of St Saviour's being suppressed and, consequently, the whole of the police administration of the parish of St Saviour being taken over by the Germans, a situation which it had throughout the occupation, ---

been the settled policy of the Insular administration to avoid.

I told Centenier Garden that I was not disposed to give him an order one way or the other in a matter into which considerations of conscience entered so strongly and that he must decide with his own conscience where his duty lay.

I added that if I did receive a formal police report from him I would have no alternative but to forward it to the Occupying Authority. Centenier Garden subsequently informed me that he had put the matter to his colleagues at a meeting of the St Saviour's police and that their unanimous opinion was that the duty of the police was to the community rather than to the individual and thus he should therefore report.

(Signed) C. W. Duret Aubin.

Attorney General for Jersey.

August 4th 1945.

. . . .

Comment. It seems that some person or persons reported the above facts to the British Liberation Forces (M.1.19. Counter - Intelligence) in May 1945. So it seems that the Attorney - General C. W. Duret Aubin had to explain in a written report to the M.1.19 Officers why he informed and sent in a report to the German Occupying Authorities, which led to Frederick William Page ending - up and dying in a German Penal prison in Germany 5th January 1945.

Thus the date August 4th 1945.
No wonder some of our people in 1945 did not want a full and open public official inquiry on collaboration. Three times the States of Jersey turned down the inquiry.
A full public inquiry in 1945, would have stopped the press and T.V (since that date) from pointing of collaboration on all our loyal peopl

Above; Copy of Memorandum from C.W. Duret Aubin.

ENEMY LEGISLATION AND JUDGMENTS IN JERSEY.

[*Contributed by* C. W. DURET AUBIN, C.B.E., *Barrister-at-Law, H.M. Attorney-General for Jersey, 1936-1948.*]

THE Armed Forces of Germany entered into effective military occupation of the Channel Islands in 1940, Guernsey being occupied on June 30 and Jersey on July 1 of that year. The occupation continued until the Liberation of the Islands by the Armed Forces of the Crown on May 9, 1945.

On July 8, 1940, the German Commandant in Jersey, promulgated, on behalf of the German Commandant in the Channel Islands, certain orders which contained, *inter alia*, the following provisions:

"The Civil Government and Courts of the Island will continue to function as heretofore save that all Laws, Ordinances, Regulations and Orders will be submitted to the German Commandant before being enacted.

"Such legislation as, in the past, required the sanction of His Britannic Majesty in Council for its validity, shall henceforth be valid on being approved by the German Commandant and thereafter sanctioned by the Bailiff of Jersey.

"The orders of the German Commandant heretofore now and hereafter issued shall in due course be registered in the records of the Island of Jersey in order that no person may plead ignorance thereof.

"Offences against the same, saving those punishable under German Military Law, shall be punishable by the Civil Courts, who shall enact suitable penalties in respect of such offences with the approval of the German Commandant."

[The Royal Court of Jersey, by Act of August 24, 1940, enacted a penalty of imprisonment, with or without hard labour, not exceeding two years or of a fine not exceeding £500 or of either, or both, of those penalties.]

During the whole of the Occupation, therefore, two main streams of legislation flowed:

(a) Enactments of the Insular legislature (i.e. the Assembly of the States), and of Insular authorities upon which delegated authority was conferred by the States, and

(b) Orders of the Occupying Authority emanating from:
    (i   The Military Commandant in Jersey or in the Channel Islands;
    (ii The Field Commandant in the Channel Islands; and
    (iii The Military Commander-in-Chief in North-West France. [The Occupying Authority treated the Channel Isles as being, for administrative purposes, within the Zonal area of North-West France.]

Upon the Liberation of the Island it became necessary to regularise the position in so far as Occupation legislation, which would normally have required the Royal Assent, was concerned and by the Confirmation of Laws (Jersey) Law, 1945, sanctioned by Order of His Majesty in Council of August 14, 1945, it was provided that forty-six such enactments should be deemed always to have had effect as if the assent of His Majesty had been signified thereto, and to have been duly registered accordingly on the dates of their original registration by the Royal Court.

In so far as delegated legislation was concerned an entirely unexpected position presented itself to the Insular Authorities upon Liberation.

Practically the whole of that class of legislation consisted of Orders made by various Competent Authorities under Regulation 55 of the Defence (Jersey) Regulations, 1939. Those Regulations had been made by the States of Jersey in exercise of the powers vested in them by the Emergency Powers (Jersey Defence) Order in Council, 1939, which extended to the Island of Jersey certain of the provisions of the Emergency Powers (Defence) Act, 1939.

Frederick William Page was an unassuming and calm man. He made no secret to the German court that he was English and an ex-British guardsman from the 1914-1918 war. He faced the court without any fear and proud to be English. His defiant attitude to the court did not go down well with the German prosecutor, nor with the German Military judge. The Germans never liked anyone standing up to them, so all this went against Page. That's why the court gave him a heavy sentence of 21 months.

On 18 September 1943, he was deported from Jersey to Fort d'Hauteville, France, arriving at Frankfurt Preungesheim from Saarbruken prison on 6 January 1944, He was then transferred to Naumburg-am-Saale penal prison, Germany, July 1944. Dysentery and dropsy, for which there was no medication available, was rampant. Page had been through hell and back and was hovering between life and death. He passed away on 5 January 1945 at 6pm.

All the above is no secret as it was reported in the JEP in 1999 by Alasdair Crosby. The arrest of Frederick William Page was also discussed on BBC Jersey Radio one Saturday morning. Someone on the radio made the defining excuse that the Centenier and the Attorney General had no choice but to report to the German authorities these illegal radios and went on to state that had the German Military authorities found out that the Attorney General and the Centenier had known of the illegal wireless offence and had not reported it they, the Attorney General and the Centenier would have been arrested and imprisoned.

Well, I look at this betrayal as a terrible thing to do to your own people. The golden rule is - you never ever betray your own people to the enemy of your country. It does not matter what the circumstances are. We often wonder how many more of our loyal people were betrayed. It was not just the run-of-the-mill informers who betrayed them.

One very important local official reported to the German authorities that a man named Connor had been found by the local police with gelignite at his home. We old survivors and ex-political prisoners of the Occupation years always had a suspicion that someone in authority was passing on information to the Germans. This information always resulted in local people being arrested.

When the last of the wartime files are released in years to come we do hope that local historians will publish the true facts. We were betrayed by a local chemist, and by two women neighbours of ours - one was a dance teacher. She was the girlfriend of the head of the German Secret Field Police in Jersey, Richard Bode. Mind you, we cannot blame the chemist too much. He was a collaborator with the Germans and he did not take too kindly to our blowing up his shop windows with home made bombs.

I for one cannot forget or forgive these treacherous disloyal people. How many good people were they responsible for who ended up in German concentration camps dying of brutal ill treatment and I for one will try and make sure our loyal Jersey people from the Occupation years will never be forgotten.

If only the Occupation States of Jersey in 1945 with hindsight would have held an inquiry on collaboration and disloyal people at war's end and brought it all out in he open, the good and the bad parts, we would not have to defend the good name and honour of our Island and very loyal Jersey people. Every now and again a book is printed, followed by press and TV programmes on collaboration in the Channel Islands - and on and on it drags.

We do know that some of the collaborators were just scrounges and self preservation type of people and some out to profit from the misery and shortage of food. However, no Channel Islander served in the German forces, not as in the German occupied countries of Europe. Please remember that war brings out not only the strong but also the weak in people.

CLARENCE AND PETER PAINTER

Arrested with his son, Peter, by the German Feldgendarmerie in November 1943 for being in possession of a German pistol, a wireless, camera and photographs of German military objects and radio parts. Before Christmas 1943 the Painters, father and son, were deported to the Cherche-Midi prison in France. On 6 January 1944, they were sent to the German Natzweiler-Strutthof concentration camp in Alsace. On 19 April 1944 they left for Wohlau in Silesia, then Dietzdof, a Krupp factory, then onto Gross-Rosen concentration camp.

Young Peter Painter, suffering from pneumonia, died in his father's arms 27 November 1944. His body was cremated in Gross-Rosen. Clarence Painter was then sent to Dora Mittelbau concentration camp, but on the third day of the journey, suffering from a very severe case of erysipela, died on the way. His body was incinerated in the crematorium at Dora Mittelbau in February 1945.

EMILE PAISNEL

Arrested by the German Feldgendarmerie, he was charged with receiving stolen military goods and military larceny. Emile Paisnel had bartered wheat for some coal with a British and Dutch national who had stolen the coal from German stocks. But Emile did not know the coal was stolen German goods. He was sentenced to ten months imprisonment 19 February 1944. In May 1944 he was deported to St Lo prison in France, later transferred to Fresnes prison, then Karlsruhe prison, then onto Frankfurt prison in May 1944. Then to the penal prison at Naumburg-am-Saale where he died on 29 August 1944. Emile is buried at the British cemetery in Berlin.

CLIFFORD BOND QUEREE

Arrested by the German Military Police June 1943. Charged with serious military larceny. Sentenced to two years imprisonment. Deported to Fort d'Hauteville, France, 13 July 1943. Then to Saarbrucken prison, then Frankfurt-Preungesheime on 6 January 1944. In July 1944, he was transferred to the German penal prison at Naumburg-am-Saale. On April 16 1945 the prison was liberated by the Allied Forces. Clifford Querée was admitted to hospital but the strenuous efforts of the American doctors failed to improve his sinking health and he died on 1 May 1945. He is buried at the British cemetery in Heerstrasse, Berlin.

MARCEL FORTUNE ROSSI

Arrested with his father, also called Marcel, for acts of sabotage. They were deported on 25 February 1943 to St Lo in France. Marcel Junior was transferred to Kreuzburg, Oppeln, Germany. No trace of him since. The last sighting of him was in Flossenburg concentration camp in 1945. His father survived and returned to Jersey.

JUNE SINCLAIR

She was a half Jewish orphan from London. She came to Jersey in 1939. For a time she was our next door neighbour at 27 Midvale Road, St Helier. At the beginning of the German Occupation she worked in one of the hotels the Germans had requisitioned - the Continental Hotel in St Saviour's Road. She told my mother that all her family had been killed during a German air raid on London.

One day at the hotel where she worked, a fat German Officer tired to kiss her and passed rude remarks about her. She retaliated by slapping his face. The next day she was arrested by the German Military Police, imprisoned and before she knew it, she was deported to the Fresnes prison in France. Later on she was transferred to the concentration camp at Brens, near Baillac, France.

Later she was put on a transport to the concentration camp at Ravensbruck where she was killed by brutal guards in 1943. She was 23 years old. After the war, a French lady, Madame Marie Boudoin who was from the north of France, wrote to my mother in 1946. This French lady had been in Ravensbruck with June Sinclair and informed my mother about the last days of June's life in the concentration camp. June had told the French lady all about her friendship with the Mière family. It is a pity that my family lost Madame Boudoin's letter when my mother died. We have tried many times to trace documents about June Sinclair but no luck as yet.

JOHN JACK SOYER

On 29 August 1943 he was arrested by the German Military Police on information supplied by an informer. Charged with being in possession of a wireless and for spreading the BBC war news he was sentenced to one years imprisonment and deported to Fresnes penal prison France. He escaped from the prison and made his way to Brehal in Normandy. He joined the French Resistance - the Maquis. On 29 July 1944 he was killed fighting with the Maquis against the Germans. A German spray of bullets smashed his spine.

John Soyer lurched sideways into the dust and as night fell he was still there. The villagers carried his body into a cottage and covered the bier with flowers. By the next morning the Germans had left Bréhal, and at noon the first Allied tanks moved into the little town. In the town square battle weary Americans stood to attention as the Frenchmen carried John Soyer's body into the church. On 1 August the whole population of Bréhal followed the funeral procession to the cemetery.

His grave is still tended and cared for by the people of Bréhal. John Soyer's name is on the war memorial at Bréhal and a street is named after him. This very brave Jerseyman's name is also on our own lighthouse memorial in Jersey.

Young Roger Laubel, a friend of John Soyer, had climbed the church belfry to ring a passing bell for his old comrade. But as he peered through the belfry louvres to watch for the funeral bier, down in the square someone called out "snipers." In a split second bullets were crashing into the stonework of the church tower and through the louvres. One bullet struck young Roger Laubel in the neck. As he fell, he clutched the bell rope and the bell tolled once for his friend, John Soyer. John was 43 years old when he was killed. His young French friend, Roger Laubel, was only twenty. Two very brave men.

Funeral and grave of John Jack Soyer.

JOE TIERNEY

Arrested by the German Secret Field Police, 3 March 1943. Charged with manufacturing and distributing news leaflets and for spreading the BBC war news. He was one of eighteen people arrested in what was known as the St Saviour's Wireless Case. He was sentenced to two years imprisonment. He was deported to Fort d'Hauteville near Dijon, France. Transferred to Frankfurt, then on to Naumburg, then Saarbrucken prison, then on 6 January 1944 to the prison at Frankfurt-Preungesheim. After a failed escape attempt he was recaptured. He died at Celle concentration camp April 1945, after collapsing on a route march to another camp. He is buried at Kaschitz.

LORD PORTSEA

A very distinguished Jerseyman who fought tirelessly for the constitutional rights and privileges of his native Island. He served as a Major in the Royal Field Artillery in France in the 1914-1918 war.

His constant harangues in the House of Lords on behalf of his beloved Channel Islands were partly instrumental in getting Red Cross life-saving food parcels to the Islands when we were starving towards the end of 1944. Although 80 years of age, he twice offered to lead a relief expedition. When the British Government warned him that the Germans would shoot him, his reply was: 'I'll take that risk gladly.'

He once in the House of Lords asked why was the British Government feeding the Greeks, 'What about our loyal Channel Islanders?' he demanded. 'We should be sending food to them first before feeding other people. And what about our 10,000 Channel Islanders in the British Forces?'

Lord Portsea was certainly one of our greatest Jerseymen. We should always honour his name. Even today there is a Lord Portsea Gift Fund for people under 25 years born in the Channel Islands (or having a parent born in the Islands). The money is intended as a help for young people needing extra funding when going into the British Armed Forces, the Merchant Navy, the Civil Service of the Channel Islands or the UK Civil Service, or training as teachers or medical staff.

This great Jerseyman passed away in Jersey, 1 November 1948 in his 88th year. I feel very sad that at the Liberation Day anniversary, there is no mention of Lord Portsea in the local press or TV programmes. But we old survivors of the German Occupation years remember him as our voice in England, fighting for us, and we shall always honour him in our hearts as our champion in those dark days of 1940-1945.

EUGENE MIERE AND HIS FATHER RENE MIERE

Father and Mother were very strict Roman Catholics. Every Sunday morning all the family would troop down to St Thomas's church for the nine o'clock mass and receive holy communion. But sometimes the Germans held a service at St Thomas's for Roman Catholics in their armed forces - with civilians sitting on one side of the church and Germans on the other. We tried to avoid going to this German mass but sometimes we forgot.

One Sunday as we were sitting in our family pew, Father Maré requested all to come forward to receive holy communion. Our family knelt down at the altar rail waiting our turn to receive the host wafer when I noticed that another priest with very cropped hair was someone I had never seen before. As this priest advanced along the line of the kneeling congregation towards us I noticed the bottom of his trouser legs were German green army trousers and German Army lace-up officers boots.

I nudged my father's elbow and nodded towards the priest's trouser legs, and whispered 'German.' Father looked towards the priest, saw what I had seen, got up from the altar rail and walked back to our family pew, followed by my mother, my two sisters and our grandparents and myself - all in silence.

After the service Father Maré, a very old family friend, stopped us outside the church and said in French to my father: 'Eugené, that was not a nice thing to do to the German Army priest who was only assisting us with the mass. After all, he is a Roman Catholic and a good man of God.' My Father said to Father Maré: 'Well, Mon Père, he serves the Nazis and wears the crooked cross on his uniform. It would be wrong for me and my family to receive holy communion from a German while my sons in the British Army could be killed by these Nazi swine.'

'But,' said Father Maré, 'if this German priest turned on the Nazis they would shoot him.'

My father had his answer for that. He looked Father Maré in the eyes and said:'you, Father and your German priest forget that your boss, Jesus, died on the cross because he opposed evil. So your German priest should not just preach but act like a man of God.'

Father Maré who had a short fuse walked away. Strangely enough, as we were leaving the church grounds, the German Army Chaplain priest came out of the side door of the rectory and as he passed I could not help but notice that he was carrying a neat small side arm attached to his brown belt by a small brown holster. One Sunday my father told Father Maré that we had seen the German priest armed with a side arm. Father Maré told my father that before coming to Jersey all German officers wore a side arm in France because the French underground movement had shot many German officers even if they were army chaplains. So in Jersey obeying orders army chaplains still carried side arms the same as all the German army officers did. Since the wars end I have checked up and have seen photographs of German army chaplains wearing side arms. And the German army doctor who examined us at the German prison also carried a side arm.

Above: Father Maré of St Thomas's Church

Left: My Father, Eugené Mière

Right: My grandfather, René Mière

DEPUTY EDWARD LE QUESNE

On 7 August 1940, Deputy Edward Le Quesne the President of the Labour Department States of Jersey was ordered by the Germans to send an architect and men to enlarge the Jersey airport runways, to paint the airport buildings green camouflage and to prepare gun emplacements. Deputy Le Quesne refused to carry out this order because the Jersey airport was now a military base. The Deputy protested that this was work of a military nature, and he refused to send men.

The Germans informed the Deputy that, as an alternative, they would conscript men between the ages of 20-30 to carry out the work. The Germans would have conscripted all the men they needed without even giving a second thought to Article 52 of the Hague Convention which stipulates that no one residing in an occupied territory can be compelled to carry out any work of a military nature which is against the interests of his own side.

But the Germans demanded more and more men. Time after time Deputy Le Quesne protested. Some of the men from the labour force had flatly refused to work for the Germans, even under threats of imprisonment. In the end these men worked on the new North road - La Route du Nord which was being constructed from La Saline to Sorel Point. In the car park at the Sorel Point end of the road there is a granite memorial stone dedicated to the people of Jersey. In my mind (and many others think the same) this memorial stone should have been dedicated to the men who worked on this road.

What is very sad is that on any Liberation Day, 9 May, any year, you will not find any flowers or any wreaths on this memorial stone. I often wonder when passing there of how many people stop and think about the loyal Jerseymen that worked on this road. What price loyalty!

In May 1945 many States of Jersey employees presented Deputy Edward Le Quesne with an illuminated address, and it was signed by the workers from all departments of the Labour Force. At the end of the German Occupation Deputy Edward Le Quesne was not given any official recognition by the States of Jersey, or by the British Government for all his hard work. Others received honours but there was nothing for a fine Jerseyman like Deputy Edward Le Quense who had served his fellow Islanders, not only during the years of the German Occupation but before and after the 1939-1945 war.

There were certain high up local officials who did not like his straight-forward attitude and his remarks when he thought they were going too far in trying to please the Germans. The Bailiff and Deputy Le Quesne were the two leading people who stand out in their long and hard battles with the German officials, protesting on behalf of their fellow Islanders.

Even at this late date, the States of Jersey should give Deputy Edward Le Quesne some official form of recognition posthumously which he richly deserves. He was not everyone's cup of tea, but he helped many people in those dark and uncertain German Occupation days. He helped me get a job, and saved me from being taken by force to work for the Germans.

Extracts from:
The Occupation of Jersey
Day by Day,
The personal diary of
Deputy Edward Le Quesne

Tuesday 29 July 1941 (Page 85)

A terrible case of a local important official reporting to the German Police that a local man had been found with gelignite was reported to me today. In as much as the penalty is death or imprisonment for life the seriousness of such reporting is apparent and more will certainly be heard of this Quisling attitude.

Friday 24 September 1943 (Page 206)

The body of an American was found at Bonne Nuit. The Germans plus our fearsome Attorney General (C.W.Duret Aubin) are frightened of a popular sympathetic demonstration similar to that which took place when the bodies of two British RAF pilots were buried. I was ordered to place the body in a zinc lined shell and to enjoin secrecy on all men concerned in the coffining and burial. Disgusted with this cowardliness on the part of our Attorney General (C.W. Duret Aubin) I broadcast the information and soon everyone knew of the occurrence. We have not been informed of the date of the funeral.

Monday 27 September 1943 (Page 206-207)

The funeral of the American airman took place in secrecy at 7.45am. The burial place is near that of our own men at Mont à l'Abbé and the grave will be attended as is that of our men.

Wed 12 Jan 1944 (Page 223)

I entered a protest against the paid police assisting the Germans in finding the addresses of girls who were shorthand typists. The object of this enquiry is fully apparent because of previous experience and the police should never have been instructed to assist. At a meeting of the paid police committee the Attorney General (C.W. Duret Aubin) who had given instructions to the Connétable of St Helier to carry out this work was ordered to stop it at once. He stated that he had seen no sinister design in this order.

With thanks to Frank Le Quesne, grandson of Deputy Edward Le Quesne, for allowing me to publish these extracts here.

ALFRED LE HUQUET

My cousin Alfred Le Huquet and two other young lads broke into the German Army quarters in Kensington Place, St Helier one day in 1944. Unknown to them it was the German Army Paymasters office quarters. Through the window Alfred passed down a large jar of jam and other bits of food. He was about to leave the office by the window when he noticed a safe with the safe door open and a key still in the lock. Going to the safe he saw there was large bundle of German Occupation marks with a paper band around them. He put the notes into a small sack he was carrying then he and his pals headed for home, not knowing that a young woman who lived in Kensington Place and was very friendly with the Germans saw Alfred come out of the window of the paymasters office. Worse still, she recognised him.

Alfred's uncle was a policeman, and by chance he was in the duty police sergeant's office when this young woman reported what she had witnessed. She also gave Alfred's name to the sergeant. However, the next morning a police van followed by a German police car pulled up outside the cottage where Alfred lived at Springfield. Alfred saw a local policeman point to the cottage. He had come along to show the German police where Alfred lived - which was very obvious .

The Germans and local police searched the cottage and after finding the bundle of notes which were under Alfred's mattress and after talking to Alfred's father, they left.

'This was strange they have not arrested me' thought Alfred, They just took the mark notes and were gone.

We think the Paymaster was only too pleased to get the bundle of marks returned. He must have had a friend in the German police who undertook to get the notes back for him. If Alfred had been arrested it would have all come out of how the Paymaster had left the safe unlocked and open. After an inquiry the Paymaster would have been court martialed.

One day this cousin, Alfred Le Huquet, was passing the Ladies College (now called the Girls College) and at the lower gate two Germans were unloading loaves of bread from a truck and taking them on trays into the College. When Alfred saw that the coast was clear he jumped onto the tail board of the truck, and was in the act of passing down loafes of bread to a small group of school children who had gathered around when the two Germans returned and caught him red handed. With the help of two other Germans from the College they laid Alfred face down on to the tail board of the truck, and with a pick handle they proceeded to lay into him.

As the blows came fast and heavy he screamed out in pain. The four Germans took no notice of the screams. Three Germans were holding him down while the truck driver applied the punishment. When they had finished they threw Alfred onto the pavement. He was in a bad way, so battered that he could not stand up but when at last he could it was very painful.

After some time he made his way to the hospital, half walking, half crawling along. At the hospital they found that one of his knee bones was protruding through the skin. It took many weeks before he could return to work. From that date on something changed in him. He was a big man, strong as an ox and, like many big men, positive and kind by nature but after that beating the balance of his mind seemed to go. He thought only about himself, imagining that he was ill and, at one point, that he was dying.

In the year 1999 he took his own life. He hanged himself in his garage at Five Oaks. So sad an end for a fine man.

PETER GRAY

Peter Gray was an old school pal who was arrested and imprisoned with us Jersey lads in the German prison in Gloucester Street, St Helier. Peter told me that he was not arrested by the German police at first but by a local policeman and taken by the same policeman to "Silvertide" the German Secret Field Police head-quarters. This local uniformed policeman handed him over to the Germans. Even after all these years have passed Peter is still angry. He stated to me that the local policeman arrested him on behalf of the Germans. He still feels that he was betrayed by our own police. Peter is writing a book on his German Occupation days in Jersey. He now lives in France and his address is La Campagne, 50190 Nay Normandy, France.

PHILIP CHARLES PALLOT

Jerseyman ex-British soldier. Superintendent of St Helier Cemeteries. Born in Trinity, Jersey 15.1.1897. Arrested June 1944 by the German Feldgarmerie and imprisoned in the German prison St Helier. *This report was compiled by his son Robert Pallot;*

At the time of his arrest at the end of June 1944, Mr Pallot (known generally as Philip Pallot) was employed by the Parish of St Helier as Superintendent of Cemeteries and was resident at the Lodge, Mont a L'abbé, with his wife, three sons and two daughters (a further daughter was married and the eldest son was serving with the Royal Air Force). He had called each evening, in company with one or two neighbours, at the house of Mr Charles Bull for the purpose of listening to the BBC 9 o'clock news but unfortunately was spied upon and reported.

Two members of the Feldgarmerie duly called at midnight and after questioning and a house search, he was arrested. I well remember my mother waking me and sending me downstairs to investigate. Needless to say I was escorted back upstairs, feeling the cold revolver in my back. His sentence was five months with a months remission but during the time of his imprisonment, and with persistent badgering of the German authorities he convinced them that important admin work was required particularly for the Strangers Cemetery, (now the site of the crematorium) and as this work specially called for by the Island Kommandant, he was allowed out on parole for three days each month. In the true fashion of the Jerseyman of the time, this "important work" that he pleaded was usually non-existent, but he managed somehow to convince the authorities otherwise. Mr Philip Charles Pallot died 5 November 1953.

Peter Gray

Reply to:
50190 NAY
NORMANDY
FRANCE.

The Director,
The Imperial War Museum,
Lambeth,
LONDON.

April 7th. 1995

Subject; Jersey Occupation Exhibition-The Political Prisoners

Dear Sir,

I am writing to you in the earnest hope that you may be able to intercede with contacts that you may have in Jersey or at least point me in the right direction in respect of the total lack of any form of commemoration or even recognition of the some 2500 political prisoners who passed through the doors of the German Military Prison during the Occupation.

Inasmuch as some ended their lives in concentration camps in Germany and many others were only saved from this fate by the Island being cut off after D-Day I am ashamed to learn that there will be no place for these lost people during the celebration of the fiftieth anniversary. I have written to the Co-ordinator of the various functions but have not had a reply, and my fellow-prisoner Joe Miere, retired director of the St. Peters' Hospital Museum has been continually stonewalled in his attempts to mount some form of commemoration to properly honour the prisoners that are still alive and in Jersey.

Whatever our motives in committing the offences against German authority we succeeded in tying up their officialdom all the way to Berlin and so in our way we did our bit in helping the war effort, and some did a lot more than that. I am only an O.A.P. and have very little resources but I have commisioned a small souvenir medallion for each of the ex-prisoners that can be found during my proposed visit from May 6th. to 10th.

Can you help me at all or is this to be just the story of the forgotten and very brave people whose efforts are to be swept under the carpet like other aspects of the German Occupation. Thank you anyway for taking the time to read this letter.

Peter Gray.

P.S. List enclosed of people who were with me at the end of the War.

Occupation and Liberation Committee

States Greffe, Jersey, JE1 1DD, Channel Islands

Tel: 0534 502000   Fax: 0534 502098

18th April 1995.

Dear Mr Gray,

Thank you for your letter of the 8th April received today, the 18th April 1995. I am sorry that you do not like my reply but I am afraid that there is not much that we can do about it at this stage. The plain and simple fact is that it has taken a considerable amount of effort both by myself and by Joe Mière to get the political prisoners recognised at all. As no doubt you are aware, in the past, there has been considerable reluctance by the Government of Jersey to recognise political prisoners at all. I am not party to the reasons for this but I did sympathise with Mr Mière when he made his approach and so steered this particular issue through my Committee to its successful conclusion. Therefore you will get recognition at last. However, there will not be large social event surrounding this Official recognition although both the Lieutenant Governor and the Bailiff will be present at the unveiling on the 27th April.

I am afraid that we had to choose a date. I asked Joe Mière for his advice on a suitable date, one that would not clash with other events. It was he that chose April 27th. He did so because, as I explained before, this was the date of the last piece of real savagery by the German occupying forces ie; the shooting of one of their own for attempting to escape. It is certainly significant to Joe Mière and as he has been the driving force behind this whole scheme I felt that it was only right that we accede to his advice on this occasion. Again the date is set and that is it.

Your last paragraph referring to dedicating a memorial to the Escapees has me confused. You say that ' a number failed to make it and were arrested '. Those who failed to make it, and there were nine who died, are recognised by having their names on the plaque which will commemorate the bravery of all those who escaped or who attempted to escape. Again as I explained to you there will be a Book of Remembrance which will be placed in the Town Hall which you can look at next time you are over.

Thank you for your letter. I am sorry if you are still disappointed but I am afraid that there is little that I can do about it at this stage.

Yours sincerely,

Bruce Willing,
Co-ordinator,
Occupation and Liberation Committee.

Mr P.Gray,
La Campagne,
50190 Nay,
France.

ALFRED JAMES CONNOR

Thirty year old Jerseyman, born Jersey 22 February 1913, St Helier. Arrested by the local police in 1943, reported to the German authorities by a local important official. After a search of Alfred James Connor's home, the local police found explosives (dynamite).

Alfred James Connor was handed over to the German Military Police. After facing a German Military Court he was deported under armed escort to St Malo, then to Fort d'Hauteville prison, France, 21 December 1943. Then transferred 27 December 1943 to the penal prison at Saarbrucken, then to a penal prison at Zweibrucken. On 17 April 1944 transferred to the penal prison at Bochum.

Alfred James Connor ID card No 28879. (January 27 1941).
Nationality British.
In 1941 he lived at number 20 Pier Road, St Helier, Jersey.
Trade or Occupation. None. Status. Single.
His registration form signature is marked with an X.
Alfred returned to Jersey in 1946.

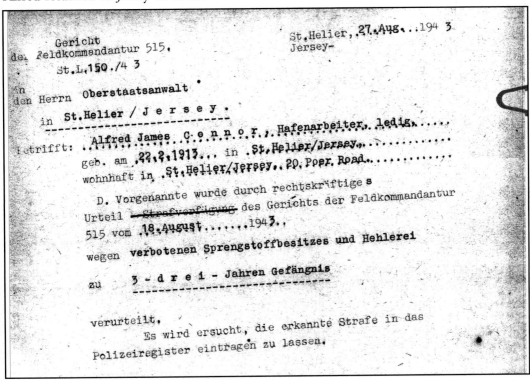

169

Attorney General's Chambers,

Jersey.

28th August 1943.

Dear Mr. Constable,

I have today been informed by the Court of Field Command 515

of the following convictions by that authority:

CONNOR, Alfred James, harbour worker, single, born 22.2.1913 in St.
    Helier, of 20, Pier Road, St. Helier, Jersey.

    Sentenced by proceedings of 18th instant to three (3) years'
    imprisonment for unauthorised possession of explosives and
    receiving stolen articles.

Gericht
der Feldkommandantur 515.
    St.L.150./43

St.Helier, 27. Aug. 1943
Jersey-

An
den Herrn Oberstaatsanwalt

in St.Helier / J e r s e y .

Betrifft: Alfred James C o n n o r , Hafenarbeiter, ledig,
geb. am 22.2.1913 in St. Helier/Jersey,
wohnhaft in St. Helier/Jersey, 20, Pier Road.

    D. Vorgenannte wurde durch rechtskräftiges
Urteil ~~Strafverfügung~~ des Gerichts der Feldkommandantur
515 vom 18.August 1943,

wegen **verbotenen Sprengstoffbesitzes und Hehlerei**

zu   **3 - d r e i - Jahren Gefängnis**

----

verurteilt,
    Es wird ersucht, die erkannte Strafe in das
Polizeiregister eintragen zu lassen.

A.A.

Heeres- Justizinspektor.

Yours faithfully,

C. J. Cuming, Esq.,
Constable of St. Helier.

Attorney General.

MINISTERE DE LA DEFENSE

SECRETARIAT D'ETAT AUX
ANCIENS COMBATTANTS

37, rue de Bellechasse – 75700 PARIS 07 SP
Tél. 01 44 42 10 00

RÉPUBLIQUE FRANÇAISE

DIRECTION DES STATUTS, DES PENSIONS
ET DE LA REINSERTION SOCIALE

Caen, le **3.1 JUIL. 1997**

SOUS-DIRECTION DES STATUTS ET DES TITRES

BUREAU DES ARCHIVES
B.P. 552 – 14037 CAEN CEDEX
TEL. : 02.31.38.45.00 TELECOPIE 02.31.38.45.69

N° d'enregistrement : B.Arch./97/DH/ML **№ 3 9 9 0 4**
AFFAIRE SUIVIE PAR Mme HIEBLOT
Poste 4549

Monsieur,

Vous avez bien voulu intervenir auprès de mes services afin d'obtenir des renseignements concernant vingt-et-une personnes en provenance de Jersey qui n'auraient pas survécu à leur déportation durant la seconde guerre mondiale.

J'ai l'honneur de vous faire connaître que les renseignements succincts que vous avez fournis sur ces déportés ainsi que la nature souvent parcellaire des archives en ma possession n'ont pas permis de faire aboutir l'ensemble des recherches.

Cependant, vous voudrez bien trouver ci-après les informations qui ont pu être collectées.

1·) Internés au fort d'HAUTEVILLE

M. Cliffords COHU, né à Catel le 30 décembre 1883 ou 1985
Marié, pasteur, domicilié à Saint Saviour (Jersey), arrêté en 1943 pour détention de tracts.
Arrivé à la prison de Saarbrücken le 21 décembre 1943 et transféré le 6 janvier 1944 à celle de Preungesheim.

M. Frederic PAGE, né à Portsmout(?) le 20 novembre 1900
Marié, domicilié à Saint Helier. Tower road, arrêté en 1943 pour refus d'obéissance.
Arrivé le 21 décembre 1943 à la prison de Saarbrücken et transféré le 6 janvier 1944 à celle de Preungesheim.

M. John NICOLLE, né le 28 juin 1914 à Argentan (Orne)
Domicilié à La Genevraie (Orne), arrêté en 1943 pour "non exécution d'une consigne".
Arrivé le 21 décembre 1943 à la prison de Saarbrücken (noté né le 17 juin 1918 à Trinvy), le 17 avril 1944 à celle de Bochum (noté sous le nom de VICOLLE José 17.6.1918), matricule 61, et transféré le 21 avril 1944 à celle de Dortmund.

.../...

171

- **M. Joseph TIERNEY, né à Jersey le 23 octobre 1910**
  Marié, domicilié à Saint Saviour S/Jersey, arrêté en 1943 pour détention de tracts.
  Arrivé le 21 décembre 1943 à la prison de Saarbrücken (noté sur les registres TIERNY
  Josef, né le 23.10.12) et transféré le 6 janvier 1944 à celle de Preungesheim.

- **M. Clifford QUEREE, né à Saint Helier le 27 septembre 1906**
  (noté sur la liste du fort de Hauteville à GUERRE Clifford).
  Veuf, domicilié 37, Belmond road, arrêté en 1943.
  Arrivé le 21 décembre 1943 à la prison de Saarbrücken (noté sur le registre, né le
  27.09.1902), transféré le 6 janvier 1944 à celle de Preungesheim.

J'ajoute que les personnes suivantes originaires ou habitant l'île de Jersey ont également
été détenues dans ce fort :

- **M. Hubert GALLICHAN, né à La Trinité (Jersey) le 26 juin 1914**
  Célibataire, domicilié à Roteland Saint Pierre (Jersey)
  Arrêté pour détention de tracts et transféré à la prison de Freiburg.

- **M. Ronald BEER, né à Saint Helier le 4 août 1913**
  Marié, domicilié à Saint Helier
  Arrêté en 1943 et transféré en Allemagne.

- **M. Flavian BARBIER, né le 28 juin 1909 à Jersey**
  Marié, domicilié à Jersey.
  Arrêté en 1943 et transféré en Allemagne.

- **M. Thomas KOWALACK, né à Recklinghausen le 9 mai 1909**
  Célibataire, domicilié à Jersey.
  Arrêté en 1943 et transféré en Allemagne.

- **M. Johannie PINWEL, né le 6 février 1922 à Jersey**
  Célibataire, domicilié 2, place Clifton à Saint Helier
  Arrêté en 1943 et transféré en Allemagne.

M. Alfred CONNOR, né à Jersey le 22 septembre 1913
Célibataire, domicilié à Saint Helier, arrêté en 1943 pour détention d'explosifs.
Arrivé le 21 décembre 1943 à la prison de Saarbrücken, transféré le 27 décembre
1943 à celle de Zweibrücken et le 17 avril 1944 à celle de Bochum.

- **M. Norman DEXTER, né à Londres le 11 juillet 1907**
  Marié, domicilié à Saint Peter Port (Jersey), arrêté en 1943 pour "refus
  d'obéissance".
  Arrivé le 21 décembre 1943 à la prison de Saarbrücken et transféré le 6 janvier 1944
  à celle de Preungesheim.

2·) <u>Déporté à la prison de SAARBRÜCKEN sans indication de provenance</u>

– ✓ M. Georges FOX, né le 12 ou 22 mai 1896 à Saint Helier, domicilié à Jersey. Condamné le 23 juin 1943 par la Felkommandantur 515 (Saint Helier) à deux ans de prison (extrait d'une liste de condamnation établie par le tribunal de Francfort-sur-le-Main) et interné à celle de Naumburg. Arrivé le 21 décembre 1943 à celle de Saarbrücken et transféré le 6 janvier 1944 à celle de Preungesheim.

3·) <u>Déportés au camp de concentration de NATZWEILER–STRUTHOF</u>

– ✓ M. Clarence, Claude PAINTER, né le 2 novembre 1893
Anglais, arrivé le 7 janvier 1944 au camp de concentration de Natzweiler, matricule 6861 (NN), et transféré le 19 avril 1944 à la prison de Wohlau.

– ✓ M. PETER, Edward PAINTER, né le 11 avril 1924
Anglais, arrivé le 7 janvier 1944 au camp de concentration de Natzweiler, matricule 6862 (NN) et transféré le 19 avril 1944 à la prison de Wohlau.

4·) <u>Internés à la prison de Fresnes</u>

– Le nom de M. Emile PAISNEL ou <u>PAISUEL</u>, 37 ans environ, figure dans un fichier indiquant son arrivée le 1er mai 1944, matricule n° 12726, venant de la prison de Saint-Lô.

– ✓ M. OGIER Lamitin (?) serait arrivé en juin 1943 à Fresnes, matricule n° 365.

5·) <u>Déportée au camp de RAVENSBRÜCK</u>

– Selon le témoignage d'une déportée de ce camp, Mme GOULD de Jersey serait décédée au mois de janvier 1945.

*camp de transit pour
p.p. français (cf. thèse Fabrique*

Par ailleurs, selon les registres du camp de Compiègne, M. James HOULLEBECQ, NN(?) né en 1927, arrivé dans ce camp le 6 juillet 1944, matricule 43832, a été déporté le 15 juillet 1944.

Un essai de reconstitution des listes de déportés au camp de concentration de Neuengamme indique que M. James <u>HOULLEBECG</u>, né le 24 février 1927, serait arrivé dans ce camp le 18 juillet 1944, matricule 37354, et y serait décédé le 20 janvier 1945.

.../...

- 4 -

Il n'existe au nom de M. Joan, Max FINKELSTEIN, né le 12 mars 1882 à Galatz (Roumanie), qu'une fiche, double de la carte qui lui a été délivrée à une date et dans un centre de rapatriement non précisés (après mars 1945), où il a déclaré notamment revenir de Laufen, et se rendre à Jersey.

Je ne détiens pas de renseignements concernant : MM. John DAUNY, Arthur DIMERY, Peter Bruce JOHNSON, Frank LE VILLIO, Maurice GOULD, Marcel ROSSI et June SINCLAIR.

Veuillez agréer, Monsieur, l'assurance de ma considération distinguée.

Pour Le Directeur des Statuts, des Pensions
et de la Réinsertion Sociale
Le Sous-Directeur des Statuts et des Titres

Jersey Archives – Service
Jersey Museum
Saint Helier
JERSEY JE 2 JNF
   (Grande-Bretagne)

JACK WALLING

Thirty one year old English born Jerseyman. Worked at Beghin's shoe shop in St Helier. Later worked for the States footwear exchange department.

In July 1944, as a result of a denunciation by a Jersey woman, he was caught listening to the BBC war news by the German Feldgendarmerie, arrested and tried by a German Military Court and sentenced to nine months imprisonment. After imprisonment in the German prison in St Helier, he was deported with other Jersey prisoners to St Malo, France. After a few days he with four French prisoners were being taken by bus to Rennes, guarded by 13 German Feldgendarmerie. The bus ran into an American combat team which immediately opened fire. The Germans piled out of the bus but the prisoners lay on the floor. All 13 Germans were killed but Jack Walling and the three French prisoners were only wounded.

Later Jack was evacuated by air to England and then on to the RAF hospital at Wroughton, Swindon. Jack returned to Jersey in 1945. He has since died. Sadly the German woman who denounced Jack Walling was married to a serving British officer but her husband was killed in the fighting in Africa.

WILLIAM ALFRED DAMARELL

Forty year old Guernsey docker arrested by the German Military Police, sentenced and imprisoned in Guernsey for striking a German officer. He was deported from Guernsey to a German penal prison in France, November 1943. In 1944 he was transferred to a penal prison in Germany. Then transferred to Laufen internment camp. Two days before Laufen was liberated on 4 May 1945, William Damarell escaped from the camp with seven other men and two Australian soldiers. After stealing a German lorry they drove through Germany and France. In May 1945, William Damarell was reunited with his wife and family in Bolton, England. He and his family returned to Guernsey in June 1945. A loyal and brave Guernseyman.

GRAHAM BUCKINGHAM.

Twenty four year old Guernsey sportsman arrested and imprisoned by the German Military Police July 1944, Guernsey. Sentenced to two years imprisonment Friday 28 July 1944 for acts of sabotage.

On the evening of the same day, Friday 28 July 1944, he was being escorted by armed German guards to the St Peter Port harbour and the boat that was to transport him to a German penal prison in France when he escaped from the German escort.

The German Police made great efforts to find him but he successfully evaded capture for many months but when in hiding at a relative's house, Graham fell on a bottle and badly gashed his hand. He was taken to the Emergency Hospital where he was arrested by the German Police once again . Strange as it seems, Graham was not guarded by the German Police, but by the Guernsey Auxiliary Police night and day.

Later, Graham was transferred back to the Guernsey prison where he remained until the Island was liberated in May 1945. Graham Buckingham was a very brave and very loyal young Guernseyman.

In July 1944, the Germans placed a wanted notice in the local Guernsey newspaper and it was printed in English and German.

GRAHAM BUCKINGHAM

BEKANNTMACHUNG

DER vom Kriegsgericht wegen Diebstahls zu zwei Jahren Gefangnis verurteilte Graham Buckingham, Chelsea House, Clategny Esplanade St. Peter Port der zur Strafverbüssung auf das Festland überführt werden sollte, ist am 23.7 im Hafengelände Peter Port ent wichen. Er befindet sich noch in Freiheit und hält sich auf der Insel verborgen

Die Bevölkerung wird darauf hingewiesen, dass die Gewährung jeglicher Hilfeleistung an Buckingham strengstens verboten ist, und dass sich jeder, der ihm Unterkunft Nahrung oder sonstige Unterstützung gewährt, der Gefahr strenger Bestrafung aussetzt.

Zur Vermeidung weiterer Massnahmen wird die Bevölkerung zur Mitwirkung bei der Ergreifung des Täters aufgefordert. Alle zweckdienlichen Beobachtungen über seinen Aufenthalt und sonstige Angaben, die zu seiner Ergreifung führen können, sind umgehend an die Standortkommandantur oder an die engl-Polzbehoerde zu richet.

Personalbeschreibung: Buckingham ist 24 Jahre alt. hat braune Augen und braune Haare, kleinen Schnurrbart, schlanke Gestalt und ist 1.65m gross

NOTICE

ON Friday last. 28th ultimo, Graham Buckingham of Chelsea House Clategny Esplanade, St Peter Port, escaped within the confines of St. Peter Port Harbour, whilst in the custody of the German Police. Buckingham had been condemned by Court Martial to two years imprisonment for theft. He was about being transferred to the mainland, for the execution of his sentence. Buckingham is still at large on this island He is holding himself in concealment.

The Public are reminded of the strict prohibition against administering any aid whatsoever to the fugitive.... All those giving him food, shelter or any kind of help find themselves exposed to severest penalty.

With the purpose of avoiding severer measures, the Public are expected to fully co-operate in the arrest of the delinquent.

All observations concerning his whereabouts, and all information leading up to his seizure, must be announced immediately to the Standortkommandantur or to the Inspector of the Guernsey Police.

The following is a description of Buckingham: Brown eyes and hair small moustache. height 5ft, 5ins, (1.65m). slight build, age 24. ......

JAMES THOMAS WILLIAM QUICK

A 34 year old Guernsey farmer. Arrested in Guernsey 1944 by the German Secret Field Police. Sentenced, and deported to a German penal prison in France. Transferred to Buchenwald concentration camp in Germany. Concentration camp number 77290.

He was one of the five Channel Islanders in Buchenwald concentration camp in 1944-1945. At the liberation of the camp he was repatriated to England 8 June 1945. He returned to Guernsey September 1945. I knew James Quick in 1948 and 1949 when he used to visit Jersey twice a year. After the brutal treatment at Buchenwald his health suffered and as time went on it deteriorated. He had a hard time trying to speak, his breathing was very bad. James was always a gentleman. He was married and, at the time of his arrest, his son was only 10 years old. James passed away in the late 1950's.

I know that I joke about Guernsey and my Guernsey friends pull my leg about being a Jerseyman. But there were many very brave Guernsey people in the German Occupation years and I always try to honour their memory.

ALFRED WILLIAM BAKER

It is not often that you read or hear about anyone from Sark being arrested and deported to a German concentration camp. Alfred William Baker, a 22 year old Sarkman, was arrested by the German Secret Field Police. He was sentenced and deported to the German penal prison at St Malo, France. Transferred to a German penal camp at Clairevaux, Aube, France in 1944. In 1945 he was transferred to Buchenwald concentration camp Germany. His camp number was 78441.

JOHN DE CARTERET PINWELL

Eighteen year old Jerseyman, arrested by the German Secret Field Police May 1944.

Imprisoned in the German prison, St Helier, Jersey. Sentenced and deported to a German penal prison in France 15 May 1944.

Transferred to a penal prison in Germany, August 1944. His last address before he was arrested and deported was; 2 Clifton Place, Ann Street, St. Helier.

DEATH OF MISS MILDRED WADDELL 28.12.1944

Miss Waddell was shot by a German serviceman at her home "Castel Samsufi" Portelet, St Brelade, Jersey on the night of 26 December 1944. On that night Miss Waddell heard a noise on the verandah of her house that overlooked Portelet Bay. She got up to find out what it was and, on nearing the window of her kitchenette, she saw that a German soldier was pushing his rifle though a pane of glass. Miss Waddell caught hold of the muzzle, pulling it downward towards the ground when the rifle went off and she was shot in the leg. She was losing a considerable amount of blood and was very shocked. She tried to attract the attention of the occupants of a nearby bungalow who were Germans but it was not until 9am that a German soldier heard her cries and went to get help. Two neighbours turned up and bandaged the leg as best they could. Two German soldiers were applying First Aid when the ambulance arrived.

At the hospital she was treated and had an x-ray and a blood transfusion but collapsed at 9.40pm, 28 December, 1944, dying from delayed shock and loss of blood. Miss Mildred Catherine Waddell was 52 years of age, born at Matara, Ceylon. An inquest was held on 2 January, 1945. Her mother was a resident of La Moye Nursing Home.

Heinz C Woelfe, a member of the German Secret Field Police in Jersey 1940-1945 made a statement on 30 April 1946 to the British officers who were interrogating him about Miss Waddell. He stated that in Jersey December 1944 he had tried to interview Miss Waddell in hospital but she was too weak to answer any questions. Woelfe went on to state that during his interment in Jersey at camp 802 at St Peter Barracks near the airport, a British army major from London questioned him about the case of Miss Waddell.

Woelfe goes on to state that, at the time, the murder must have been the result of Miss Waddell being shot in the leg. He said that when he was transferred to England, September, 1945 from camp 802 in Jersey to camp No 9 at Tiptree, Essex, he met an NCO whom he knew and this man had been with the Medical Orderlies in Jersey. This NCO Sgt Krah and his comrades who had been stationed at the Military hospital No 2 (which was the General Hospital in St Helier). He told Woelfe that shortly after Christmas, 1944, a member of the Flak unit had been admitted with internal injuries incurred whilst trying to obtain food. Woelfe stated that he was able to learn that the injured soldier was the suspected murderer whose unit had been based near the scene of the crime. Woelfe could not remember the soldier's name but he later deserted from his Flak Unit at St Brelade. He was shot, 27 April, 1945 on the parade ground at Fort Regent. This soldier was 23 years old Kanonier (Gunner) Nicolas Schmitz. Born on 25 June 1922 at Dusseldorf, Germany. He belonged to the Zweiten Kompanie der Flakabteilung 364 based at St Brelade, Jersey. After the execution he was buried at the Strangers Cemetery, Westmount. St Helier Jersey, Grave 13.

Please remember that this soldier, Nicolas Schmitz, was only a murder suspect. So far at this date (year 2004) we have not discovered any real evidence that he was guilty of the crime of shooting Miss Waddell in 1944.

How do I know so much about Nicolas Schmitz? He was in the next cell to mine in 1945 at the German Military Prison in Jersey and was under sentence of death for desertion. There were many Germans in the old prison block and many under sentence of death. But for some reason the Germans placed Nicolas in our block. He was court martialed and sentenced to death in March 1945. The night before the sentence was to be carried out, the poor chap was sobbing and crying all night long and calling for his mother - Meine Mutter-Meine Mutter. For a 17 year old youth like myself it was very distressing to hear him. Talk about death's row in that row of cells on the top floor, there were five people under sentence of death.

The young soldier Nicolas Schmitz was taken out of his cell on the morning of 27 April 1945. He passed my window and I could see he was handcuffed between two army guards and followed by an army sergeant armed with a machine pistol. As they passed towards the first gate in the main square of the prison, his girlfriend (who was also arrested) called out to him from a facing top floor window. He pulled back against the handcuffs and shouted up to her and then a little dirty white handkerchief waved from the cell window. He called out again and the guards pushed and pulled him forward through the gate and lead him to his death by firing squad.

The soldier's girlfriend was also sentenced to death but the Jersey Bailiff's plea to the German Feldkommantant on her behalf saved her life. Her sentence of death was commuted to 10 years imprisonment. She still lives in Jersey.

BERT CHARDINE

In May 1942, PC Bert Chardine helped three Jersey lads to escape from Jersey. He gave them petrol for their boat. The three lads were Peter Hassell, Maurice Gould and Denis Audrain. They were trying to escape from Jersey to England and were carrying photographs of the German defenses in Jersey. But their boat overturned and Denis Audrain who could not swim was drowned. The other two, Peter Hassell and Maurice Gould, were captured and sent to German concentration camps. Maurice Gould perished in a German penal prison 1 October 1943. Peter survived the war and died in Canada just a few years ago.

P.C. Bert Chardine was arrested for trying to help the three lads to escape from Jersey and he served two months in the German prison in Gloucester Street, St Helier. By 15 February 1945, he was already back in the local force when he was instructed by Police Sgt Griffin to patrol Gloucester and Newgate Streets (outside the prison) to stop any political prisoners from escaping. Bert refused to carry out this order to stop loyal British people from escaping from the prison. His report which he gave me a copy of just before he died in Jersey, 25 November 1998, is published here in full.

I asked Bert one day in 1997 if he knew who gave the local uniformed police the order to patrol outside the prison to stop our loyal people from escaping. Bert told me it was the Jersey (His Majesty's) Attorney General C.W. Duret Aubin, acting on orders from the Germans. This did not surprise me at all!

Beglaubigte Abschrift.

Gericht   St. Helier, den 11. Juni 194 2.

der Feldkommandantur 515

St. L.   Nr. 279 /1942

Strafverfügung

gegen

den **britischen Staatsangehörigen, Poliz. Constable**

Albert Alfred C h a r d i n e in Fair View Village, Grouville

geboren am 30. 9. 1916   in St. Martin, Jersey

wird wegen **Hehlerei**

eine Strafe von 2   (in Buchstaben: zwei)

~~Tagen Wochen~~ — Monaten Gefängnis — ~~Festungshaft Stubenarrest gelinden geschärften strengen Arrest Haft Reichsmark, an deren Stelle im Falle der Uneinbringlichkeit~~ treten, festgesetzt.

~~Die erkannte Strafe gilt durch die erlittene Untersuchungshaft in Höhe von als verbüßt.~~

~~Daneben wird (Einziehung; Bekanntmachung der Entscheidung)~~

Sachverhalt:

Der Bestrafte hat im Mai 1942 in St. Helier seines Vor-
teils wegen Sachen - 4 Gallonen Benzin -, von denen er

B 36 Strafverfügung (§ 48 a KStVO.) (Sept. 1941) C/1440
Verlag Franz Vahlen, Berlin W 9

den Umständen nach annehmen musste, dass sie mittels einer
strafbaren Handlung erlangt sind, an sich gebracht und zu deren
Absatz bei anderen mitgewirkt,

indem er das Benzin von einem unbekannten O.T. Angehörigen erwarb, der es sich durch eine Unterschlagung zugeeig-
net hatte, und es an den Engländer Hassalt weitergab,

~~Übertretung~~ — Vergehen — ~~Verbrechen~~ nach § 259 R.Str.G.B.

Beweismittel:

Eigene Angaben.

Diese Strafverfügung wird rechtskräftig und vollstreckbar, wenn nicht innerhalb
dreier Tage nach ihrer Bekanntgabe schriftlich oder mündlich Einspruch erhoben wird.
Der Einspruch kann bei dem Gerichtsherrn, dem nächsten Disziplinarvorgesetzten oder bei
dem Offizier oder Beamten, der die Strafverfügung bekanntgegeben hat, erhoben werden.
Der schriftliche Einspruch ist nur dann rechtzeitig eingelegt, wenn er innerhalb der drei
Tage bei einer dieser Dienststellen eingeht.
**Die Strafvollstreckung wird nach Rechtskraft dieser
Strafverfügung angeordnet.**
Der Gerichtsherr: Der Untersuchungsführer:

gez. Knackfuss   gez. Dr. Seger
     Oberst.   Oberfeld-Kriegsgerichtsrat

Die Richtigkeit der Abschrift
wird beglaubigt.
den 13 Juni 1942

Heeresjustizinspektor

183

POLICE REPORT.

DATE .... 15-2-1945 ....

TIME .... 6-50 P.M. ....

SUBJECT ...... Re. Patrolling of Gloucester St. &Newgate St. ....

.... Re. escaping of Political Prisoners. ....

SIR,

     I beg to report that at the above stated time I was instructed by P.Sgt. Griffin to patrol Gloucester St. & Newgate St. re. Political Prisoners attempting to escape from prison.

     On receiving the instructions I refused to carry them out because I dontt think it is the duty of a civilian Policeman, and I have friends who havebbeen put in prison by the Germans for very litte little reason, and Iwould not like them to know that I was outside waiting to catch them ifthey tried to escape; and as you know I, and several other Policeman have been in prison for the Germans, and Iam sure if any of us were in their today we would not like to know that onr own workmates were waiting to try and stop us from escaping.

A. A. Chardine

*I certify that the above is a genuine
copy of a Police Report by P.C. Chardine
and copied by me as Town Clerk of
St. Helier in 1945.*

W. H. Marshall

184

A letter — after 53 years

During the Occupation, Bert Chardine helped three men to escape by supplying petrol. Until this year, he never knew what happened to one of them . . .

DURING the Occupation, Bert Chardine, a member of the Paid Police, earned two months in prison for giving some petrol to a group of young men planning to escape from the Island.

The boys, Denis Audrain, Maurice Gould and Peter Hassell, made their escape carrying photographs of the Island's defences but the boat overturned and the papers washed ashore. Denis Audrain, who couldn't swim, was drowned and the other two were later captured and sent to forced labour camps.

Maurice Gould died there but Peter Hassell was eventually returned to England.

Mr Chardine has always wondered what became of Peter Hassell, who never returned to the Island, until recently when, after 53 years, he received a letter from Mr Hassell who now lives in Ontario.

He writes: 'I have had you on my conscience for 53 years, and although I knew that you had been sentenced to two months in the German lock-up I was very worried in case you also lost your position as a policeman.

'In 1942 we came to you because we knew that you were trustworthy and patriotic. You were stupefied that we were such idiots and constantly warned us about the perils of the undertaking. Despite your warnings, youthful arrogance prevailed. Consequently I am alone.

'Denis Audrain, as you know, drowned on 3 May 1942 and Maurice Gould perished in a German prison on 1 October 1943.

'I went on to survive three years in about eight or nine concentrations camps and prisons. I could not face returning to the Island as I felt very guilty, being the only one alive.

'Subsequently, I spent 25 years in Military Intelligence and the last 20 as an investigator with the Ontario Securities Commission. I find it very hard to return to the islands, but all concentration camp survivors have that syndrome.

'I have one policeman son and another who is the director of a juvenile prison — the worm turned.'

Bert Chardine pictured during the Occupation

185

JOHN HENRY INGROUILLE

John Henry Ingrouille, was born on 3rd April 1920, Guernsey, Channel Islands. He was the only child of John and Alora Ingrouille of La Miellette, Vale.

John attended the Vale School until he was 15 years old. In 1938-1939 he worked on a farm in Jersey. He returned to Guernsey in July 1940 and had to work as a cook for the German Occupation forces at Vale Mill. John was a bit of a joker and one day he pulled the leg of the Germans, telling them that he could raise an army of 800 men to fight against them.

The Germans took what John said as fact, and arrested him. They also accused him of stealing some knives and forks from his place of work, Vale Mill. John was informed against by a Guernsey woman and her daughter, December 1940. He was sent under armed escort to Jersey where he faced a German Military Court. The woman who had informed against him was also sent to the Jersey court - as a witness for the German prosecution. John Ingrouille was sentenced to 5 years imprisonment. In January 1941 he was deported to Caen penal prison in France where he remained for 18 months, then was moved to Germany. In May 1945 he was liberated from the Brandenburg penal prison. On his way back to England his health was so undermined by the brutal treatment he had suffered in the German camps and penal prisons that he collapsed at Brussels Airport. He was taken to the American hospital in Brussels where he died on 13 June 1945. John's body was brought back to Guernsey in 1946 and buried in the Vale Church Cemetery.

On Liberation Day, Guernsey 1945, the woman and the daughter who had informed against John Ingrouille were seized and had their hands tied by a large crowd of loyal Guernsey people but before the crowd could give them their due punishment British soldiers rescued them.

John Henry Ingrouille was a very brave young Guernseyman. We hope and pray that someone or other in Guernsey will remember John on 13 June each year, the anniversary of his death. I am told that he was a happy-go-lucky young man who loved life.

A Beintôt, Mon Vier.
A La Prechaine

Joe Mière

GERMAN RuSHA COMMISSION (Rasse und Siedlungshauptamt) (Race and Settlement Head Office)

Channel Islands Children born to German Fathers. 1940 - 1945.

If the Occupation of the Channel Islands by the German forces had gone on for another year or if 'D' Day had been in June 1945, and not June 1944, would we have witnessed our very own Jersey children who had blue eyes and blond hair being taken by force to German 'Lebensborn' homes in France and Germany. It could have happened. Remember that in 1942-1943 the Germans deported over 2,000 UK born Channel Islanders by force to internment camps in Germany. Among them there were many very young children. So who or what would have stopped the Germans from taking our children to Germany to be brought up as Germans?

The German Lebensborn Organisation had left it late, May 1944, to cast their net on the children of the Channel Islands. Thank God for 'D' Day, the 6th of June 1944. I don't think that many people living in these Islands these days, or those dark days of 1940-45, know or even realise that the German RuSHA Commission 'Rasse und Siedlungshauptant' (Race and Settlement) from the SS 'Lebensborn Organisation' in Germany, sent a unit to these Islands in 1944.

The SS RuSHA unit was ordered to subject to racial examination the illegitimate children born to local women that had been fathered by German servicemen of the occupying forces. Also the mothers of these illegitimate German children were also to be subject to racial examination by the SS RuSHA unit. The 'Lebensborn' records consist of 200 files containing 500 documents in each file

The Channel Islands

In one document found in the files on the Channel Islands, the RuSHA Commission Order stated; that all mothers with children already born whose fathers were German servicemen in so far as they comply with our racial specifications will be transferred to Germany. And all the women made pregnant by German servicemen will be taken to German Lebensborn homes in France. The SS Lebensborn home at Lamorlaye, north of Paris, was opened by the SS on 6 February 1944, in a château that belonged to the well known Ménier family. The officer in charge was SS Oberstabsarzt und Sturmbannführer der Schutzpolizei Dr Fritz. One of the German RuSHA documents on the children of the Channel Islands stated that not all the products of Jersey and Guernsey were equally valuable racially in the eyes of the SS Lebensborn Commission. The document stated that many mothers were not up to standard.

The 'Lebensborn' documents go on to state that in a letter dated 24 May 1944 sent by the head of the Race Office in Berlin (The Lebensborn Organisation had its headquarters in Munich). The letter and document states; according to a communication from Area Command No 515 (515 was the German Administration Headquarters at College House, St Helier, Jersey) that "since the Occupation of the Channel Islands by German Forces eighty children have been born whose fathers are unquestionably members of the German occupying forces. In view of the high Nordic component in the race of the Channel Islands' population which is substantially higher than that of continental France, the mothers and children concerned should be racially valuable and flawless. So the Rusha leader considers that the racially and genetically flawless children, and perhaps also mothers, should contribute to the desired growth of the population of the German people by being resettled in the Reich.

The document goes on to state; The situation of these unmarried mothers is very bad indeed, as on one hand they are persecuted by the rest of the civil population of the Islands, and on the other they have been refused any maintenance allowance for the children by the Military Command in France. In most cases these English mothers have learnt German so they could be transferred to Germany without difficulty. The documents go on to state; At a conference on 24 May 1944 between the Lebensborn representative and the senior officer of the SS and police in France, SS Sturmbannführer Dr Fritz and myself, it was decided that in future the Lebensborn Organisation should take over responsibility for the expectant mothers in the Channel Islands, after previous investigation by the RuSHA leader.

The documents also state; Racially, the women in the Channel Islands came halfway between the high Norwegian rating and the lower rating attributed to French women. The documents point to many instances of mothers being not up to standard. When they were, in most cases the child was taken away and placed in a Lebensborn home somewhere in Europe. The documents show, among other things, how broad was the gamut of methods employed by the RuSHA in laying its hands on children. These varied according to requirements, but the mother's feelings were never taken into account. On the 8th June 1944, just two days after the Allied landings in Normandy, France, a young woman of French origin but British nationality, made an application for nationality. Because of her antecedents she was classified in category 3, that of a woman who was undesirable - meaning racially undesirable.

The German RuSHA examiner made the following report; Yvonne S is expecting a second illegitimate child by the same German soldier, Horst B.. Nevertheless I regret not being able to place her in category 2 (possible), the lowest necessary for granting of German nationality. In spite of everything the girl makes a good impression. I therefore ask the leader of the RuSHA for a decision in relation to her and her children, who could be transferred to a Lebensborn home in France. What happened to Yvonne S? Did the father of her two children marry her before the Lebensborn office grabbed them? In Jersey there are a number of people with a name strangely resembling hers but none of these have ever heard of her. Yvonne and her two children vanished from Jersey without leaving a forwarding address. June L also had two children, the father being a German officer. She left Jersey in 1944 for Germany and, up to this date, she still lives with her her husband in North Germany.

After the end of the war in 1945, Poland and other countries requested British, American and French help in finding the 200,000 taken from Poland and the thousands taken from other occupied countries. Give the Russians credit, they made sure that 20,000 kidnapped children in the Russian zone of Germany were returned to their families. But a fact that seems incredible is that only 6,000 of kidnapped children were returned from the British, American and French zones of occupation in Germany.

At the Conference of the International Refugee Organisation in Geneva on 10th May 1948 it was decided that searches for the kidnapped children should cease in July 1949. Children found in the British zone in Germany after that date would be sent to the British colonies. In 1947 the Allies of yesterday were slowly sliding into the cold war. Poland was by then a Communist state. The Germans did not declare to the occupying authorities that they were bringing up non-German children. There were also difficulties with the children themselves who were demoralised and passionately Germanised so they denied their true nationality. The West German judges who dealt with these cases of the adoption of kidnapped children were mostly ex-Nazis so it was inconceivable that they should decide against their fellow citizens in cases involving returning the kidnapped children to their true families.

Their is no lack of examples of this post-war Nazi justice which decided the fate of innocent victims in favour of their tormentors. Only 15% of Polish children torn from their families to be Germanised have been repatriated to Poland.

References: The Lebensborn records consist of 200 files, containing 500 documents in each file.

International Search Service, Arolsen, Germany

German Trial of the heads of the Lebensborn Organisation, Munich
1950-1951.   Case No 11985/L/o/ 1955.

American Military Tribunal No 1 Case No 8 the RuSHA SS Race Office and Lebensborn Organisation 1947-1948.

Polish Commission. Warsaw. Kalisz. Katowice. Poland.

Potsdam Library Germany.

West German report on the Lebensborn Organisation. Bonn, Germany 1955.

Wiener Library. London, England.

Unesco report , Trogen, Switzerland. July 1948.

Centre de documentation. Paris, France.

The Library of Contemporary International Documention of the University of Nanterre, France.

The Joe Mière Collection. File 3982/a. Archive No 8 at the Jersey War Tunnels, St Lawrence, Jersey, Channel Islands.

German babies 'were destined for the Reich'

BY ELAINE HANNING

BABIES with German fathers born to Jersey women during the Occupation were viewed as 'racially flawless' and were destined to be sent to Germany to contribute to the racial purity of the Reich.

German documents from 1944 show that German officials recorded only 80 such births during four years of Occupation and reveal that it was proposed that the babies and their mothers should be sent to Germany.

The documents, notes from which are now in the Joe Mière collection, show that the race and resettlement unit of the SS Lebensborn Organisation, RuSHA, which resettled half-German children from occupied countries in Aryan homes, visited the Island in May 1944. Their task was the racial exami-

nation of illegitimate children born to local women and fathered by German servicemen. The mothers were also to be examined.

A letter from Feldkommandantur 515, at College House, dated 24 May 1944, carried a clear message to Berlin: 'Since the Occupation of the Channel Islands by German forces, 80 children have been born whose fathers are unquestionably members of the German occupying forces. In view of the high Nordic component in the race of the Channel Islands population which is substantially higher than that of continental France, the mothers and children concerned should be racially valuable and flawless, so the RuSHA leader considers that the racial-

ly and genetically flawless children and perhaps also mothers should contribute to the desired growth of the population of the German people being resettled in the Reich.'

The plan, which also included passing the responsibility for future expectant mothers to the SS unit, was never carried out because just two weeks later D-Day changed the destiny of the half-German babies.

● The files referred to are from the American Military Tribunal No 1, case No 8, the RuSHA-SS Race Office and Lebensborn Organisation, 1947 to 1948, the archives of the Süddeutsche Zeitung, Munich, information from the International Search Service, Arolsen, and the German trial of the heads of the Lebensborn Organisation, Munich, 1950 to 1951, collected and collated by Joe Mière.

The Germans left behind more than a few concrete bunkers in the Channel Islands,

How Jersey's Nazi children disappeared

The Westaway Crèche was once a prominent feature in the neatly manicured streets of St Helier, Jersey. But there are no references to it in the public library, and the trust that ran it is now chiefly remembered as a donor of children's shoes. The crèche, like the children it once housed, has become part of Jersey's unspoken, and controversial history.

Records released this week by the Public Records Office suggest that as many as 900 half-German babies were born to Jersey women during the occupation. The fierce denials of this fact in Jersey show that 50 years on, some wounds have not yet healed.

The children themselves – the only people who could shed light on the true figure – are unlikely to answer. They have "disappeared", or are carefully protected by the few remaining people who know their parentage.

Many residents who are old enough to remember, will tell you that such children were their neighbours, or at their school. But they will not tell you the true figure, will tell you that the past is "left well alone".

coast kept Napoleon's forces at bay but were no defence against the Nazis

Photograph: R

German Underground Hospital Museum, is widely considered to be the island's "occupation expert". He is

wept tears of anger at the latest "exaggerated" claims that most Jersey women slept with Germans

off for execution. Alice's own death sentence

Plan to make master race

Jojo Moyes and Elizabeth Wine

Children born during the Nazi occupation of the Channel Islands narrowly escaped being transported to Germany as part of a programme to produce a master race, a historian has claimed.

Joe Mière, former curator of Jersey's German Underground Hospital, says that documents from sources across Europe show that a unit from an elite SS squad visited shortly before D-Day to assess the "racial suitability" of 80 children born illegitimately to Jersey mothers.

The visit was part of the Lebensborn programme initiated by Heinrich Himmler, which produced some 7,500 children. Officers were ordered to father "perfect Aryans" in special Lebensborn homes, while in occupied countries suitable children were stolen to improve future blood stocks.

Documents dated 24 May 1944 addressed to the RuSHA (racial unit) headquarters in Berlin state: "Since the occupation of the Channel Islands by German forces, 80 children have been born whose fathers are unquestionably members of the German occupying forces ... The situation of these unmarried mothers is very bad indeed.

Mr Mière, who has studied the occupation for more than 50 years, said many mothers did in fact move to Germany.

Michael Leapman, co-author of the book *Master Race*, about the Lebensborn programme, said that the new documents showed that even at the late stage of the war, the Nazis were still being selective. "Because Himmler admired British stock the Germans were looking to increase their population by taking illegitimate children fathered by German soldiers. Whether these children had a lucky escape or not I don't know.

Articals in The Independent Newspaper
Saturday 23rd November 1996

192

ARRESTED OCTOBER 1941

My best friend Frank Le Pennec and I were walking past Burton's Corner, King Street on the morning of 19 October 1941, when we accidentally bumped against a German officer and he nearly lost his balance. We walked on but the German officer was not going to let this go before he had made a fuss. He shouted at us to stop, he caught up with us and started shouting at us in passable English. He informed us that we would have to apologise for our bad manners and disrespect to an officer of the German Army.

We told him it was done accidentally, and why all the fuss over nothing. The German officer blew his top and started to shout at us in German. We went to move on when the German called out to a local policeman who had been standing on Hettich's corner observing what was going on. The policeman had just started to move away (we think he did not want to get involved with this little farce) but came over and the German officer ordered him 'arrest these two and take them to the police station. I will follow to report and press charges.'

So off we went, the policeman (who did not look happy) walking between Frank and myself, the German officer following behind us. We arrived at the Town Hall. We were told to wait in a room full of lockers and sat on a long bench. The policeman and the German officer went in to the duty Centenier's office.

After half an hour we were called into another office. The Centenier started to lay down the law to us. How good the Germans had been and how well they had treated the local population, etc, etc, and how we should show respect to German officers. He then informed us that the officer had laid an official complaint against us and, at the officer's request, we would be held in police custody until they had checked our details, and seen if we had any police records.

After a lot of brown nosed creeping by the Centenier, the German officer shook hands with him and other policemen and parish officials, then left. We were then taken by the police van to the prison in Gloucester Street and handed over to the German military part of the prison. We were then placed in the same cell. Unknown to us was the fact that it would not be the last time we saw the inside of these cells. The other cells were full of local people.

The next morning, after a so-called breakfast, we were escorted down to the Town Hall. In an office was the same German officer and the same centenier, also another man that we took to be the Connétable of St Helier. The Centenier said that he hoped we had learned our lesson. He also informed us that the German officer was going to give us a warning that if we ever got into trouble with the German or local police we would be imprisoned and deported from the Island 'Is this understood?' We both nodded in assent.

We did not mind so much the German officer. After all, he was a German and, like most of them, he thought he was part of the Master Race but we were disgusted with the Centenier's brown nosed creeping to the German. As we left the Town Hall two local policemen gave us a smile and said to us: 'never mind lads, the day will come.' These two were two of the good and loyal policemen.

ON THE RUN FROM THE GERMAN POLICE AND ARRESTED
NOVEMBER 1944

In November 1944 I was working at Washington's Salon at First Tower when one morning one of the girls, Maud Guyoncourt, told me that my sister Marguerite was on the phone and wanted to speak to me. Marguerite told me that she was phoning from a friend's house because the German Secret Field Police were searching our house from top to bottom. They wanted to know where I was because they wanted to question me. My mother told them she did not know where I was at this time of the day. I told my sister that it would be better if I went into hiding until the hue and cry had died down. She could keep in touch with Maud if anything new turned up.

First of all, I made my way to my friend Frank Le Pennec's house which was only a short distance away from Washington's salon. I warned Frank's mother to hide any wireless sets or anything that would get them into trouble with the Germans. I had to try and get a message to Frank at his work to warn him that David Dawson had already been arrested and that the Germans were searching my home. There was a good chance that they would arrest Frank and search his home. I was very worried about David Dawson. He was a big chap but not very strong minded.

Now where to hide myself? At the back of Washington's salon there was a disused old coal store. When the Germans came to the salon looking for me Maud told them that no one in the salon had seen me for days and the last time they saw me I was cycling towards St Aubins. The Germans searched the shop and as they left they warned my boss that if I turned up he was to phone them at once. They left a note with their phone number.

What a brave and good friend I had in Maud. The following morning she brought me two old blankets and some food my sister had taken to her home. It was a very miserable place to hide away in but I had to grin and bear it. It was better than being in a German police cell and it would suit me till I found a better place to hide myself from the Germans. The floor of the store was only earth and sand, the outer walls being made of wood. It had been built on part of a small garden. The roof was not very good. One night it rained heavily and water leaked into the store. I had to move around to dodge being soaked.

I could not make any noise because next door was the German OT bread store. Good job the floor was made of earth and sand. I made a hole in one corner to use as a toilet and in the dark it was not easy to use. After six days in the old coal store I had washed but did not shave. Maud brought me a message from my sister to tell me that the Germans had been back to our house for another search, and had taken from my room my grandfather's sword that was hanging on a wall. They had also forced open the boarded up small fireplace in my room and found leaflets and some small boxes of ammunition.

They informed my mother that they were not going to waste time searching for me, but if I did not give myself up and report to them they would arrest all the family and imprison them. They also stated that I had only 24 hours in which to give myself up or they would carry out their threat of arrest. I knew that my family would not give me away but I made up my mind to give myself up for a very good reason. If my family were arrested and imprisoned who would look after our home? In no time people or Germans would loot all our goods. It was a sign of the times when people you had known for years would not think twice about stealing your furniture and household goods but these were not normal times and all that my family had worked hard for would be gone. So I decided to give myself up and try to bluff myself out of trouble. They already had arrested Frank and David and for the sake of my family I would have to face the music, come what may.

On the way to Silvertide, the German Secret Field Police HQ at Havre des Pas, I met my Uncle, P.C. René Le Huquet. I told him where I was going and he said to me 'Careful, Joe, they will hurt you.' He had seen them in action when they had arrested people late at night in town. The German police sometimes accompanied the local police when they patrolled the town after the curfew hour. Uncle René then said: 'There is nothing any of us can do to help you, so take care and best of luck, Joe.'

I made my way to Silvertide, rang the bell and after a short wait the door was opened by a German. He looked me over and said: 'What do you want?' I told him that I was told to report here. I gave him my name and showed him my ID card. He then escorted me down the hall and into a room that overlooked the beach and sea. There were three other Germans in the room, one was sitting behind a table used as a desk by the look of the paperwork on it.

I was told to sit on a chair that was facing him. Again, name and address and ID card. The German behind the table was Heinz C. Woelfe, as I would later find out, one of the best known of the German Secret Field Police - and with a Canadian accent. (He had lived in Canada for a few years.) He said: 'So you think you can make a fool out of us. We will see about that.'

Then the questions started. This went on for over an hour. In between the questions one of the Germans would punch me when I did not answer in the way they wanted. Woelfe said to me: 'We know all about you and your friends.' I asked him why all this fuss if they knew so much about us? He did not like this one bit. Then it was two of them that really started to knock me about. One blow sent me flying onto the floor. I had hardly got up when they knocked me down again. I was beginning to think that it was not such a good idea to have given myself up to these brutes.

Woelfe said something in German to the two men who were giving me a hard time. They escorted me out of the room, down the hall and out to a waiting car. By this time I was in a real daze so I do not remember which route they took to the prison. There I was put in a cell. The next morning I was taken out to the guardroom where, waiting for me, were the German Navy Harbour Police. They took me on foot to their HQ which was at the corner of Weighbridge Place and Mulcaster Street - part of the Pomme d'Or Hotel.

There they started to question me, the questions always accompanied by blows to the face and body when they could not get any information out of me. I did think:"What the hell has the German Harbour Police got to do with all this." They started to shout and rave about us having weapons and wanted to know where we had hidden them. I felt like a ping pong ball caught between the German Secret Field Police and the German Harbour Police. After about two hours they took me back to the prison.

Two days later the German Secret Field Police again came for me and took me back to Silvertide. This time three Germans had a go at me and kept knocking me down with nearly every blow. And before I knew it I was spitting out blood, I reached into my pocket for my handkerchief and I wiped my lips. I could feel bits of teeth in my mouth and as I spat into my handkerchief there were bits of teeth in the saliva. My lips were cut and I could feel that some of my front teeth were missing. I placed the handkerchief with the bits of teeth in it back into my pocket. I do not remember much after this, being in a state of shock, and found myself back at the prison. Otto, one of the German prison guards, brought me water and a rag to wipe my face. The brutal treatment and questions went on for weeks. With one day the German Secret Field Police, another day the German Navy Harbour Police. The Navy Police were worse than the Silvertide lot.

One morning in the prison Otto and Ludwig, two of the German prison guards, escorted me to the hospital, took me to the top floor to a small room where a German Army dentist treated me. He removed the bits of broken teeth that were in my gums but he never even asked me how I had lost my teeth, nor was he very gentle with his treatment. He spoke to the two prison guards so I take it they must have told him all about me.

On the way back to the prison Ludwig said to me: 'Don't judge all Germans the same.' I did know what he meant because the German prison guards had never ill-treated me in any way, and were always correct towards me. All of a sudden, the brutal treatment from the German Police stopped. They still shouted at us and still demanded answers to their questions but no more beatings. I found out later that my mother had been to see the Bailiff of Jersey and she had informed him how the German Police were treating us. The Bailiff told my mother that he would look into the matter. And he did. He complained to the German Kommandant, explaining how two young Jerseymen were being treated by the German Police.

If you read Sinel's Diary you will see on page 264, dated 31 January 1945, that two boys had been beaten up by the Germans. We did find out later why both German Police forces (the German Secret Field Police and the German Naval Harbour forces) were so angry with us. If was because one night a group of us had tarred the houses of the girlfriend of the head of the German Secret Field Police, Bode, and of the girlfriend of the head of the German Naval Harbour Police, Kohler. Now we know why the German Police treated us so brutally.

We were pleased when at least in February 1945 we were sent before a German Military Court. No more getting woken up late at night to be questioned and ill-treated. They used all the old tricks of their trade, even telling me that Frank had signed a statement, I asked them to show me this. They refused because he had not signed anything. They told Frank the same. He also asked to see my so called statement and again they refused and again because I had not signed anything. They had no proof.

What we were charged with at the Military Court was only guess work on their part, and information from their paid informers. These informers were paid about 100 marks every time they reported anyone to the German Police. There is a list of these informers at the Jersey Archives but these documents are closed till the year 2045, as some of these informers are still alive and living in Jersey. Ref: Documents DZ/D/2/H9/2.

THE BLANK STARTING PISTOL AND GERMAN POLICE

Bode. Head of German
Secret Field Police

H. Woelfe

Karl Lohse/Lose

German Naval & Marine Police HQ.
Pomme d'Or Hotel, Wharf Street
.Rebuilt in the late 1970's

Wilmelm. Mitz-Steinkat

Grosskopf

In November 1944, I and my pals Frank Le Pennec and David Dawson were arrested by the German Secret Field Police (Geheimefeldpolizei) and taken to the German Military section of the public prison in Gloucester Street, St Helier. Most days we were taken from our cells one at a time and brought under armed escort to the notorious German Secret Field Police HQ at 'Silvertide,' Havre des Pas, for interrogation. The German Harbour Navy Police (Hafenueberwachungsstelle) were also taking a hand in interrogating us at their headquarters which was on the corner of Weighbridge Place and Mulcaster Street, (The Pomme d'Or Hotel).

Sometimes you were taken out for interrogation at 11pm. You were hardly returned to your cell when the German Navy Police arrived and took you to their headquarters to be interrogated. It seemed a if the two police forces were in a competition to see who could get a signed statement from us. Well, poor old David broke down and signed a statement. They had knocked him about so badly that he just signed anything they asked him to sign.

They also got him to pick us out at an identity parade. This took place at a Harbour Police room at La Folie Inn at the South Pier. Frank and myself had to stand facing the wall, and we were told not to turn around. But out of the corner of my eye I saw it was poor old David. We never held this against him because we knew he was not strong minded, and we knew he did not know about us having hand guns. We had never told him too much so we knew he had no knowledge of Frank's pistol or the hand guns I had hidden at my grandmother's cottage. After a year we felt sorry for him. He was always having treatment for mental stress The poor chap died many years ago when he was still very young.

At one time Frank and I were very close to breaking point but the thought of dishonour to our families and ourselves made us strong - and as we both came from Norman and Breton stock we were very stubborn minded. During our interrogations by the Secret Field Police and the Navy Police, both of them kept on about a pistol and other firearms. The questions were always accompanied by blows to the face and body. A kick in the crotch was very painful. Those German police knew how to hurt you.

I was getting fed up with this brutal treatment and there was plenty of time to think when you are locked up in a small cell for nearly 24 hours a day. So how, I asked myself, do we find some way to get the German police off our backs. Frank and I could not chat about this problem because they kept us apart in separate cells. One day after much deep thinking I devised a plan in my head. Sometimes a little simple plan can work if every one keeps to the plan but they must have faith and trust in you.

I remembered that my sister Marguerite's boyfriend, Johnny Hoar (whom she helped to escape from Jersey in 1944) possessed a small starting pistol which fired blanks. So one day I wrote instructions to Marguerite on an old piece of paper and tied the note around a stone I found in the exercise yard. When next out on exercise I threw it over the wall into the civilian prison yard.

Luck was on my side that day. A prison warder, Frank Veron, found it and he was a friend of my family. When he went off duty that night he took the note to my sister. It was a great risk. If he had been caught with the note he would have lost his job and the Germans would have imprisoned him. The note ran as follow.

Dear Marguerite,

Please go to Johnny Hoar's house and find his little starting pistol. And please take it to Frank Le Pennec's home at First Tower and ask his mother to sew the starting pistol in the bottom lining of a mack or old overcoat, and hang the coat or mack behind a bedroom door. Please Marguérite, on no account must my instructions be changed in any way. It is a matter of saving Frank's and my life, and tell Mrs Le Pennec that when the Germans search the house again she is to show them where the starting pistol is hidden. So please, Marguerite carry out my instructions to the letter. And tell no one of all this. And please burn this note. One day I will tell you what it is all about, and do this as soon as possible.

With love, Joe X X X.

The one person to be trusted in carrying out this task was my sister. She was a very brave girl and had been arrested before by the Germans so she knew I would have the understanding if she did not want to act as the link between me and Frank's mother. I did not stop to think of anyone else finding the note in the prison yard. Three days later when in the yard I threw a note in to Frank's cell window. Again it was not easy because there were bars on the outside, then a small glass window partly open, then another set of bars on the inside - so it was luck that the note went through the small opening.

In my note to Frank I explained to him my little plan to get the German police off our backs regarding the pistol, and he was to tell them the next time he was interrogated where he had hidden the so-called pistol. I assured him that the blank pistol was a starting pistol and could only fire blanks because the barrel was solid steel. Knowing Frank so well, I was sure he would want to start arguing that the plan would not work. Dear old Frank, even when we were in the German Military Court waiting room he was not convinced that the plan would work. He said 'What about if the German Court placed other real pistols alongside the blank pistol' and 'How would I know which was the blank pistol and I pick out the wrong pistol.' I told him that I had seen the blank pistol many times at Johnny Hoar's house - and he was to look at the wooden butt plates, the plate on the right hand side had a piece missing. Also the trigger folded up and there was no German Occupation law in force stating you could not own a sports blank pistol. Besides, when his hand pointed out or touched the blank pistol I would cough loudly.

A few days later Frank and I were taken one morning to the German Secret Field Police HQ. Frank told them, after being knocked about, where he had hidden the pistol. The Germans looked so pleased with themselves, thinking that they were going to find the real pistol. They took me back to my cell at the prison, then took Frank by car to his home at First Tower and he showed them where the pistol was hidden. They were not very pleased to find not a real pistol but a blank starting pistol. Then they went mad and started to hit him. As the blows came fast and hard, he let out a cry. His mother was in the room and she screamed 'What are you doing to my son!' One of the Germans shouted at her: 'Be quiet, otherwise you will get the same.' These methods were seen by one of Frank's sisters who was in the room.

The Germans then took Frank back to the prison. I was taken from my cell to the guardroom where the Secret Field Police were waiting for me. They called me all the names under the sun, then started to push and punch me about. One said in English: 'You and your friend think you are smart' and with that a few more blows before I was returned to my cell. They were angry with us, they did not like to be made to look like fools. The plan must have worked in some way because after this last lot of brutal treatment they never asked any more about the pistol.

One morning in February 1945, we three, Frank, David and myself, were taken from our cells and into the guardroom. There was a four man escort, fully armed and waiting to take us to the German Military Court at Avondale, Lower Kings Cliff. The guards gave us a warning: 'If you try to escape we will shoot you.' Three of the escorts were armed with machine pistols, and one was armed with a rifle.

We left the prison by the main side gate and were marched up Gloucester Street, through the Parade Gardens, then into Lower Kings Cliff. They took us into the back entrance of Avondale (it is still there) then up the back stairs and into a small room which we took to be the waiting room for the Court - and so it was.

As we were getting marched along the route to the Court, Frank and I tried to chat, but the guards ordered us to keep silent and not to speak to one another. But in the Court's waiting room we did have a chance to chat. Frank was still very worried that the plan of the blank pistol would not work. 'If this doesn't work, Joe, we will be in a right mess.' I told him to have a little faith and to wait and see. He once more said to me 'What about if I pick out the wrong pistol?'

I repeated again for him to look for a small pistol that had a folding trigger and that one of the butt plates had a part missing. I also repeated that if his hand touched the blank pistol I would cough loudly. Frank was still not convinced that it would work. After waiting for a quarter of an hour we were marched into the court room.

This long room had three windows all facing the front of the house. At a long table sat three German officers. The officer sitting in the middle was wearing a monocle. And on the right of the table sat a German Army corporal who was to be our defence counsel. And a lot of use he was! Every time he stood up to speak he was told to be quiet by the officer wearing the monocle. On the wall behind the three officers was a big photograph of Hitler. Facing the three Judge's table were four rows of chairs and we were told to sit in the front row.

One of the three Judges read out the charges against us all in German. We could not understand one word of what he was on about. After a lot of old bull from the three German military judges Frank was called to the Judges' table, and, in English, one of the Judges asked Frank to point out the pistol found in an old coat at his home.

I must say that Frank had been right in one way because the Judges had placed in a neat row seven small pistols and automatic hand guns. From where I was sitting I could see the small blank starter pistol which had been placed in the middle of the row. Frank's first try went to the wrong pistol but as his hand moved along the row of hand guns and touched the blank starting pistol I gave out a loud cough. With his finger, he moved the small trigger and told the Judges 'This one.' 'Are you quite sure?' asked one of the Judges. Franks reply was: 'Yes because I remember that part of the wooden butt plate was missing.' He was told to look again, Frank made out to have another look and stated that it was still the same one. All the Judges looked over the blank pistol, each in turn, then Frank was told to return to his seat. They then returned us to the waiting room. About half an hour later, were marched back into the court room. We had to stand in front of the three military judges and they informed us of the court's findings. They then read out the charges against us. And one by one we were sentenced. At the start of the sentencing they began in German. *'Feld-Urteil; im Namen des Deutschen Volkes'* (Field Judgment, in the name of the German people).

In our court martial documents No. 46/45 dated 14 February, 1945 (I have copies) the German Military Justice Inspector states that the blanks gun was confiscated by the Truppenkriegsgericht. So the plan did work. The Germans never found the real pistol or the three handguns that were hidden at my grandmother's cottage. They knew they had somehow been had but they could not prove anything. The strange thing is that I never knew Frank had the real pistol. I had never seen it. And Frank never knew that I had three German hand guns.

After our court martial we were marched back to the German prison in Gloucester Street and in the guardroom the German Secret Field Police and the German Navy

Harbour Police were there waiting for our return. Heinz Woelfe tried to be friendly to us. Funny people these Germans! Only a few days before they were knocking us about. They said that they hoped there were no ill feelings now that we had been tried and sentenced (what cheek) One of the German Harbour policemen, Schraeler, from the Hafenueberwachunsstelle had lived in the USA and was at one time in the New York police. He told us that they knew we were telling a pack of lies about the pistol and they were very angry with us. He said: 'When we get you to Germany you will be sorry!' He was a very nasty and unpleasant man.

We asked Woelfe who had informed on us. He smiled and said 'You must be joking. We have our sources of information.' After this we were taken to our cells. When I think back on all this it is as if we had taken part in a film. But our experience at the brutal hands of the German police has left a deep mental scar in our minds. Even after all these years I sometimes wake at night in a cold sweat.

Frank was a very brave man and very intelligent. He had an alert mind, but he was never the same man again. As the years passed the brutal treatment we received from the German police took its toll. He was my best man when I married his lovely sister, Marie, in 1954. He was also godfather to our son, Jean-Pierre. Frank passed away in 1990. He was a well loved uncle to our three children, Jean-Pierre, Martine and Michael.

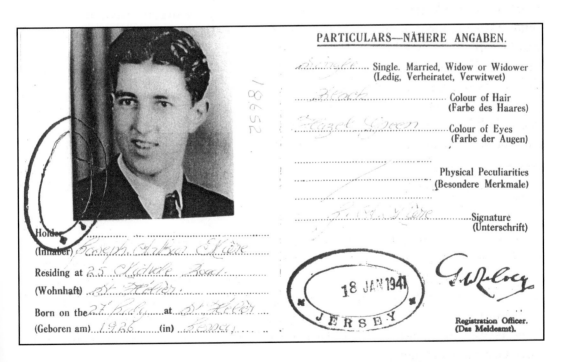

I lost my first ID card. Here is a copy of my second one.

3.

German Secret Field Police and Military Police, and Naval Police.

· ·

Geheimefeldpolizi. German Secret Field Police.

Bode.

Dusterhoft.   H.Q. Silvertide. Hame-des – Pas.

Grosskopf / Grosskapf.

Lohse / Lose.

Steinkat.

Wolfe / Woelfe.

· ·

Hafenueberwachungsstelle. German Naval and Marine Police.

Bootsmaat / Boottsmaat.   H.Q. Pomme D'or Hotel.

Kohler.

Kracht.

Krahl.

Schraeler / Schreler.

Von Cleve.

· ·

Feldgendarmerie. Military Police.   (H.Q. Bagatelle. St Saviours.)

Diechmann.

Engel / Engel.   Gelkler.   Kaufmann.   Roeder.   Weggermann.

Feckler.   Gossets.   Mohr.   Schneider.

Forster.   John.   Nichles.   Treutin.

   Karie.   Ricker.   Weekber.

· ·

Luftaufsichtsdienst. Air Force Police.

Hoffman.   H.Q. St Peters.

Heusinger.

Klopper.

Mueller.

Peiper.

· ·

Organisation Todt Polizei. O.T. Police.

Hauser.   H.Q. Midvale Road.

Heider.

Krans.

Weinert.

· ·

Polizeistandgericht. German Military Court.

     H.Q. Avondale. Lower Kings Cliff. Queens Avenue.

LETTER TO MY FATHER FROM GERMAN PRISON, 21 FEBRUARY 1945

My letter to my father was passed out of the prison by a very kind German prison warder.

Dear Dad,

Just a note to let you know I am still alive, lips badly cut, one eye closed, head getting fuzzy, 53 days of this so far. Feels funny without my front teeth. Please don't tell Mother she will only get upset. German guards not bad chaps in their own funny way, but Gestapo police real big soulless brutal pigs. Had to let you know dad just in case anything happens to me. Young German soldier in the next cell cried all night for his mother, yesterday he was sentenced to death.

Give my love to all at home, we will all be together again one day. (good night dad).
Love Joe

PS. Please take care of my little dog. X

FOUR GERMANS DROWN AT LA ROCQUE

After 'D' Day, 6th June 1944 the Germans in Jersey were on invasion alert. They did some strange things when it came to carrying out strict orders, sometimes causing tragic results.

On the early morning of 9th June 1944 four German soldiers of 10/Gren Rgt 582 were drowned at La Rocque where they were on guard duty. The tide gradually covered a rock on which they were standing. Although they could have been rescued by a La Rocque fisherman, the Germans would not allow it. Inexperienced German soldiers manned a boat at Gorey, but the four soldiers on the rock had drowned before the boat arrived.

The four soldiers were fully equipped and wore great coats. Their bodies were found at low water at the foot of the rock on which they had been standing. They were listed as follows.

Oberfeldwebel Paul Huebner. Born 13 July 1915. Grave 145.

Obergefreiter August Schaefer. Born 26 March 1904. Grave 146.

Gefreiter Josef Borowaki. Born 6 September 1919. Grave 147.

Grenadier Leo Dobrzewinski. Born 15 September 1919. Grave 148.

They were buried at the German Military Cemetery, St Brelade's Bay, Jersey.

All the above and others were exhumed in 1961 and taken for re-burial at the German Military Cemetery at Mont de Huisnes, La Manche, France.

SEARCH OF OUR HOUSE, NOVEMBER 1944

When the German Police were searching for me in November 1944, they closed off the top and bottom of Midvale Road. They were not just looking for me but also for some other person who could be hiding out in one of the big houses in the road.

It was a matter of German routine to take the opportunity of having a look round to see if anyone had stowed away a radio set - or wireless, as we called them in those days. Listening to the BBC news was forbidden by the Germans who realised that the progress of the war (with their forces retreating on all fronts) gave heart to us and made us more difficult to govern. The possession of a radio set would certainly get you into prison or worse - a concentration camp in Germany.

When the searchers came towards our house it was our little Grandmère who dealt with the crisis. She left the house by the basement door, taking her home-made push cart with its Victorian pram wheels and the radio set covered over with laundry. As Grandmère reached the bottom of the road the German Police stopped her and demanded to know where she had come from and where was she going.

The questions were in bad English and as Grandmère did not speak English or understand it and only spoke Norman French, they could not make her see what they wanted to know. At last they got fed up and let her pass. The funny thing was - they paid no attention to her little push cart and its pile of laundry and the radio set underneath.

However, the Germans rang our door bell, and Mother let them in with the words 'It's you again. What do you want this time?' They had looked over the house before, but only to open doors and look into rooms - not a full search. But this time they opened cupboards and drawers, garage and garden and even the loft.

In the basement they found the under stairs semi-cellar door locked and demanded that it be unlocked. Mother tried to tell them that it was only a children's play-acting toy shop, but this made them more keen to have it opened. When Mother had unlocked the door and switched the light on the faces of the Germans changed into big smiles and the reason was that, on row after row of wooden shelves, neatly stacked was what the German police thought was an 'Aladdin's Cave' of branded boxes of food of all kinds, packets of green label tea, packets of sugar, tins of 50 cigarettes, and in the wine racks were bottles of what looked like wine and brandy.

I must inform the reader of this fact. Before the war, say 1937, my two sisters and I used to play at shops, so we used to save most of the empty food packets and fill them up with sawdust. My sisters would re-seal the packets with glue. When the Occupation started we locked the door and forgot all about our play room.

The two Germans called out to the others who were searching upstairs. Soon there were five or six German police gazing at what they thought was a hoard of food. They shouted at my mother and wanted to know why this stock had not been declared to the authorities.

Mother took hold of a packet of tea and tore it open and all the sawdust fell out. She did the same with two other boxes and again the sawdust fell onto the floor. Then Mother said to them 'My children used to save all the old packets. You can take the lot if it makes you feel any better.' Two of the Germans opened some more packets and their faces dropped. They gave up and moved over to our now empty pantry, boot cupboard and so on.

But in searching my attic bedroom and after removing the sealed board from the fireplace and poking around, they found in a recess two small boxes of German 9mm rounds of ammunition. And in an oilskin wallet they found some leaflets that had been dropped years before by the RAF. They also took away a sword that was hanging on the bedroom wall which had belonged to my great grandfather.

Mother told me after the war that the German police had been very polite, calling her Madame. The one that was in charge spoke with an American or Canadian accent (this must have been Woelfe). They informed her that when they found me I would be in big trouble - and it would be better if I gave myself up because there was a chance that all the family would be arrested. 'It's not the first time your son has been in trouble with German police,' they said to her. 'Or your family.' They were referring to my arrest in 1942 and to my father and grandfather, both having been arrested before.

The British M19 officers at Liberation time tried to find my great grandfather's sword, but no luck. I always hoped to find it one day. It could turn up in a second-hand shop.

After the German police search of our house, all the dummy packets from our toy shop store went to keep our fire gong to be able to cook food.

GERMAN SOLDIER SENTENCED TO DEATH 1945

One morning I was in No 2 solitary confinement cell in C Block, lying on my bunk when the door was unlocked by Fritz, a German prison guard who had been a farmer in Thüringer, Germany. He told me I was getting moved. I had nothing but what I stood up in so off we went up the stairs and along the long corridor. We stopped outside cell 19. Fritz unlocked the heavy cell door and in I went.

A big German soldier with short blond hair was sitting on the only single bunk bed in the cell. 'Good morning to you,' he said in better English than I can speak. 'Good morning to you,' I replied. We exchanged names, then he asked me when my big day was. Thinking he meant my birthday, I told him it was the 27th July. He got up from his bunk bed and said: 'That's strange, very strange. You mean to tell me they will not shoot you till July? And it is very strange that my birthday is the 27th July but in 1917.'

My word, I thought they were going to shoot me - but why? I got quite worried, then it dawned on me. I explained to him the mix up. He then started to laugh and told me we had something in common. Born same day, same month but not the same year. He told me he was under sentence of death and when they placed me in this cell he thought we were in the same boat.

We were both puzzled why they had put me here. His name was Karl Lohmann. He was born in Berlin and was married with three children. He was under sentence of death for striking an officer and for spreading anti-Nazi and anti-Hitler discontent among the men in his unit. His father had been a Communist, had been arrested and had died in a concentration camp in 1937 in Germany.

I informed him of the latest war news and told him that the war would soon end. 'But too late to save me,' he said. He asked me if I would write to his family if he was not around anymore. Before we could continue our interesting conversation the guard, Ludwig, came to escort me back to my cell.

Karl Lohmann asked for something in German. I think it was a request for paper so that he could write down his wife's address for me. On the way to my cell I asked Ludwig why I had been moved. He told me in a low voice that the Secret Field Police had placed under arrest a German officer. The prison staff wanted a single cell to put him in, and my cell was the only convenient one that the prison chief could think of at the time. I had gone to Karl Lohmann's cell as a temporary measure. I asked Ludwig if he did not find it unusual to place a political prisoner in the same cell as a condemned German soldier. His reply to my question was that the death sentence had not yet been confirmed by the Military Court and they did not want to mix the condemned soldier with the other military prisoners as he might cause trouble. Having been put once again in my solitary confinement cell and thinking of what had taken place that day, I thought about the German officer who had been arrested. In a low voice (even prisons have ears) Ludwig told me that two officers from the Kommandantur had arrived and collected the officer, and so far as Ludwig and the prison staff knew the officer was now under house arrest. I would have loved to find out why he was arrested and placed in the German prison.

The condemned German soldier, Karl Lohmann, survived the war. I did check at the end of May 1945 and the British officers at the prison informed us that all the military prisoners had been returned to units in the Island, then transported to prisoner-of-war camps in England. So, on my birthday, I sometimes think of him and I often wonder if he was ever reunited with his family in Berlin.

MOTHER AND FLORENCE LE PENNEC INTERVIEW WITH GERMAN KOMMANDANT

My Mother. Mrs Elizabeth Marie Mière

Florence Le Pennec.

My torn shirt stained with blood and bits of teeth were smuggled out of the prison by a German guard and by a friendly civilian warder from the public prison side, Frank Veron, a friend of our family for many years. The small parcel was addressed to my father. I did not want my mother to know because of what she might do. But, it was mother who opened the parcel. Naturally she was very upset and thought the Germans were killing me. She was not a woman to hide her feelings and her anger was up to boiling point.

After phoning the family of my friend, Frank Le Pennec, at First Tower, she found that he was getting the same police treatment as I was. A joint approach to the situation was obviously needed.

My mother and Frank's sister, Florence Le Pennec (Flo) made their way together to the headquarters of the German Kommandant with the object of demanding some action on his part. The sentry on the door would not at first not let them in. But mother made such a fuss that a German officer came out, wanting to know what the disturbance was about. Mother and Flo were trying to explain while the officer was telling them to go away. But they were so persistent that he eventually said that they would have to wait.

After ten minutes he returned, took their names and details and, some time later, escorted them to the Kommandant's office. My mother explained the facts but the Kommandant refused to listen. She then burst out with accusations about his 'brutal military police.' That did it. He told her that I had committed acts of sabotage, had insulted the Führer and the German armed forces and had sided with the enemy of the Third Reich.

According to Flo, my mother blew her top and threw every insult she could think of at him. She told him that her two soldier sons would settle with him one day if anything should happen to their young brother, Joe. Flo thought that they would be arrested on the spot. She later told us how frightened she was at my mother's outburst. What added fire to her fury was the memory of her two brothers dying in the Great War of 1914. My father and my grandfather had been wounded three times in that war and on her side of the family there were many deaths.

The German thought that my mother was mad and said so. Mother and Flo were then escorted out of the building by two officers and an armed guard. Thinking back over those years, most probably what they thought was the Kommandant was a high ranking officer on the Kommandant's staff. Florence (Flo) Le Pennec (now Mrs Corfield) is still living in the Island, at St Brelade.

INTERROGATED AT THE GERMAN PRISON BY TWO GERMAN OFFICERS

Being warned by one of the guards, Ludwig, that there was a Kommandant investigation going on regarding the German police treatment of prisoners during interrogations, I waited with an apprehensive mind for that day. It came on one cold morning. I was in solitary confinement when the cell door was unlocked by one of the German prison guard, and Big Heinrich and Oberwachtmeister Heinz Woelfe from the German Secret Field Police walked in, followed by his side kick and lap dog, Karl Lohse Lager. I noticed that, lurking in the corridor, was Wilhelm Mitz, one of the strong arm boys from Silvertide. Woelfe and Lohse were dressed as always in long leather coats to look like the Gestapo which they were not, but very close in many ways.

Woelfe looked at me and in a gruff voice asked: 'How did your mother get a parcel from you from this prison. Which one of the prison guards smuggled it out?' I thought to myself - here we go again. They did not bring in the strong arm man, Wilhelm Mitz, to play cards. It looked as if I was in for a right old bashing.

'I do not know anything about a parcel or any smuggling' was my reply. Woelfe's eyes lit up and smiling he said: 'If you did not smuggle out a torn shirt with blood on it, then that means you have not been beaten up by any of my men or beaten up by the Harbour Police.' I said to Woelfe: 'I do not know what you are talking about and I do not know anything about a parcel.' Woelfe was grinning all over his face. 'Then your mother must be seeing things. Is she just mad or disarranged.' Lohse chipped in and asked if my mother was simple minded or just anti-German.

I told Woelfe that my mother was at the end of her tether with worry. With two sons at the war and me in this prison, my poor mother was close to breaking point. 'Right' said Woelfe in his Canadian accent and, still smiling, he looked at my cut lip and swollen eye. 'You want to be more careful' he said, 'when you walk into these heavy prison doors.'

I nearly blew my top, but thought better of it. Woelfe would only call in Mitz to bash me up. And I thought the British would soon sort these brutes out at war's end. I think it was the relief of not being bashed about on this visit by the Silvertide gang that made me feel cheeky. 'From now on,' I told Woelfe, 'I will name the door after your bully boy, Mitz, who is standing in the corridor.' Woelfe turned round and said: 'Now don't start with all that cheek again or have you forgotten already where your cheek got you last time?' He was no longer smiling as he left my cell.

But that was not the end of the police visits to the German prison. The very next morning after so-called breakfast the cell door was unlocked by Ludwig. He had come to escort me to the prison guardroom. Ludwig said to me: 'It is the Kriegsmarine Polizei come to question you about the parcel. Please remember we have families in Germany and if you say anything about us smuggling your parcel out of the prison they will suffer. You don't understand these Nazi police.' I told Ludwig not to worry. 'By the way, how did the singing go last night?' Ludwig was the conductor of the German army choir in Jersey. 'It was only a practice but it went well.' he replied.

As we entered the guardroom my heart nearly stopped beating and for a minute I started to feel fear. Standing there were Kohler (sometimes called Kranke) and Schraeler (some- times called Scrieber) two of the most brutal men you could ever meet. Kohler was a an ex-policeman from Berlin. He came towards me, his ugly face full of hate. You could see he was trying to control his temper. He took hold of my jacket and raised his fist. I thought - here we go again. I hope he hits me hard with the first blow and puts me out cold like he did once before. Schraeler put an arm out to Kohler and said to him something in German, a few words I could understand like, 'careful, think well. Don't forget the warning etc.' (Now when I think of it - they must have been warned from the Kommandant's Office to cut out the rough stuff).

Kohler and Schraeler who had been in the New York police turned to me and said: 'So smart guy, are you like the smart ass of a Bailiff of yours, trying to make trouble for us? You wait, you little shit, we will not forget this. We have not finished with you yet. We will be back and that mad mother of yours - you will have your whole damn family in here one day and when we win this war we will show you what real treatment is.' I could not help but smile at his reference to them winning the war. 'And wipe that smile off your face, you are just a small fry. When we get you over to Germany, you wait and see.' he said. 'You won't talk now but over there you will, I assure you.' And with these last words they both left the guardroom.

Ludwig came to return me to my cell. He asked me what had taken place. As he escorted me back he said: 'The chief told us you were frightened but do not let them get you down and please do not judge us all by these Nazi police.'

At the Liberation of Jersey British officers took our statements and details about these German police. They locked them up in the same cells that three days before had been occupied by political prisoners. And only a week after the British released them, they were sent to prisoner of war camps in England. The following week the German prison guards were sent to North Yorkshire prisoner of war camps. Most of the Field Police went to camps in Essex. The German Harbour Police with other Naval personnel were sent to camps in Scotland.

The Bailiff's intervention on our behalf did stop the German Police from ill-treating us - because one morning two German officers arrived at the German prison to interview me. At this time I did not know that my mother had been to see the Bailiff. Later on, I found out from Ludwig that two German officers had been sent to investigate the Bailiff's complaint to the Kommandant. These two officers were very correct and polite in their manner towards me. First of all they wanted to know how a torn shirt with blood stains wrapped around bits of teeth had found its way out of the prison. At first the question threw me off balance. 'Was it a German prison guard or a Jersey prison warder who took the shirt out of the prison?' asked one of the officers. In fact it was Ludwig who passed the shirt out of the prison but I was not going to let him down. He would have been in great trouble. And as always, I acted as the dumb country boy when being interrogated.

I told the two officers that I did not know who had taken the shirt out of the prison, and I thought it had been stolen from my cell. The next question was who beat me up - was it the German Secret Field Police or the German Harbour Police? When and how did it take place? Or did I fall and put the blame on the German Police? They could see that my face was still bruised. Who were these German officers fooling, they could very well see that the bruises were not caused by a fall. I told them that their police were very good at knocking people about and the day would come when they would be held responsible for their brutal treatment of prisoners.

On the face of one of the officers there was a flush of anger but otherwise they ignored my outburst of attempted bravado. The next question was - is your mother right in the head? I asked why. 'Well, your mother went to the Kommandant's office and insulted one of the officers.' Later I found out that she had gone with Flo Le Pennec to find out what had become of me. I replied to the question by saying: 'If my mother seemed to you disturbed it's because she has a lot of worry on her mind - with me in prison and my two brothers in the army and no news of them. My father is at home, still suffering from three wounds in the last war. My mother's two brothers were killed in the war of 1914-1918. No wonder she is upset. I am sure that your own mother must be worried about you as well.'

The two officers smiled at my reply. One of them said: 'You are not such a fool as you make out to be. But next time your mother insults a German officer or soldier she will be arrested and imprisoned - and that's a warning. And as for you, you are a stubborn young man. We are here to help you, but you reject our help, and will not help us in our investigation. Remember we are not policemen. Inspector Bode from the German Secret Field Police warned us that we would be wasting our time with you.'

I thought to myself - that brute Bode from the German Secret Field Police is trying to protect himself and his bully boys. As the two officers were leaving the guardroom, one turned around and said: 'The prison chief informs us that you are in solitary confinement until you behave yourself and show him some respect.'

As I was taken back to my cell by Ludwig, he thanked me for not saying that the guards had taken my parcel out of the prison. Poor old Ludwig with the buck teeth, he like the other German prison guards seemed to have a great fear of his own police. One must remember that if they had been arrested not only they but their families in Germany would have been arrested too.

I had, like the other prisoners, run into trouble with the prison chief and the prison guards but the punishment was always light - put in solitary confinement for a few days or weeks - in other words treated like naughty boys. To us young ones German prison guards were old men, yet they were only between 30 and 40 years of age.

My sleep that night was very disturbed and I was fearful of what tomorrow would bring, thinking that the German police would arrive and start knocking me about again and take it out of me as a revenge. But no, they never put a hand on me again. As a matter of fact, a few weeks after the German Military Court sentence when I had been transferred over to the civilian side of the prison, some of the German police passed by me in the exercise yard and they asked me if I was all right and was there anything that I needed. I thought 'what bloody cheek.' I walked on and ignored them. We do not know what the two German officers put in their report but it certainly put the wind up the bully boys. After the Jersey Bailiff's complaint to the Kommandant, it goes to show that someone at the Kommandant's office or even the Kommandant himself would not tolerate gangster methods among their military police forces.

People will and do wonder how can I remember all this after many years have passed. Well, when we were sent over to the civilian side of the prison after being sentenced, one could get hold of pieces of paper inside the covers of books, etc. The prayer books in the prison chapel were a good supply base. The prison chaplain tried to find out who was taking the blank pages out of the prayer books on a Sunday when we all attended the chapel service. We had plenty of time on our hands to record what had taken place. Some of the lads used to pull my leg about always writing on bits of paper. One or two have said since that they wished they had put down the events of that time.

Over on the civilian side of the prison we were not guarded by the German military but our own people - HM prison warders. Some of them were real shit hawks, but most of them were very kind and would take out letters or bring you in food, sometimes writing paper. Mind you it was very strange being guarded by your own people. These local prison warders took their orders from the prison governor who in turn took his orders from the prison board and the States of Jersey. Orders also came from the Jersey Attorney General. We even had local uniformed policemen who had been arrested by the Germans and imprisoned with us.

MOTHER AND WOMAN FROM UPPER MIDVALE ROAD

A woman who lived at upper Midvale Road met my mother one cold December day in 1944. She said with a smirk on her face: 'Your son Joe was seen walking between two German soldiers along Colomberie. I did not know your son was so friendly with the Germans - to be seen walking with them.'

My mother who was not slow or backward in a reply to any suggestion of a slur on her loyal family, said to the woman; 'You silly old woman, how dare you! My son, Joe, is imprisoned in the German prison and if whoever told you about seeing him walking between two Germans, if that person had looked more carefully he or she would have noticed he was handcuffed to one of the Germans who were taking him to be interrogated at Silvertide, the German Secret Field Police HQ at Havre des Pas. Would you like my son, Joe, to come and have a chat with you after the end of the war?'

The poor woman went white. 'I am so sorry, Mrs Mière. I did not mean to harm your son's good name. I will today inform the person who saw your son of the true facts. Please do not tell our son. We do not want any trouble from him and his friends.' And off the woman went, no longer a smirk on her face.

My mother must have been in a good mood that day otherwise the woman would have had a slap, and I can tell you after a slap from my mother, you could hear the bells of St Luke's days later. She was very patriotic. She would take our two dogs for a walk down Midvale Road with red, white and blue ribbons tied to their collars. And on the walk back she would always walk the dogs through the terrace of Portland House (now the Portland Hotel) which was the Organisation Todt HQ and she made sure the dogs did their business in this terrace.

Many times Mother was shouted at by the German OT staff for her dogs fouling the German occupied terrace. In the end they gave up shouting at her. They thought that Mother was a little mad but Mother was not mad. She knew what she was doing (so it seems did the dogs). One German OT officer, trying to tick her off about her dogs, made the understatement of the Occupation when he said to her (in good English); 'Madame, I take it you do not like us Germans!'

Saturday 5TH May 1945

Dear Joe (Kid),

Great news is circulating around the town everyone seems to be going mad — long queues are waiting outside of Laurens trying and fighting to buy UNION JACKS I reckon that it will be over any minute now I am sure waiting to see you out again — I am prepared to greet our troops with a Super new American Flag (Stars & Stripes) also a pretty large French & Belgium but I don't seem to be able to get a Onion Jack — Mrr Dawson took back the one you had in your house yesterday to put on his flag-pole so we're stumped for one.

The B—?!!? Huns sure ~~look~~ look down in the dumps — damn good job — they wanted this war, and they're sure getting it plus a bit extra for which they never bargained for.

Old Ma Robin the Bitch is scared to hell with the thought of the Great Fuhrer pegging out — never mind she'll have the runs after we've finished with her — also she's not sleeping home now someone might try to cut her throat when she's sleeping.

Went down to your house last night and was very surprised to see an old friend ...he's sure looking O.K.

was very dissapointed at not being able to come down on Tuesday because I was looking forward to seeing you — never mind some things can't be helped — I see a good lot of Red ✝ Cross Clothing has arrived in the island — but I don't think we ought to trouble about it we'll soon be wearing His Majesties Forces rigouts — and be earning the kings shilli: g — I hear that we're all going to be conscripted from the ages of 18 — 31 it suits me — any moment now

Captain Lootenant Flying Officer Sergeant Instructor Major General Colour Colonel. Lord Louis Moyse — D.S.O. V.C. D.F.C. M.M. M.C. Croix de Guerre and Order of St Michael of the Garter, ◦ Boss of the Undersea Air Raid Shelters — with folding Wings sends his greetings from the Battlefield of St Helier

"Love to all the Boys" and one and all your affectionate pal

John ("SLUG. V.C. D.F.C. RAF)

R. N
R. A. F
R. A.

(THUMBS UP!)

ALSO COMMA-NDER IN CHIEF OF THE FLYING DUST-MEN

87

ESCAPE FROM THE PRISON, 1945

Donald Bell and Frank Le Pennec were both in the next cell to mine, No 1 of Block C. I was in No 2 of the same block of the military prison in St Helier.

Donald and Frank had been planning to escape for about two weeks and one day Frank told me to hold myself ready to join them. Blankets were to be put round their cell window which would muffle any sound that might reach the guard. On one of his visits he would be pushed into No.1 cell and locked in. All this meant overcoming him in the first place and stopping him from raising an alarm. Once out of the main door of the cell block, we would run to a large ventilator pipe at the end of the prison yard that was covered with rings of barbed wire, then across the roof of the prison block, then to drop over the high wall into Newgate Street.

But two days before this could take place, Richard Williams, another inmate in a separate cell, attempted to escape. He was caught but, as the Germans did not have a spare cell in our solitary confinement area, I was moved out as Richard was brought in. I just had time to warn him of Donald and Frank's escape plans. I think he caught on to the idea that he was to take my place. Two nights later there were sounds of gunfire coming from block C. Everyone near where I was wondered what was going on. I knew but kept silence, praying that the lads would make it.

The next morning at about 7 am I was taken to the guardroom and found myself facing Oberwachtmeister Heinz Woelfe, his side kick Karl Lauger and Wilhelm Mitz (strong-arm man of the Secret Field Police) with Krank and Scriber of the German Water Police (the Water Rats). They wanted to know what I knew of the escape plans because, as Woelfe reminded me, two days before I had been in the next cell. Were the escapers making for any particular place, the address, etc.?

I spent a very hard hour in that guardroom. Krank, Scriber and Mitz started to punch and push me around. Then for some reason Woelfe stopped them and said: 'As you can see, the lad is not all there.' With the German police I always acted the real dumb country boy, so after one hour they were getting nothing out of me and I was sent back to my cell. Brian Bisson, another inmate, and his brother were there and saw that I had been beaten up.

It was only three years ago that Brian Bisson told my wife, Marie, how they brought me back into the cell in a bloody mess. Brian is still alive and can confirm all this. Two days later I was taken to my old cell in block C. Later that day they brought in Richard Williams. Poor old Richard - he was not able even to walk. I had to carry him on my back to the WC.

For some reason I was very angry with him - I suppose because he had taken my place in the escape and had been caught. But as Frank told me after the war, Richard most probably saved my life by taking my place. It was just fate. I will never forget Frank who became my brother in law and godfather to my sons, and will never forget Donald and Richard, three very brave young men, with whom I was privileged to be imprisoned. The three of them were my inspiration for the Joe Mière Collection. Many times I would have given up my research and recording work on our loyal political prisoners but thoughts of their bravery made me carry on this lonely task.

Most of the above is taken from my notes on the Occupation made in 1945-46 when my mind was still young and fresh.

GERMAN MILITARY COURT

C.J. Cuming, Constable of St Helier, was instructed by the Attorney General (C.W. Duret Aubin) to register all Jersey political prisoners who had been sentenced by the German Military Court in the local Jersey police register. By this order the Attorney General treated loyal Jersey people as if they were criminals.

| | | HANDTÜBERWACHUNGSSTELLE. | CASE |
Name of Accused.	Charge.	Sentence.	Source of
MIÈRE, Joseph Arthur, Washington, FIRST TOWER.	Unauthorised possession of weapons. Insulting	Prison 1 yr 3 mo	"V Mann"
DAWSON, David, 28 Midvale Rd., ST HELIER.	the Wehrmacht. (Smearing houses of pro	" 1 yr 6 mo	
LE FEUVRE, Frank, Manchester Ho. FIRST TOWER.	Germans with Swastikas)	" 1 yr.	

THE GERMAN UNDERGROUND HOSPITAL

IDENTITAESKARTE
Joseph Arthur MIERE

Identity cards were issued from 1941 onwards by the German *Feldkommandantur* and all persons in Jersey aged 16 years and over had to carry a card to be produced on demand. The originals were beige in colour with a black and white photograph stapled in place.

Jersey-born **Joe Mière** was 15 years old when he was first arrested in October 1941 for insulting a Wehrmacht officer. He was fined and held in custody for four days. He was arrested again in September 1942 for demonstrating against the German occupying forces (he and others led the singing of "There'll always be an England" as English-born people were being deported). Released after two days with a final warning he was arrested once again in November 1944 on the much more serious charges of being in possession of weapons and arraigned for trial before the Truppenkriegsgericht (the War Court Martial). He was detained in custody in the Public prison. In his report to the court of 12 February 1945, Feldpolizeiinspektor Bode of the Secret Field Police stated that 'his record shows that he has consistently insulted the occupying forces and carried out acts of sabotage. He refuses to admit to his crimes. He can be violent and when interrogated by the Field Police he had to be restrained by force but continued to insult the interrogating police officers'.

Joe Mière was sentenced to 18 months imprisonment and released from the Public Prison on the evening of 7 May 1945. After a career in local commerce Joe became the curator at the German Underground Hospital and has devoted himself to building his photographic collection - on display in the visitor centre - and keeping alive the memories of his turbulent youth. Joe has now retired and still lives in Jersey with his wife Marie.

Copied from the Counter Intelligence closed files held by the Public record Office. (Translated by Captain B. Richards 1945)

Report on Channel Islands. Jersey. M.1.19. (R.P.S) W O - 392A / 3789.

This German document number 293 a k - PG. The Geheime Feldpolizei 644. (Secret Field Police) 131 az / 3122b. and German Military Court activities Jersey 1940 - 45.

. . . .

Report by Feldpolizeiinspektor Bode, of Gruppe Geheime Feldpolizei 644 Jersey to the Truppenkriegsgericht (Troop War Court Martial) on the prisoner Josef Miere. Born 26 - 7 - 1926 in St Helier Jersey. Residing at 25 Midvale Road St Helier. Police record of the accused prisoner Josef Miere. No 27638 ak. He had been arrested on the 19 of October 1941, for insulting a Wehrmacht Officer, given a fine then released with warning 23 October 1941. Arrested with others on the 16 September 1942 for demonstrating against the German occupying forces, and refusing to obey an order given by a Wehrmacht Officer, imprisoned and released with second and final warning, 17 September 1942. Arrested with two others 14 November 1944, and detained in prison awaiting Trial by Troop War Court Martial, for being in possession of weapons and insulting the Wehrmacht. His record shows that he has consistently insulted the occupying forces. Carried out acts of sabotage against the Wehrmacht. He refuses to admit to his crimes, which were committed against the occupying forces in Jersey. He can be violent, and when interrogated by the Field Police he had to be restrained by force by the police, but continued to insult the interrogating police officers. His bad behaviour while under detention awaiting trial by the Troop Court has been submitted in a separate report by the prison authorities. (Signed by) Bode. Feldpolizeiinspektor.

des Festungskommandanten Gruppe Geheime Feldpolizei 644.

Truppenkriegsgericht den. 12 Februar 1945. Jersey.

Jersey. St L/PG. 46/45.

Gerieht
des Festungskommandanten
J e r s e y

St.L. 46/45

Beglaubigte Abschrift !

F e l d   -   U r t e i l
im Namen des deutschen Volkes

In der Strafsache die brit.St.A. 1.) Josef Miere, geb.am 26.7.1926 in
St.Helier, wohnhaft ebend., Midvale Road 25 2.) David Dawson, geb.am
geboren dem 1.2.1924 in Grouville, wohnhaft in St.Helier, Midvale Road 28
3.) Frank Le Pennic, geb.am 4.10.1920 in St.Aubins, wohnhaft in St.
Helier, First Tower

wegen fortges.gemeinschaftlicher deutschfeindlicher Kundgebung u.a.

hat das am 30. Januar 1945   in St.Helier /Jersey

zusammengetretene Feldkriegsgericht

für Recht erkannt: Die Angeklagte Miere, Dawson und Le Pennic werden
unter Freispruch im uebrigen wegen fortgesetzter gemeinschaftlicher
deutschfeindlicher Kundgebung in Tateinheit mit fortgesetzter Beleidi-
gung der Besatzungsmacht, Le Pennic ausserdem wegen Nichtablieferung eine
Radiogeraets und zwar Miere zu 1 -einem- Jahr 6 -sechs -Monaten Gefgs.
Dawson zu 1 -einem- Jahr 6 -sechs- Monaten Gefaengnis, Le Pennic zu ins-
gesamt 1 -einem- Jahr 6 -sechs- Monaten Gefaengnis verurteilt. Der Detektor
Apparat und die Schreckschusspistole werden eingezogen. 2 Wochen der
erlittenen Untersuchungshaft werden jeder Angeklagten angerechnet.
Bestaetigungsverfuegung: 1.) Jch bestaetige das Urteil. 2.) Die Strafen
sind zu vollstrecken. 3;9 Die nach der Urteilsverkuendung weiterhin
erlittene Freiheitsentziehung wird der Verurteilten auf die Strafzeit
angerechnet. O.U., den 13.Februar 1945. gez.Heine, Oberst

Die Richtigkeit der Abschrift wird beglaubigt und die Vollstreckbarkeit des Urteils bescheinigt.

O.U.,den 14.Februar 1945

Heeresjustizinspektor
als Urkundsbeamter der Geschäfts-
stelle.

Court of the
Fortress commander
Jersey

St.L. 46/45

Certified Copy

Field Judgement
In the name of the German People

In the criminal matter concerning the British nationals 1) Josef Mière, born 26.7.1926 in St. Helier, resident there, 25 Midvale Road, 2) David Dawson, born 1.2.1924 in Grouville, resident in St. Helier, 28 Midvale Road, 3) Frank Le Pennic, born 4.10.1920 in St. Aubins, resident in St. Helier, First Tower

On account of continuous joint anti-German declarations and other offences

The field court-martial assembled in St. Helier/Jersey on 30th January 1945 has reached the following verdict. The accused Mière, Dawson and Le Pennic will be sentenced on account of continuous joint anti-German declarations con-comitantly with continuous insult of the occupying force, Le Pennic also on account of not handing in of a radio as follows: Mière 1 – one – year 6 – six – months imprisonment, Dawson 1 – one – year 6 – six – months imprisonment, Le Pennic in total 1 – one – year 6 – six – months imprisonment. The detector apparatus and the blank gun will be confiscated. 2 weeks of the detention while awaiting trial will be taken into account for each of the accused.
Confirmation order: 1) I confirm the judgement. 2) The sentences are to be executed. 3) The imprisonment after the pronouncement of judgement will be taken into account for the sentences of convicts. O.U., 13th February 1945. Signed Heine, Colonel

This copy is certified and the judgement is confirmed to be enforceable.

O.U., 14th February 945

Military Justice inspector
As the registrar of the office

O.U., 14th February 1945

Court
Of field post number 43 507

Troop War Court-Martial Jersey

St. L. 46/45

To the
Public Prosecutor in St. Helier

In the criminal matter against the British national Josef Mière, hairdresser, born 26.7.1926 in St. Helier/Jersey
Resident in St. Helier, 25 Midvale Road
On account of continuous joint anti-German declarations and other offences, the certified copies of the sentence and the confirmation order are sent with the request to execute the sentence in the British penal institution in St. Helier.
The convict will serve his prison sentence in the penal institution in St. Helier.

Start of sentence: 13.2.1945, 0?.00 am * (*figure illegible)
End of sentence: 15.7.1946, 12.00 midnight

It is requested to inform the convict of the confirmation order – execution decision – and the committal notice – length of sentence and to send the release notice after serving his sentence to the above mentioned court.

A.B.

Military Justice inspector

Form 6

Attorney General's Chambers,

Royal Square,

Jersey.

Wednesday, 7th March, 1945.

The Viscount.

I have been informed by the Troop Court that, by verdict of that tribunal dated 30th January 1945, the British national, Josef (Joseph) Miere, born on 26.7.1926 in St. Helier, Jersey and residing at 25, Midvale Road, St. Helier, was sentenced to one (1) year and six (6) months' imprisonment for continual anti-German demonstrations in company with others and continually insulting the Occupying Forces.

It is requested that this sentence be executed in the Public Prison where Miere is already incarcerated.

Sentence is to date as follows: (Four weeks' detention are taken into consideration.) -

Commencing on 13th of February 1945 at 0.00 hours

Concluding on 15th of July 1946 at 24.00 hours.

Will you please make the necessary arrangements to have this sentenc executed as requested and will you also, please, inform me in due course of the prisoner's release.

Attorney General.

Granted remission & released at 6 p.m. on May 7th, 1945.
(See 32)

My Comment: "What a cheek" we were not given remission by the German Court. It was Liberation time so the States of Jersey and the Attorney General had to release us.

THE GERMAN PRISON, GLOUCESTER STREET, ST HELIER

One of the two prison blocks in Gloucester Street and Newgate Street taken over by the Germans had been reserved for women before the Occupation. It had steel doors and cells measuring ten feet by eight. It was here that the Germans put their political prisoners - that is, Jersey civilians caught in anti-Nazi activities by the German Secret Field Police, the German Feldgendarmerie or the Kriegsmarine Polizei (the Naval Police, known as the Water Rats).

The other block was used mainly for German servicemen held in detention for various military offences such as desertion. It backed on to a yard and Newgate Street. There were twenty cells altogether, measuring nine feet by nine - sixteen for service prisoners and four for political prisoners sentenced to solitary confinement. If you stepped out of line or refused to obey orders or upset the guards you were put in one of these solitary confinement cells.

Three times I had solitary confinement and it was quite an experience. Instead of your own people in the building, you had a block full of Germans and your exercise time was only twenty minutes a day. There was also the big old prison block, not part of the German area, which in pre-Occupation days held the debtors cells, the prison chapel and the hospital cells.

Some German prison guards, we noticed, were armed with a very old type of side arms with a bore of .38, six of them in large brown leather holsters. These had been kept in the governor's office until the Germans arrived and then they took possession of them. None of the new prison staff or the public seemed to know anything about these pre-war revolvers or would give out any details concerning any arms kept in H.M. prisons - which is only right - but all I wanted to know was whether the six revolvers were returned to the civil prison governor at the Liberation of Jersey in May 1945.

When the Germans were cut off from the French coast in late 1944 they could not ship over any prisoners for their prisons and concentration camps in Germany. So because of overcrowding, they ordered the States of Jersey to build a large wooden hut in the garden facing the civilian prison governor's house. It contained three rooms - first room six beds, second room six beds, third room ten beds. We were transferred to the new hut on the civilian side of the prison which was run by the Jersey Prison Board.

To be fair to most of the prison warders, they did not treat us as criminals and many of them smuggled out our letters, told us the war news and did their best to make life in prison more bearable but there were two or three that were real shit hawks, always reporting you to the prison governor. The boys soon sorted them out - even a policeman who had been arrested by the Germans got hold of one of the sneaky warders and gave him a rough time. But apart from that we did not like being guarded by our own people wearing the British Crown on their caps.

Whoever gave the order for this should have been arrested at war's end and asked to give an explanation as to why loyal political prisoners sentenced by the Germans should be in the control of the British Crown and the States of Jersey. What I protested strongly against was having my finger prints taken by a warder as if I were a criminal.

One evening in the hut, as it was light outside, we thought we would like to know what was at the back of the hut. We forced a back window and three of us climbed out while the others kept watch. We made our way into a small yard and through a door that, strange as it seems, was not locked. Beyond this was another small yard - and not one civil or German warder in sight. After this we moved into a strange big yard which, as we found out later, was called 'Bradley's Yard.' It seemed that this was the execution yard and in the middle was a large brick-lined open-top pit. This was the old hanging pit of former years.

It made the yard look more gloomy than ever. In the corner was another pit with raised sides made of brick and covered by a wooden top and galvanised iron. We lifted the lid and found it full of lime powder. South of the yard and at the base of a very high wall (it was the prison wall in Newgate Street) were several small grave headstones. These marked the graves of prisoners who had been executed by hanging many years ago, their remains buried at the foot of the wall. Now we knew why there was a lime pit in the yard - the lime was to put in the graves. We made our way back to the hut and told the other prisoners what we had discovered.

There was talk of some of us escaping by this unguarded route to the high outer wall. Plans were put in hand by a small group of us but events overtook the escape plans. The war ended. Every time I have to visit the hospital I think of that yard and those headstones. As you enter the hospital from Newgate Street and on your left hand side, now built on, was where the yard and pits were situated in 1945.

BRITISH FLAG IN THE GERMAN PRISON

Who in this day and age would believe that a Union Jack was on display in the German prison in St Helier in April 1945? But it is true and we should like to record this fragment of Occupation history before we all pass on. It took place about three weeks before Adolf Hitler's birthday inside our room in the new prison hut.

This little flag has a history. It was given to me by my grandmother and was about 16 inches by 24, made of art silk and cotton. It could pack up very small and I always put it in the top pocket of my jacket. When arrested by the Germans and searched they went wild when they found the flag. Being true to form, they listed it with my other goods - wallet, pen, etc. Strangely enough these items, except my identity card and pen, were sent over to the civilian side of the prison and finally came back to me with the flag.

One of the political prisoners in our room was Jack Dingle who had been caught for sabotage and possessing a wireless. He suggested putting the flag over the top of the door leading into the next room - which we did and another inmate, Bernard Hassall, painted in white letters on the flag the words 'political prisoners Jersey 1945'

On this particular day in April there was a big flap going on in the prison. Word got round the grapevine that some big German General was expected on a tour of inspection. (See Leslie Sinel's "Occupation Diary" page 279). The civil governor of the public prison was 47 year old Ernest Briard - and he had a shake on. He came into our room with Packer the head warder in tow and told us to hide all knives, books, etc, before the General arrived.

Briard was about to leave the room when he spotted our Union Jack draped over the door. No need to tell you that he nearly passed out with shock. Poor old Briard - he could already picture the firing squad.

'Get that flag down at once,' he shouted, his face red like a turkey. We told him in plain English that we were not deaf. The flag was a British one and it would stay where it 'bloody well' was. All the lads shouted out 'we are all King's men in here.' Briard said that one of his staff would remove it by force if need be. Being young and, like most Jersey lads, strong headed, I was having a go at this very unpatriotic governor and things were   starting to hot up when Jack Dingle came forward, looked at me and said: 'OK, Joe. Keep your cool, son.' I have always looked on him like an uncle and have always had a great love for him and his family.

Now Jack Dingle has never been a big man physically but in pure guts Jack is ten feet tall. Turning round and rolling up his shirt sleeves, he said to the governor: 'If anyone tries to take down this flag I will knock him down - and up went Jack's fists like an old time boxer. Vic Webb, Alan Costard, Bernard Hassall, Tim Volante and myself stood behind Jack. Briard saw trouble ahead and, shaking his head from side to side, he turned round and walked out, followed by his staff. A cheer went up from the lads. We felt good and proud and we had every right to be.

Later that day the German General arrived at the prison. When it was our turn to be inspected we all stood by our beds. The General had a good look around, looked at the flag, went into the next and last room, came out, walked a few feet and stood there looking at our flag. He was wearing the very smart uniform of a German general, with red lapels and a red stripe running down his trousers. In our drab surroundings he was a splash of colour.

All of a sudden the General gave us a very smart salute and, turning to Governor Briard, said in English: 'These boys are British all right.' As they all departed from our room there was silence for a while. The general was man enough to see that we loved our country and he was big enough to accept it.

Later on we discovered that our visitor was Major General Wulf, the new fortress commander of Jersey - Inselkommandant. Outside the Governor's house the General was shaking hands with old Briard who was bowing two or three times to the General. All the lads were looking out through the windows of the hut (they were sealed shut, even on a warm day because Briard refused to have them unsealed). Bob Lawrence got one window unsealed, and all the lads shouted at Briard who was still bowing to the General. 'Why don't you kiss his bloody arse.' Even the General as he left had a big smile on his face. The day we were let out of the prison must have been a great day for old Briard.

But no wonder the Governor was in such a flap. On 31 March 1945 he was sentenced by the German Military Court to a fine of 60 Reichmarks, in place of a sentence of 3 weeks imprisonment (in his own jail) for negligently allowing a prisoner to escape. It would have been funny having Briard in a prison cell.

I have all the above signed by five witnesses who were there when the event took place - all ex-political prisoners.

WE THE UNDERSIGNED DO STATE THAT THIS IS A TRUE ACCOUNT OF THE INCIDENT THAT TOOK PLACE IN APRIL 1945 AT THE GERMAN PRISON, ST HELIER, JERSEY, C.I.

THAT TOOK PLACE IN APRIL 1945 AT THE GERMAN PRISON St HELIER JERSEY . C.I.

Joseph. Miere.. *Joseph Miere* ...... P.P.: 18503 .Known as Joe.

John. Dingle... *J. E. G. Dingle* ....Known as Jack

Victor. Webb.. *V. G. Webb* ....Known as Vic.

Alan. Costard.... *A. Costard* ....Known as Alan.

Bernard. Hassall *Bernard E. A. Hassall* P.P. 12504. ....Known as Berni

Top Left: Ernest Briard, The Prison Governor. **Top Right:** John (Jack) Dingle. **Above:** The Prison in the 1960's showing C block on the right & the guard room & wash house in the centre. **Below:** Side door, Gloucester Street. & C block cells for Solitary confinement.

Top :Showing A block and wooden hut to the left placed by the States to house political prisoners. To the left is B block. **Inset** Cell door. **Bottom :** To the left is the Governors house and X marks B block.

GERMAN SOLDIER SHOT, 27 APRIL 1945

'Meine Mutter, meine Mutter'
Kanonier(Gunner) Nicolas Schmitz

In Block B of the German prison in St Helier, cell number 14, were two Jewish French ladies who were under sentence of death. They were Lucy Schwob and Suzanne Malherbe. In the next cell to me was the young German serviceman, Kanonier (Gunner) Nikolaus Schmitz who had deserted and was suspected of murdering Miss Mildred Waddell although this murder was never proved. He had certainly deserted and been given shelter by a young woman originally from Guernsey named Alice, her brother, Peter and their family. I will never forget the day this young German serviceman arrived in our block and was put into the cell next to mine. That day he had been sentenced to death by a German Military Court. As a rule the Germans keep all their servicemen in block C. We surmised that after being sentenced to death, to return him to Block C would have upset other German servicemen awaiting sentence in Block C. This young German was born at Dusseldorf on 25 June 1922.

That night the poor chap was sobbing and crying and calling for his mother. 'Meine mutter.' It was very heart rending and distressing to hear him. I still get upset even after 58 years have gone past. Writing this part of my book, I still have to stop and control my feelings. A 77 year old grandfather should not cry but I am not ashamed to admit it. After all, German or no German, he was someone's son. The day he was sentenced I spoke with him all day and long into the night. He spoke a little English. My German was so bad that I made him chuckle when I tried to speak a few words.

The next morning Otto, the German guard, opened the cell door of the two French ladies so that they could put out their night pot that was collected and washed by the Russian prisoner, Michael. (Poor old Michael did all the dirty work in this block.) Both French ladies saw their chance and quickly passed my cell and spoke to the young soldier who was awaiting execution. They could speak German and they gave him words of comfort and tried to give him hope.

His girlfriend, Alice who had given the young German shelter was also under sentence of death and had been put in the women's section on the civilian side of the prison which was not guarded by Germans but by Jersey prison warders. Her brother, Peter, was still in our block.

On the morning of 27 April, 1945 at about 7am I was looking out of the hut window when I saw four Germans heading for the inner lodge door. I recognised the young German serviceman. He was handcuffed to two army guards and followed by a German army sergeant who was armed with a machine pistol. As they approached the inner lodge door, Alice called out 'Nicky' to him from a facing top floor window. Then she waved a little white hanky while being held up and supported by Belza Turner and Evelyn Janvrin (two women whom the Germans had arrested). The young soldier shouted out something. When he called out again to Alice the guards pulled and pushed him to the prison lodge gate. I knew this was the final chapter for him and, being a Roman Catholic, I crossed myself.

Kanonier Niklaus Schmitz, from the Zweiten Kompanie der Flakabteilung 364 and based at St Brelade's, Jersey was executed by firing squad on the morning of 27 April 1945, at the parade ground at Fort Regent, St Helier, Jersey. He was buried at the strangers cemetery at Westmount, St Helier in grave number G13.

Strange people these Germans. They allowed Alice, accompanied by her mother to attend his funeral service. The remains of Niklaus Schmitz now rest at Mont des Huisnes, near Mont St Michel, France. It was the Bailiff of Jersey who saved Alice's life. He wrote a moving plea to the German Feldkommandant. Her sentence of death was commuted to ten years imprisonment. At this date Alice still lives in Jersey.

Bailiff's plea saved woman

Case history 2

ON APRIL 23, 1945, a month before the end of the war, the Jersey Bailiff, Alexander Coutanche, wrote to the German commandant on the island appealing for mercy for a 20-year-old woman.

She was called Alice and she had been condemned to death by a court martial for harbouring a German soldier who had deserted in the final months of the occupation.

It had become clear to the Germans that they had lost the war and as food and clothing supplies ran out, they became increasingly desperate. The troops of the garrisons were reduced to eating nettle soup and killing birds for food. Several Germans deserted and were hidden by their girlfriends.

The bailiff wrote to the German commandant: "I have seen the father of this young woman and he has told me that for some four or five months a great friendship had arisen between his daughter and the German soldier.

"Alice was, it would appear, passionately in love with this soldier. A young woman in love does not always weigh the consequences of her acts, when they are dictated by what she believes, however wrongly, to be for the welfare of her lover. I appeal for mercy."

The intervention was successful and the death sentence was stayed. Alice remained in prison until the liberation of the islands by the British a few weeks later, but they arrived too late to save her German boyfriend, known as Nicky. He was shot.

Joe Miere was in the same prison as the couple after being arrested for minor resistance activities. He remembers them well. "Nicky was in the next door cell to me. I heard him crying all night, 'Meine mutter, meine mutter,' [My mother, my mother].

"On the other side of me were two French ladies, Suzanne Malherbe and Lucille Schwab, who had been arrested for attempting to incite mutiny among the Germans. They spoke to him in German.

"I saw him the day the guards took him out and took him along the yard outside my window. He pulled back and shouted something up to the cell where Alice was. She shouted back and then a little grey handkerchief appeared as she waved goodbye. Within half an hour that chap was dead."

After the war Alice, daughter of a local fish merchant, remained on the island, married an islander and had a family. She has always shied away from talking publicly about her affair.

Deutsche Dienststelle

für die Benachrichtigung der nächsten Angehörigen
von Gefallenen der ehemaligen deutschen Wehrmacht

VI/23

Deutsche Dienststelle (WASt), 13400 Berlin

Herrn
Joe Miere
4 Warren Court
La Folie
Millbrook
Jersey
Channel Islands JE3-1JX

Geschäftszeichen:
(Bei Rückfragen bitte Geschäftszeichen,
Namen und Geburtsdaten angeben)

Bearbeiter/in:

Zimmer:

Telefon: 169
(0 30) 4 19 04 (Intern 99 61 94)

Telefax:
(0 30) 4 19 04 (Intern 99 61 94) 100

Datum:
23.08.01

Sehr geehrter Herr Miere,

auf Ihr Schreiben vom 29.03.01 teilen wir Ihnen mit, dass es uns <u>leider
nicht möglich war</u>, noch lebende Angehörige des

Schmitz, Nikolaus, geb. 25.06.1922 in Düsseldorf,

zu ermitteln.

Der Todesfall des Herrn Schmitz ist uns seit 1952 bekannt. Die Eltern und
die Schwester wurden seinerzeit vom Ableben Ihres Angehörigen in Kenntnis
gesetzt.

Anfragen bei den Einwohnermeldeämtern bezüglich einer heutigen Anschrift
seiner Angehörigen verliefen jedoch ergebnislos.

Wir bedauern, nicht helfen zu können und bedanken uns für Ihre Bemühungen
in dieser humanitären Angelegenheit.

Mit freundlichen Grüßen
Im Auftrag

Fr. Wengel

Dienstgebäude:
Eichborndamm 179
13403 Berlin
eMail:
wast@com-de.com

Fahrverbindungen:
Bus 125, 221,
U-Bhf. Rathaus
Reinickendorf (U8)

Sprechzeiten:
Mo.-Mi. 9.00 - 14.00 Uhr
Do. 9.00 - 18.00 Uhr
Fr. 9.00 - 13.00 Uhr

Zahlungen bitte
bargeldlos an die
Landeshauptkasse,
10789 Berlin

Kontonummer
58-100
Kapitel 1167

Geldinstitut
Postbank Berlin

Bankleitzahl
100 100 10

WASt 121 (5/01)

Volksbund Deutsche Kriegsgräberfürsorge e.V.

German War Graves Commission
Service pour l'Entretien des
Sépultures Militaires Allemandes
Servizio per le Onoranze
ai Caduti Germanici

Bundesgeschäftsstelle · Postfach 10 38 40 · D 34112 Kassel

Mr.
Joe Mière
Number 4, Warren Court
La Folie, Millbrook
St. Lawrence

GB- Channel Islands/Jersey JE3 1 JX

**Bundesgeschäftsstelle
Werner-Hilpert-Straße 2
D 34112 Kassel**
Telefon **(0561) 7009-0**
Telefax **(0561) 7009-246**

e-mail   gn@volksbund.de

Ihr Zeichen	Ihre Nachricht vom	Unser Zeichen	Durchwahl	Kassel,
	21.02.01	GN 2.1 Ka	7009 -197	22.03.2001
				KA002733.SAM

**Nikolaus SCHMITZ, * 25.06.1922 Düsseldorf + 27.04.1945 Insel Jersey
Deutscher Soldatenfriedhof MONT-DE-HUISNES/Frankreich,
Gruft 53 - Grabkammer 65**

Sehr geehrter Herr Mière,

wir danken für Ihr Schreiben und müssen Ihnen leider mitteilen, daß in unseren Unterlagen keine
Adressen von Angehörigen des Nikolaus Schmitz enthalten sind.

Vielleicht ist es möglich, beim Standesamt der Stadt Düsseldorf evtl. Verwandte herauszufinden:

> Stadtverwaltung/Standesamt
> Marktplatz 5
> D - 40213 Düsseldorf

Unter Umständen kann Ihnen auch die

> Deutsche Dienststelle (ehemalige Wehrmachtauskunftstelle/WASt)
> Eichborndamm 179
> D- 13403 Berlin

Auskunft erteilen.

Wir bedauern sehr, Ihnen nicht weiterhelfen zu können.

Mit freundlichem Gruß

ABTEILUNG GRÄBERNACHWEIS
UND ANGEHÖRIGENBETREUUNG

Im Auftrag

Kalbhenn
Sachbearbeiterin

FIVE BODIES IN A SECRET GRAVE IN FRANCE

We have never found where the Germans buried the Jewish couple, the Kleinsteins, in 1941. But the following could be of interest as it shows how people can be buried in secret.

On the tiny Island of Batz, just five miles off Roscoff on the north coast of France, a grave was uncovered by French police 2 years ago. It was found by a boy who was digging in the sand when he unearthed a human skull. The grave was 30 ft long and, lying there, head to toe in a line, were five skeletons. These were the remains of four young men and a girl aged between 20 and 25 but there was nothing to identify who they were. There were no signs that they had been killed by either bullets or blows and they had been lying there since 1940.

The small Island had been occupied by the Germans. In 1940 a group of five youngsters had set out from Carantec, a town that was ten miles along the coast from Roscoff on the French mainland. Nothing was ever heard of the five young people - no one knows if they ever reached England. They vanished without trace like so many during the war years. There was a large rock lying beside the skeletons. And what became of their small boat? None of the five was an Islander. Yet the Mayor of Batz stated that in all the years there has not been a single unsolved case of missing people.

TERRIBLE SACRIFICE 1943-1944 R.A.F.

On the night of 28 January 1944, 432 Lancaster and 241 Halifax crews took part in an attack on Berlin. 20 of the Lancasters and 26 Halifaxes failed to return. This raid was one of a series between November 1943 and March 1944. The last raid in the series against Nuremberg resulted in the greatest loss suffered by any air force in World War II. Of 572 Lancasters and 214 Halifaxes taking part, 95 failed to return. Each bomber carried a crew of seven, which means 665 airmen failed to return that night.

By the end of the war, almost 8,000 bombers had been lost and 55,573 aircrew; 44.5 per cent of all men who flew with Bomber Command had died. Thousands more were wounded or taken prisoner after being shot down. Despite this terrible sacrifice, the men of Bomber Command were denied a Bomber Offensive Campaign Star, and their Commander-in-Chief, Sir Arthur Harris, was the only senior commander denied a peerage in the victory honours. These omissions were unworthy of a great nation. Source of information: John Hampton.

GEORGE D. SMITH'S LEAFLET SENT AROUND ISLAND

AN OPEN LETTER
From a Jerseyman to The Members of The Jersey Public

30, Manor Park Estate,
La Pouquelaye.
8th. April,1944.   St. Helier.

Dear Reader,
Have you been cold this winter? Then read this account of an attempt to discover why one man has not shared our privations.

I received clear evidence that on January 20th 1944 a lorry load of sawn blocks was delivered from the States Labour Dept. depot at No. 53 Esplanade to the residence of Mr.F.M.Burrell, the manager of the Electricity Coy. As this appeared to constitute an irregular transaction, I decided that my duty as a citizen was to request the competent officials to investigate the matter. The next two months were spent in unremitting but fruitless efforts to obtain a satisfactory explanation.

On January 22nd 1944 I interviewed Mr.Popin, the Fuel Controller, and two days later laid the case before him in writing; he replied that Mr.Burrell had not been supplied with wood in excess of his ration --- a deliberate falsehood. Being dissatisfied with this bald denial, I called on Mr.C.W.Duret Aubin, the Attorney-General; he had been informed of the matter and supported the Fuel Controller's contention. On my insistence, he suggested that I write to Mr. Popin for further information. This I did, and after seventeen days received from him certain explanations, which in the opinion of the Attorney-General negatived any suggestion of illegality.

These explanations I considered inadequate. I informed Mr. Aubin, and he declared that if I persisted in my allegations, the matter would have to go to court, and requested me to state my case in writing. I submitted to him a long questionnaire, which, had it been answered, would have elucidated the whole matter. For the next fortnight I heard nothing more than a formal acknowledgement, and I spent the following week in fruitless attempts to see Mr.Aubin. Finally, on April 1st (April Fool's Day), I received a letter saying that after mature consideration he was of the opinion that " the transaction in question is not one which calls for the institution of judicial proceedings against either of the parties concerned therein".

Here the matter rests for the matter. This is the result of more than two months assault on the armour of officialdom, the ultimate haven of seventy days' journeying on the uneasy seas of bureaucracy. I have received no answer to my questionnaire, and no explanations, either verbal or in writing, which I can accept as conclusive ---- very little, in fact, beyond a bland assurance that everything is to the ultimate benefit of the public, and a suggestion that I shouldn't worry my little head about these delicate matters.

That would you do?

Yours truly

George D. Smith

P.S:- Anyone interested is invited to examine the lengthy correspondence summarised above.

239

TWO BLACK EYES FOR A COLLABORATOR

Collaborator
John George Lingshaw

During the German Occupation years, local people used to hold dances at the Chelsea Hotel in Gloucester Street, St Helier. Also at the upstairs showroom at Boudains cycle shop in Bath Street. One evening there was a dance at the Chelsea Hotel. A big party of us were there, I with my young girlfriend, Irene Bisson, whose father ran the Commercial Hotel on the corner of Commercial and Conway Streets. The doorman for that evening was an Irish boxer called Eddie O'Connor (He now lives in London). Eddie recognised John Lingshaw who was a well known collaborator and German police informer trying to come into the dance. Eddie without any fuss or commotion threw Lingshaw out into the street with the words 'You are not welcome here.' Half an hour later just as the dance was warming up, Lingshaw returned with the German Military police. Lingshaw pointed out Eddie O'Connor and others to the Germans. At once the Military Police closed down the dance, and everyone had to go home. Feelings were running high against the informer, Lingshaw. Eddie and Irene and I with three or four other friends left to go home. Outside the Chelsea Hotel we spotted Lingshaw walking up Gloucester Street. Eddie called out 'Lets get the sod.' Lingshaw spotted us and took to his heels. The chase went through Cannon Street and Minden Place and into Bath Street, but by that time there were only three of us left. As we ran down Stopford Road we spotted Lingshaw crouching behind the steps of the Masonic Temple. Eddie dragged Lingshaw out and turned to me and said 'Joe, you are a Jersey boy. Give him a good thrashing.' He added 'And my boy, if he lays a hand on you I'll break his jaw.' I did hesitate. After all, Lingshaw was much smaller than me.

But Lingshaw struck out at me and I caught the blow on my chest. That did it. I hit him twice, once in each eye, and down he went. Lingshaw got up in a daze, then we could hear jackboots coming down the road. Eddie gave Lingshaw a right hook and down he went again. We then went off. I arrived home well after curfew. But by a strange coincidence the matter did not end there. My mother scolded me for being so late, and told me not to make any noise, because a young man who had been mugged by six big men was in the small top room. Being a guest house we often had people stay overnight. Mother told me that the young man was only staying overnight as he could not get home before the curfew hour.

The next morning as I started to come out of the bathroom which faced the bottom of the stairs, the overnight lodger was coming down the stairs. Straight away I recognised Lingshaw. He had two black eyes which were nearly closed. He did not see me as I jumped back into the bathroom. It's a good thing he did not see me because if he had seen and recognised me I would have been in deep trouble. The local police would have arrested me and I would have been given six months imprisonment. Then to be followed by a trial in a German Military Court and I could have even be sent to a concentration camp in Germany. I would have loved to tell him after the war that he spent the night only two rooms away from one of his attackers. It must have been fate that sent him to my mothers door that night.

Lingshaw was disliked even by the Germans with whom he collaborated as an informer against his own people. On his identity card it states that his address at one time was 'Silvertide' the German Secret Field Police HQ in Jersey. I think this says it all. And what was Lingshaw's reward from the Germans? They deported him with the UK born residents in February 1943. These deportees objected to the informer being put among them so he had to have special protection. He was removed from the camp and went to work for the Germans in Berlin.

When the war ended Lingshaw was arrested and convicted at the Old Bailey of 'doing acts with intent to assist the enemy' and was given four years in prison in England. He never returned to Jersey.

DENNIS JOHN ALFRED LEISTER

Born London 19 June 1922. His father was of German descent. He lived with his German born grandmother in Tufnell Park and visited Germany with her every year on holiday for two years, 1935-1936. He lived in Germany, attending school and learning to speak fluent German. In 1939 he joined the "Peace Pledge Union" scheme, providing agricultural labourers for the Channel Islands. He arrived in Jersey 27 May 1940. When the Germans occupied the Channel Islands in July 1940, Leister became an interpreter for the German authorities in Jersey.

Then came his experiences with Eric Pleasants, their deportation to France and Germany and their enlistment in the British Free Corps of the Legion of St George.

He married Lena Jurgens (she worked in Zehlendorf at the headquarters of the Kurt Eggars Regiment) and he was attached to the Regiment's "Skorpian West" operation. Lena and Leister did not want to get caught in the Russian advance on Berlin so they set out for Italy in April 1945 and hid out in Bressanone until the American forces arrived. In Milan he had dumped his British Free Corps uniform. On being repatriated to England in June 1945 he was arrested and convicted of treason. He was sentenced to three years penal servitude by Mr Justice Croom-Johnson at the Old Bailey, London.

Most of the British Free Corps of the Legion of St George were eventually brought to trial at the Old Bailey, charged with high treason under the Emergency Powers (Defence) Regulations Act 1939, sections 2A and 90. Section 2A made it an offence which could be punishable by penal servitude for life for anyone intending to assist the enemy by an act likely to aid the enemy or that was prejudicial to public safety, the defence of the realm or the efficient prosecution of the war. 57 British and Commonwealth citizens joined the British Free Corps between 1943 and 1945. Thank God that no Channel Islander ever served in the German forces.

The source of my information is Eric Pleasants. He used to correspond from his home in Kettering in Norfolk until he passed away. I still have his long letters in my files. They are so interesting to read and are now in the Jersey Archives Service (September 2003) under Eric Pleasants letters Joe Mière.

ERIC PLEASANTS

Born Norfolk, England 17 May, 1910. His father was a gamekeeper on a large estate. With the patronage of the Bowes-Lyon family he was able to attend Loughborough College where he obtained a diploma in physical education and physiotherapy, and he made his living as a PE instructor and professional wrestler using the name "Panther Pleasants." He joined the British Union of Facists as a bouncer for their protection squad at their meetings.

When war started in 1939 he was considering registering as a conscientious objector but joined the Peace Pledge Union scheme, which was sending parties of agricultural labourers to the Channel Islands. He arrived in Jersey in May 1940 where he met John Leister. Whilst serving a 14 day sentence in Jersey he also met the notorious safecracker, Eddie Chapman who later boasted the dubious distinction of becoming a double agent for both the German and British secret police. Chapman, Pleasants and John Leister became involved in black market activities, acquiring much of their stock by raiding the many large houses left standing empty, their owners having left for England just before the Germans arrived to occupy the Island. They also entered the house of the Bailiff of Jersey, Alexander Coutanche. Breaking into one large manor house, they stole a collection of six miniature paintings which Pleasants buried beneath the floorboards of the old chalet in which he and Leister were living in the grounds of the Panama Hotel in Green Street, St Helier.

In about 1978 Pleasants and John Leister revisited Jersey but when they came to the place where they had buried the six miniatures they found a large new building on the spot where the chalet had been. Eric Pleasants told me that the miniatures may have been the work of Jersey miniaturist, Philippe Jean. When breaking into a house in Grouville in 1940 he stole some very old Jersey silver which he then buried in the garden of a house called "The Pebbles" in La Grande Route de la Côte in the parish of St Clements. Again the garden had been built on. Pleasants told me that he never recovered any of his buried loot.

It was soon after the beginning of the Occupation that he, John Leister and Keith Barnes attempted to escape to England in a stolen boat and were caught by the German Military Police while trying to rob a petrol store for the voyage. Pleasants and Leister were deported to a German penal prison at Dijon, France. At the end of their prison sentence they were sent to the civilian camp at Kreuzburg. Both attempted to escape but were caught and were sent to a German penal prison at Breslau. Six months later they were transferred to a prisoner of war camp at Marlag-Marlag. It was here that Pleasants and Leister joined the British Free Corps of the Legion of St George, a military body formed by traitors and turncoats in the pay of the Germans, with a base at Hildesheim. After refusing work on a sports field they and other soldiers were arrested and despatched to an SS punishment camp at Schwerin and then returned to their unit at Dresden. Pleasants was once again put in charge of PT and he was chosen to box for the SS Pioneers against an SS police unit.

In February 1945 Pleasants married his German girlfriend Anneliese Nietscher. On the evening of 12 February of that same year the British and Americans started the heavy bombing of Dresden. His wife's family lived just outside of Dresden. There was a good chance that the British Free Corps would be sent to fight the Russians. Pleasants was sent to Stander's peace camp and spent his time giving exhibition boxing bouts against Max Schmeling. In Berlin Pleasants and his wife Anneliese were trying to escape from Berlin before the Russians encircled the city. Pleasants changed his British Free Corps uniform for a Wehrmacht one. As they made their way out of the city, they were stopped by two Russian Military Police. Pleasants killed them both with his bare hands and he and his wife made it to his wife's family home outside of Dresden. Later the Americans pulled out of East Germany and the Russians moved into Dresden. Pleasants and his wife stayed in the Russian zone, Pleasants working as a strongman act to entertain the Russian troops. In 1946 they were both arrested on suspicion of spying. After they were arrested, Pleasants was sentenced to 25 years imprisonment and sent to a penal labour camp at Vorkuta in the Russian Arctic. He spent seven years at this camp and never saw his wife again. In1952 Eric Plaisants was repatriated back to England.

MRS BAUDAINS AND HER SON, GEORGE

Forty one year old Alexandriene Baudains and her 16 year old son, George, were collaborators and informers for the German police in Jersey. On the eve of Jersey's liberation in May 1945, they both went to the local police station in St Helier and requested that the police give them police protection. The local police placed them both at the Little Sisters of the Poor at St Johns Road in St Helier. They were there only a few days when the Little Sisters of the Poor asked the police to take them away because the old people in the home were starting to attack the Baudains.

The local police collected them from the home and placed them in a cell at the local public prison in Gloucester Street, St Helier under protective custody. Their cell door was not locked and Mrs Baudains' husband was allowed to bring food and goods they needed to the prison. For eleven months Mrs Baudains and her son, George, stayed in the public prison. The public feelings against these two collaborators and German police informers remained very high. The Jersey public were out for blood.

The Jersey authorities did not know what to do with them even after eleven months had passed since the liberation of Jersey. On the morning of 23rd March 1946, the police escorted the two Baudains to the boat in St Helier harbour. They were each given £5 and placed on board the boat that would transport them to England. Mrs Baudains asked the police for a cabin for herself and her son. The policeman's reply was not recorded.

Once in England the Baudains made their way to Bristol and as time went by they set up there. A few years later George married an English girl and they had a daughter and a son. In 1985 George's daughter, now married, paid a visit to Jersey. The poor girl had quite a shock when, on a visit to the German Military Underground Hospital Museum she saw her father's and grandmother's photographs and collaboration history on display. She made contact with me, as it was my collection.

At first she was very reluctant to tell me who she was. Finally she told me that she knew nothing of the past life of her father and it was quite a shock to her to know that he and his mother were collaborators and German police informers. She knew that her father came from Jersey, but he never spoke of the German Occupation years. It was while watching the TV and Bergerac that she made up her mind to visit Jersey and find out why her father and his mother had left. She also stated that when she was very young, her father left home, leaving her and her brother and their mother. She told me she did not know where he was living. I did not press her on this but I think she knew where he was in England. I did not believe her when she told me that he had visited Jersey two or three times, although he used a different name when booking in at hotels. So how did she know about his visits to the Island?

In 1986 she wrote and told me her father, George Baudains, had died in July 1986. She kept in touch with me for a few years and even sent me a photograph of her two little children. But since 1993 there has been no more news of her or her family. In a letter in 1989 she informed me that her grandmother, Mrs Baudains had died 26 May 1975, and she was buried in Bristol, England.

I have always kept my word to George Baudains daughter and not told any press or TV people her address. After all it is not the daughter and her family who are to blame for the father's and grandmother's sins. She did tell me that her grandmother, Mrs Baudains, was a very wicked old woman. Even today there are many old Jersey people who still hate the name of Mother Baudains.

The Baudains leaving prison

Never to be Forgotten

PEARL JOYCE VARDON

Jersey woman Pearl Joyce Vardon, born 5 April 1915 at St Matins, Jersey. One time school teacher in Jersey, at Halkett Place primary school, and for a short while teacher at the Jersey Ladies College. She lived for a time at 'Gwendoline', Bellozanne Road, St Helier. Her address in January 1941 was number 7 Grosvenor Terrace, St Helier. In 1941 she was an interpreter for a German building firm, Theodore Elsche. The head office was on Victoria Avenue. The building firm was part of the Todt Organisation, in Jersey. She fell in love with a German officer, Captain Siegfried Schwatlo. In March she travelled to Paris looking for employment as a radio announcer. Later she moved to Radio Luxembourg and then she worked for the German Broadcasting Service where she broadcast German propaganda.

After the war's end she was arrested in Germany and in February 1946 she was flown back to England. She was tried at the Old Bailey 27 February 1946. She was sentenced to nine months imprisonment. After serving her time in prison, she moved to Wales where her lover was held as a prisoner of war. On his release they both returned to Germany.

RAID ON CHEMIST SHOP IN BATH STREET AND - 3 COLLABORATORS WITH THE GERMANS

Mrs Marjorie Robins

Joan Robins

Josie Lillicrap

Our little resistance group decided to do something about three families in Midvale Road. They were letting the side down and were collaborating with the Germans.

One of these collaborators lived right opposite our house in Midvale Road and they ran a chemist shop in Bath Street. Every weekend they held a party for their German friends. The German servicemen singing at the top of their voices kept us and others awake till the early hours, and looking out of our windows one could see Germans come and go from the house.

So one day we had our carbide bombs that some of the Spanish workers showed us how to make. We used carbide, tar, sawdust, sand, weed killer and water. You had to use very thick glass bottles, and not to add the water till last because you had to shake the mixture which with water made the gas thus formed expand. When the bombs hit a wall there was explosion. One fine late evening four of us arrived outside the chemist shop. The first bomb hit the big glass window but bounced off and exploded in the road. The next two bombs hit the large windows and exploded, smashing them. Four more bombs were thrown into the shop, and they went off with a big bang.

We then ran through the old fire station into James Street. But as we left the scene of the wrecked shop another group arrived. They were led by Denis Geary. This group was armed with bricks, etc. They also intended to wreck the shop but were just too late. We called out to them to run fast because the local police would soon be arriving, followed by the German Military Police.

The next morning at about 7.45 on my way to work I stopped for a short time opposite the wrecked chemist shop, it was in a mess. The police had placed wooden barricades around it to keep away the large crowd that had gathered. The local police and German Military Police were both there in force. It was like a scene from a film set. As I stood there a tall chap came alongside and whispered to me that the night before a truck had pulled up outside the shop and hand grenades had been thrown at the shop. 'I cannot tell you anymore,' said this silly twerp. He was foolish enough to hint that he was involved and with a wink he was off. I had to smile. An old school pal, Doug Bacon who had his own little resistance group came along to watch what was going on. It was only two weeks before that I had showed Doug how to make carbide bombs, but at that time Doug told me that he did not think our home made bombs would work. However, on this day he was very impressed because he said: 'I see they did work, Joe.' Doug then left the scene. We did not want to hang around too long, and I had spotted the collaborator and owner of the wrecked shop walking towards it with a local policeman and a German officer. If he had seen me (he knew me by sight) he would have put two and two together and had me arrested on the spot. But as time went on he was one of the informers who reported us to the Germans in 1944. How do I know who reported us to the Germans? One day in November 1944 Frank and I were being interrogated by the German Secret Field Police at their HQ. Four German police were standing around a high desk. A German Police officer asked us in German if we understood

German. We made out we could not understand what he was asking. Then he asked in English and we stated we knew no German.

He returned to the other three Germans at the high desk and started to read a letter. At the end of this first letter he read out the name 'Le Poidevin, Chemist.' Frank and I were standing not far away with our heads turned towards the wall, but out of the corner of my eye I could see the four Germans. The German officer then started to read a second letter again in German. At the end of this letter he read out the name 'Josie Lillicrap.' One of the three Germans asked the officer what the name 'Lillicrap' meant. The officer told him it meant flower shit. This brought out a burst of loud laughter from the three Germans. Even Frank and I had to smile. A third letter was read out, and at the end the name Robin was read out. So we now knew who had informed on us.

Josie Lillicrap ran a dance school in Midvale Road not far from our house. She was the girlfriend of the head of the German Secret Field Police in Jersey, Feldpolizeiinspektor Bode. On Liberation Day in Jersey he was seen going into Josie Lillicrap's house in Stopford Road dressed in civilian clothes. The British liberation forces soon had him behind prison bars.

One of the other collaborators in Midvale Road was Mrs Majorie Robins and her daughter Joan Robins. They, like their next door neighbours, used to have all night parties with their German friends, singing Nazi songs till the early hours. Not only were we kept awake by the noise, but those Nazi songs got under our skins. It was about time that someone paid them a visit.

One night after the curfew hour we waited till Mother Robins had called out good night to her German friends as they left her house, then we blew in her windows with our carbide bombs. It was only later on that we found out that her prized bamboo encased piano had been wrecked by our bombs. There was no more playing or singing from that house for a few weeks. Mother Robins was an informer for the German police. And to think that there were 10 Jersey boys from Midvale Road in the British forces. And yet there were these collaborators entertaining the Germans in their homes.

However, at war's end, Mother Robins got her deserts. The Bailiff of Jersey on the night before Liberation Day came to the prison and released us with the words 'Do not kick a dog when it's down and no trouble please.' On the way home my sisters and I and friends had just got to the top of Midvale Road when we saw a crowd a little further away. 'What's going on?' we asked one group of people.

A large crowd about a hundred strong had assembled outside Mother Robins house in Midvale Road. They broke in and dragged her out. They tied her hands and feet, then placed a noose around her neck and then threw the rope over the tall gas lamp outside the house. They were just about to hang her when the local police arrived. She was screaming her head off. There were so many people in the road that the police could not get past with their van, they had to park it at the bottom of the road. They then ran up to the crowd. They were just in time because she was already dangling from the lamp post.

The police got her down and took her in the police van to the Town Hall for her own protection. It was Dr Shone from Royde House in Midvale Road who had phoned for the police. Later on, Mother Robins and her daughter left the Island to live in the West Country in England. Her daughter still lives there. We think the States of Jersey and the British Government were pleased that most of the very well known collaborators left Jersey. These collaborators should have been tried in public and then deported to Germany. After all they were an embarrassment to the Island and the British race.

BAILIFF OF GUERNSEY

Victor Carey, Bailiff and official representative of the King in Guernsey, tried to suppress the use of 'V' signs, this manifestation of hope for the loyal Guernsey people. He had the following notice published in the local newspapers aimed against his own fellow countrymen. At war's end Victor Carey was honoured with a knighthood, 12 December 1945.

Reward of £25.

A reward of £25 will be given to the person who first gives to the Inspector of Police information leading to the conviction of anyone (not already discovered) for the offence of marking on any gate, wall, or other place whatsoever visible to the public the letter 'V' or any other sign or any other word or words calculated to offend the German authorities or soldiers.

Signed: Victor G Carey
Bailiff of Guernsey
This 8th day of July 1941

The above notice was published in the local Guernsey newspaper, below the coat of arms of Guernsey showing that this was a notification of La Gazette Officielle.

A copy of the above notice was smuggled out of Guernsey by escapee Guernseyman, Wilfred Renouf, and given to the British intelligence M.I.19 in 1944. The copy is still in their files. Most loyal Guernsey people were very upset by this offering of a reward against their own people. At war's end all attempts to have a full investigation into the above reward notice and on the collaboration in Guernsey were quashed by the same local authorities that ruled in the Occupation years.

LETTERS TO THE EDITOR

How Sir Victor resisted the Hun

SIR — I recall discussing the German occupation of the Channel Islands (report, Dec. 2) with my grandfather, Sir Victor Carey, in the 1950s, when I was about 16.

He was well aware of the criticism of his role as Bailiff of Guernsey, but asked me not to enter into any debate on it, something I have respected until now.

My grandfather told me that when he was first asked to sign a proclamation, shortly after the Germans had landed, he refused. But he was summoned back to the Military Commander's office to be presented with a list of some 30 names, and told to select 20 who would be shot the next day if he persisted in his refusal. All those on the list were known to him, and he was "charming and weak" enough to sign.

A lawyer, my grandfather told me that he and his staff tried repeatedly to delay publication of the frequent orders and proclamations by redrafting them in the hope of softening the invariably harsh and domineering tone of the documents. With a wry smile he would recall, "In that, sadly I failed."

He often asked that, when I came to judge the facts which one day would emerge, I should remember that the Germans took over the islands by the simple expedient of landing at their air and seaports. The softening-up process, by Stukas bombing the harbour at St Peter Port (which I personally recall experiencing as a seven year old), was over.

The islands, on orders, were demilitarised; and the Third Reich was there in a "paternal guise", promising that the traditions and way of life would in every way be "honoured and respected" by the 20,000 troops stationed on the island of six miles by nine.

Since my grandfather had reached retirement age, he only reluctantly took on the additional job of acting Lieutenant Governor after the declaration of war. He said that, despite all this and the studied "charm" of those in command who first arrived, he never consciously did anything to co-operate unless he felt it was in the best interests of the islands and the islanders.

He told me many times that on every occasion in which he had any personal dealing with the Germans he stated that they were, and would always be, the hated enemy.

I only hope that I am forgiven, after all these years, for breaking my promise of silence.

PETER DE VIC CAREY
Isleworth, Middx

(Grandson of the Ex-Bailiff) Peter De Vic Carey's letter to the Telegraph, Mon 7 Dec 1992 defending his grandfather's actions. It is only fair to publish this here but the Germans would have never shot people just because he refused to sign. This is a load of old bull.

BAILIFF'S ADDRESS TO THE MEMBERS OF THE STATES ON MARCH 21.

Gentlemen,—I have called you together at short notice, which I am empowered to do, on a very serious matter which has arisen in the last few days and which I desire to bring to your notice as well as to that of the whole population of this island.

NOT ONLY STUPID—BUT CRIMINAL.

A few days ago an ill-disposed person or persons deliberately and maliciously cut a telephone cable in two places in the neighbourhood of the Airport which belonged to the German Military Authorities and thus performed an act of grave sabotage. Such an act was not only stupid but criminal, as it involved those who were participating in it with the penalty of death but it also brought the population of the whole island under the grave displeasure of the German authorities and in danger of the loss of their liberties.

I think you will all agree with me that since the Occupation the German Authorities, both Military and Civil, have treated us with humanity and consideration and have gone out of their way on several occasions to help us in these difficult times, and it is our duty and obligation to co-operate with them in carrying out their Orders and Regulations. Those of us who have had to meet the German Officers from time to time have always been treated with courtesy and consideration.

APPEAL TO EVERYONE.

I will therefore ask you and the people of this island to govern themselves in such a way that there will be no recurrence of such an incident as that to which I have just referred. Such incidents only make the task of those in authority more difficult, and the Controlling Committee of the States who are faced with such grave economic problems for the well-being of the community should not be hampered in their work by these criminal acts. I should also like to add that it is the duty of any individual who has any information with regard to the perpetration of this act of sabotage to inform the police immediately, as unless the culprit is brought to justice we do not know what further penalties the population may incur.

ENDANGERING LIVES OF ISLANDERS.

I may say that I am glad that the great majority of the inhabitants have conducted themselves with propriety and dignity in these difficult times and it is only a very few who do not appear to have realised the grave situation in which the people of this island are placed by such a senseless act of sabotage which places not only the property but the very lives of the islanders in danger.

I can assure you that I will take all possible steps to bring the perpetrators of such acts to speedy justice, so that the safety of the population as a whole may be safeguarded. I am also sure you will wish to join with me in a declaration of our abhorrence of this and any similar acts which I hope will not recur.

I should like to inform you that the duty of providing the required guard for night duty has been imposed by the German authorities on the five parishes nearest the Airport.

EXTRACT FROM
JURAT LEALE'S SPEECH
IN THE
STATES ON MARCH 21.

Mr. Bailiff and Gentlemen,—On the question of the cutting of the telephone wires by some foolish and dangerous person, I should just like to put the position exactly as I see it. In June of last year any of us who wished to do so could have left the island. Two very large vessels left on the Saturday evening of evacuation week; one of them practically empty, the other entirely so. We stayed here knowing full well that German troops could, without any resistance, occupy the island whenever their Command ordered them to do so. Our staying here meant that we accepted that position and were prepared in the event of occupation to act as good citizens. That being so, it is entirely wrong that anyone should now think he has the right to do this kind of thing. We made our choice last June and we must not now think we can do things which may have the most serious consequences for the rest of the island.

We must face the fact that the German authorities are bound to take a most serious view of such incidents and to insist that they do not occur. If continued, the penalties imposed will inevitably be more severe. There has never been an army of occupation in history which could have taken other than a serious view of such an occurrence.

CONDEMNATION.

I feel, therefore, that the States have the right as well as the duty to condemn such acts, as on the one hand utterly foolish, for they do no sort of good to anyone, and on the other hand as wicked, because they bring in their train inconvenience and maybe sufferings imposed on everyone.

In staying on here, we trusted all the other people who stayed with us not to get us into trouble. Those who even contemplate committing such acts betray the confidence we, and our womenfolk, too, placed in them. Surely we have enough difficulties to surmount without anxieties of this kind being thrust on us. If the responsibility for condemning this act rests on us today as an official body, let us leave it at that. Let us shoulder privately the responsibility of condemning them in like manner and brand those who do them as both very stupid and very dangerous.

As everyone knows, as a consequence of this incident the curfew hour has been put back again to nine o'clock in the evening and the States have been ordered to provide sixty men between the ages of 18 and 45 each night for patrol work.

DUTIES TO BE SHARED BY ALL.

Now probably we could, from those who are in one way and another on our payroll, obtain these 60 men by telling them that it was as much as their job was worth to refuse. But I am sure that no one would wish the burden to be borne by certain classes of the community to the exclusion of others. To do so would be grossly unfair. It is therefore essential that powers should be taken so that the burden may be spread without distinction of class or calling; and we are introducing this session a Projet enabling us to do this.

As to the machinery to be set up, it is this: Each of the Constables of the parishes concerned will furnish to a representative of the Labour Office a list of the men from his parish who are eligible and suitable for this duty. We do not want men mentally unfit. Each parish will contribute its quota daily.

DISCRETIONARY POWERS FOR SPECIAL CASES.

The Labour Office representative will then serve on the person concerned a notice informing him of the date on which he is to serve. The only reason for noncompliance that can be accepted will be medical, and of course it will be the duty of the men concerned to notify the Labour Office immediately of his inability to be present on his appointed night. The Labour Office will, however, have discretionary powers to deal with special cases.

I may say that hours of duty are from 8.30 to 8.30 with two hours on duty and four hours off. Suitable shelter has been provided.

COLLABORATORS AND FRATERNISATION

Yes, only a foolish person would deny the fact that we did have some collaborators in Jersey during the German Occupation 1940-1945. There were not many real collaborators, and most were mainly people out for themselves, black market racketeers, scroungers, and people who traded with the Germans. And there were some short sighted people who were playing safe just in case the Germans won the war. We also had some informers in Jersey. Their behaviour was really disgraceful and amounted to treason.

The German Secret Field Police had dozens of letters every month from informers. There were no known Gestapo units in Jersey but people always called the German Secret Field Police the Gestapo. In the German Underground Hospital Museum archives are many files with the original informers letters. Some informers were paid between 20 and 50 German marks for each person they had informed on, leading to the arrest and imprisonment of the people.

Why did people inform on their own people to the German police? Some informed to get extra cash, others from malice, spite, a grudge, or just plain envious jealousy. These hateful informers should have been hunted down at war's end and tried in public. In the closed files at the public records office in London there are some on the informers in the Channel Islands 1940-1945 who informed on their own people to the German Secret Field Police, reference KU4/78/65169/315F. I have some copies of some of the closed files. I also have copies of the British counter intelligence reports for the Channel Islands 1940-1945.

At the Jersey Archives Service in St Helier, Jersey, are closed files DZ/D/H9/2 on the source of information, names and addresses etc of some of the informers. But I have been refused permission to see and read these closed files. I was informed that it is possible, if not probable, that some of the people who are named in the records may still be alive and living in Jersey. And Human Rights (Jersey) Law 2000 Article 8 of the convention provides that everyone has the right to respect his/her private and family life, his/her home and correspondence.

So now we all know that the German collaborators and informers are protected by our laws. At war's end the States of Jersey did have enough proof to take legal action against the collaborators and informers for their treachery and treason, and also their scandalous behaviour during the German Occupation of Jersey 1940-1945. We the loyal Jersey people were informed in January 1946, that no retrospective legislation was possible owing to the absence of the necessary legal machinery, so that persons concerned cannot be brought to trial in Jersey or in England. It was also stated that it would not be in the interest of the Island that consideration of this subject should be prolonged. In other words a cover up by the British Government and the States of Jersey. At war's end, we asked the British M19 officers who interviewed us political prisoners 'When were they going to arrest the collaborators and informers of the Occupation years?'. They informed us that everything was in hand once they had taken statements from the ex-political prisoners, and those who had proof of the people who informed on them. Also they were investigating and interviewing people who had been accused of being collaborators or accused of being informers for the German Secret Field Police.

Well, these British M19 officials did take statements from these people in Jersey. And their findings and statements and the results of their investigations are recorded in the closed files, to be opened in 50-75 years time. I doubt if I will be around by that time. It is a great shame because it means that the loyal Jersey people were arrested on the information given by informers to the Germans and sent to brutal treatment in concentration camps where many died, while the collaborators and informers got away with their disgraceful treason, and are protected by our laws.

As for the women and girls that collaborated with the Germans (called Jerrybags), the behaviour of these woman was disgraceful but it's the same in any country that is occupied by troops from another country. In England they have never as far as I know ever published numbers of how many allied soldiers, mostly American, got English women pregnant, or how many illegitimate children were born to these women of American and other allied fathers. I was in the army in 1945 in England and at weekends in the towns that were close to prisoner of war camps, German POWs with yellow letters painted on the back of their jackets, were walking about the town and chatting up the young English girls. I often wonder how many German POWs got girls pregnant in England. It would be very interesting to know how many children were born with German or Italian POW fathers.

The German records for the Channel Islands found in the Lebensborn files in Germany state that, up to May 1944, 80 illegitimate children were born whose fathers were German servicemen. In all the Channel Islands, at the most 120 to 130 children were born of whom the fathers were German servicemen, from 1941-1945.

Not all the illegitimate children were registered in the Islands, as the following case will show. A few years ago a good friend of mine who was born at home in 1944 asked me to help him to get his birth certificate. We checked all the records for births etc, but could not find his birth registered anywhere in Jersey. It was only when his mother died that he found out that who he thought was his mother was really his grandmother. Her daughter had fathered a baby by a German soldier in 1942 so his grandmother brought him up as her son.

His sister admitted to him that she was his mother. He had a shock to find out that the one he called his sister was really his mother. She even had a photo of his German father. But the nice chap that he was he never held it against her for not telling him about his birth. She told him he was born at home and the birth was never registered. There could have been a few like him that were never registered. He died only a few years ago and at his funeral I met his mother/sister, but did not let on that I knew all about her secret affair with a German that led to the birth of my friend.

People often ask me how many women went out with members of the German forces in Jersey 1940-1945. I can only guess the total, and from what I saw during the Occupation, I would state about 300 women and girls went out with members of German forces in Jersey 1940-1945. I know and see many of them that still live in Jersey. Some of these women had husbands in the British forces serving overseas. These women came from all walks of life, two had policemen fathers. And these women did not all come from working class families.

Most of our loyal Jersey women and girls kept faithful to their husbands or boy friends and 95 per cent of our women and girls stayed loyal to King and Country, bless them. In the German prison in St Helier in 1944-1945 we had 14 Jersey women arrested by the Germans. They were brave and wonderful, really nice decent and clean living women, and I am still very proud to call them dear friends. We still keep in touch, it's a bond that nothing can break. I am glad to state that the men and boys in that German prison treated these brave and loyal women with great respect. Even the German Military prison guards treated these ladies with respect. In the row of cells I was in there were two French ladies and one Jersey girl, all under sentence of death. They did not moan or cry out. They kept cheerful, heads held high. It was a great honour to be with them. They set an example to us all. When I came out of 20 days of solitary confinement those dear ladies cheered and shouted out 'Joe's back.' I will never forget them.

FRENCH COLLABORATORS

How did the French deal with collaborators after the liberation of France 1944-1945? The deaths of resistance fighters - 10,842 were killed without due process of law, 6,675 during the Maquis struggles before the liberation - the rest afterwards during the course of reprisal actions. 779 more men were to be executed as a result of sentences that were pronounced by the courts of justice and the military tribunals.

By the middle of 1945, 60,000 guilty or suspected collaborators had been arrested in France 39,900 were given prison sentences. Two thousand and seventy-one death sentences were passed by the courts. They granted pardons to 1,303 condemned men. 768 appeals from condemned men were rejected by the courts. The death sentences passed on all women and minors by the courts were commuted to prison sentences. The examining magistrates decided that there were no grounds for prosecution in 18,000 cases.

By September 13 1944, the Free French Government had set up special courts of justice provided for by the decree of 24 June 1944. In each region there was to be a tribunal presided over by a magistrate and including a jury appointed by the President of the Court of Appeal. The lists of the citizens qualified to serve on this jury were drawn up by the Commissioner of the Republic. This tribunal was to judge cases of collaboration with the enemy under legal forms and guarantees the right to a defence counsel.

In the realm of public office, resentment was particularly sharp, for Vichy had cashiered more than 50,000 people and, furthermore, certain officials had displayed odious zeal in the service of the invader. Out of a staff of 800,000, only sanctions were pronounced, of which scarcely 5,000 resulted in dismissals. With the co-operation of a considerable number of Vichy officials and a mass of informers, 60,000 persons had been executed, and more than 200,000 deported of whom a bare 50,000 survived.

A further 35,000 men and women had been condemned by Vichy tribunals; 35,000 officials cashiered; 70,000 'suspects' interned; 15,000 officers degraded under suspicion of being in the Resistance. Local atmosphere made itself felt. Sometimes the sessions were disturbed by mob interventions. In several regions there were even riots to snatch the prisoners from the courts. This was the case in Nîmes, Naubeuger, Bourges, Annecy, Alec and Rodez. In fact about twenty unfortunate prisoners were lynched throughout the country. It was necessary that the men who had taken responsibility in the highest office for the acts of the Vichy regime should appear before a jurisdiction established for this purpose. The courts which judged them had to be politically qualified to do so. The court was installed in the Palais de Justice.

The first trial to come before the High Court was that of Admiral Esteva, Resident General in Tunisia at the time of the Allied landing in North Africa. Following Petain's orders, he had allowed the Germans to disembark, had ordered the roads to be opened to them and had forbidden the French forces in the country to join the Free French fighting the enemy. Admiral Esteva was sentenced to solitary confinement. General Dentz was next to stand trial. As High Commissioner in the Levant, he had in 1941 allowed German squadrons to land on Syrian territory in accordance with Vichy's orders, had established the points where the Wehrmacht was to disembark and had used the forces under his command against the Free French and British forces. General Dentz was sentenced to death.

Pierre Laval was sentenced to death. Joseph Darnand was also sentenced to death. Marshal Philippe Petain was sentenced to death by the courts but he was reprieved and confined on the Ile d'Yeu. So it went on and on in war torn liberated France. There were 55,000 sentenced in Belgium, and more than 50,000 in Holland.

CHANNEL ISLANDS BLUFF FAILED TO FOOL THE GERMANS

A plot to bluff the German Commander of the Channel Islands into surrendering soon after D-Day collapsed in a farce. Secret documents released in November 1996 revealed that, had it worked, the Islanders would have been spared six months of their grim German Occupation.

A British intelligence agent tried to land on Guernsey in September 1944 with a 'turned' captured German General to persuade the occupiers that a liberating invasion was imminent. But the plan, code named 'Operation Nest Egg,' failed when his boat was intercepted by a German naval patrol and his captors refused to believe him. 'Nest Egg' was the brainchild of the Supreme Headquarters Allied Expeditionary Forces Psychological Warfare Unit, run by, among other intellectuals, Richard Crossman who would later become a Labour minister.

From the start its planners admitted they were embarking on a bluff. In a memorandum dated 10 August 1944 and marked 'top secret' they said: There is no assault force available. After 20 August, an occupying force will be available to accept surrender but not to fight for the Islands. The plan was to put a captured German General on the telephone to the garrison commander General Oberst Graf von Schmettow. He would call from France to arrange a parley, possibly at sea under a white flag. This memo continued: 'The German general would then be used to lay the facts before the commander. He should be able to persuade Von Schmettow that large scale operations were imminent, thus obviating the necessity for deception by physical evidence of impending attack. If it becomes clear that Von Schmettow is a 'fight to the last cartridge' man all further propaganda operations should be discontinued. If he agrees to negotiation, then the details can be worked out on the spot. The German negotiator General Bassinger, an Afrika Korps veteran, said he doubted that the plan would be a success. The Chiefs of Staff refused to consider anything other than unconditional surrender.'

The plan went ahead anyway. On 22 September 1944, Major Alan Chambers embarked in an air-sea rescue launch, flying a white flag, with General Bassinger. Letters inviting Von Schmettow to the rendezvous had been dropped by the RAF the previous night. Near St Peter Port, Chambers was climbing into a dinghy to row ashore to find Von Schmettow when a German motor boat arrived.

Chambers stayed on board the motor boat for an hour and a half, trying to persuade the Germans to take him to Von Schmettow. His report states: 'I was offered a cognac. Unfortunately none was to be found and coffee was finally produced. This was of very inferior quality. After some fumbling, a package of two cigarettes was produced and one was handed to me. On leaving, after being refused permission to go ashore, I said in German to the naval lieutenant - "Are you quite sure you realise the consequences which will follow your refusal to let me see the Commander?" The naval officer made no reply and appeared unaffected.'

On their way back to France, the British party was fired on by the German guns on Guernsey. One member was wounded. The following month, the chiefs of staff told Churchill's war cabinet: 'We are recommending to you that no food supplies should be sent to the Islands at this stage'

The Channel Islanders were to continue to suffer hardship, as predicted, for another eight months before their belated liberation.

LIBERATION - JERSEY, 9 MAY 1945

Joe Mière was a
political prisoner
who was a thorn
in the side of
the German
authorities

My story

JOE MIERE

'ON Liberation Day, I
went down to West
Park. I had been in
prison as a political
prisoner for about seven
months and we were released
from prison the night before.

The Bailiff came and re-
leased us — but he warned us
not to kick a dog when it's
down.

Gloucester Street was full of
people and my family came
down with a handcart but they
couldn't get a Union Jack,
they could only find a Belgian
flag.

I felt excited when the
troops arrived — I was ready
to go and do that, go and fight
the Japanese, but I was too
skinny and small.

The first place we headed
for was the German court
martial building at Kingscliff
to see if we could find any
documents but all we could
see were burnt ashes in the
fireplace.

We were young and you
know what youngsters are
like.

They call it hooliganism
today but then it was called
patriotism.

Out of all the people that
need a medal it's the mothers
who should have got them —
many times you'd say, oh the
rations have increased this
week — but of course,
your mother had given
you part of hers.'

We had been released from the German prison
in Gloucester Street by the Bailiff early
evening, about 6.30pm on 7 May 1945. Outside
the main gate in Gloucester Street there was a
crowd of people, family and friends, waiting to
welcome us as we regained our freedom. The crowd
cheered us as we came through the prison side gate.
With family and friends we made our way home to
25 Midvale Road.

The next day we went to Conway Street, the
liberation troops were making their way up the
street to the Parade Gardens where some of them
halted and placed their kits down on the grass by the
Westaway Crèche. They were very kind and they
filled my old pipe with tobacco.

On Liberation evening my pal Frank Le Pennec
and I went to the Weighbridge. A little old man was
standing between Frank and me when all of a
sudden a shot rang out from the Pomme D'Or
Hotel. The little old man cried out in pain and told
us he had been shot. We lifted his trouser leg and
saw blood running. Two local policemen took him
by car to the hospital. With all the goings on we
clean forgot about the little old man.

In the 1950's we wanted to check with the
hospital for their records of Liberation evening, but
they would not bother to look for that date. If only
you could be allowed to check the hospital records
of years ago you would find out about things that
nobody has gone into before and it would be so
interesting. That Liberation evening we thought we
would look at the Royal Square. As we got there we
heard a lot of shouting in German. Just about
standing and drunk up to his eyeballs was a tall well
built German in the black uniform of the Panzers
(tanks) and by his rank badges he was an NCO
(Sgt). He was calling out that it was his birthday. In
his right hand was a pistol held high in the air.

Very quickly we formed a plan to disarm this happy German. We three, Frank, George Le Pennec and myself went towards him, singing happy birthday to you, etc. Then Frank made for his legs, George his left arm, and I, being tall, the pistol. We all ended up in a heap and I passed the pistol to Frank who then tried to find the safety catch. Then, like a bolt out of the blue, a boy about ten years old snatched the pistol out of Frank's hands and made off towards Snow Hill. George went after the boy but could not find him.

Now the German was fighting mad. He took a big swing at Frank who blocked the blow and let the German have one of his right hooks. The poor German went flying, right on top of three people who had been leaning on their bikes watching the goings on. They all went down, bikes as well in a heap.

The German just about got to his feet and was going to swing again at Frank when out of a doorway came two local policemen. They took hold of the German and, with his arms pinioned up his back, marched him towards the Town Hall. The two policemen must have been in the doorway a long time and did seem to resist arresting the soldier because of the pistol in his hand. As the years went by the soldier must have thought back many times of the day of his birthday when he got drunk and was arrested by the local police.

The next morning, 9 May 1945, Frank and George and myself made our way to the Weighbridge, then on to West Park. The BBC took photographs of the large crowds in front of the Grand Hotel, I still have the photo they gave us later on. We are on the right hand side. How we got hold of a large Union Jack and a long pole, goodness knows but we marched up town. I carried the flag on the pole followed by a large crowd. I gave the flag to someone else and he went off, with the crowd following, towards Halkett Place.

Then in Amy and Sons doorway we saw five or six big chaps kicking and raining blows on a young girl (who had been consorting with the German soldiers). We stopped them from ill-treating the girl and we told them that was enough. At first they turned on us until two of them recognised us, then they ran off. The poor girl got up and ran down French Lane. We then walked up Queen Street. We stopped outside the front of Boots. We filled up our pipes. In those days Boots had a sort of open arcade. We had just got our old pipes going when this very young girl ran past us. She was about 16 years old and was naked as the day she was born. Her nose was bleeding, her hair, what was left of it, was covered in blood where the scissors for cutting off her hair (the punishment for girls going with Germans) had dug into her head and the blood was running down the side of her face. She went into a corner by a door, crying like a trapped animal. She had been badly knocked about.

We told her she was now safe, but as we approached she cried out, thinking, it seemed, that we were going to hit her. I will never forget the look in her eyes - pure terror. We stood her up and put my old military style raincoat on her. Doing up the buttons, I thought - why the hell was I carrying a raincoat on such a fine and warm day? We told her to run home and she bolted towards La Motte Street. I loved that old mac and I called out to her not to forget to return it to me. It was the only one I had. Frank turned to me and said 'Are you mad Joe. Do you know where she lives and does she know where you live?' I replied 'no.' 'Well, how the hell are you going to get your mac back?' said Frank. He was right, I never saw my mac again.

She must sometimes on Liberation Day think of how she was attacked by a wild mob and how two young Jerseymen helped her, one of them giving her his raincoat. We had no time for collaborators but, having felt the brutal blows of the German police, I knew what she had gone through. She was about a year younger than me, and seeing her with that fear in her face brought back a dark part of my young life.

The next evening walking down by the harbour I met a very nice young lady. We were both looking at a Royal Navy ship that was tied up alongside the harbour wall. Life can be strange because, in talking, we discovered that she was the sister of Brian Bisson who had been imprisoned by the Germans and, best of all, we had shared the same cell. I walked the young lady home to her house at Georgetown. We got on very well and she was very pretty and attractive and charming to talk to. I would have liked to make a date with her, but being very shy of asking, it was only a goodnight and see you sometime.

At the Liberation of Jersey, many of the young men and women in the Island volunteered to join the British forces. The Yacht Hotel, being used as a temporary Naval office, was besieged by hundreds of young Jersey people wanting to sign on for the Royal Navy. A young naval officer, Jerseyman Bernard Le Cocq who had arrived with the liberation forces, informed us that the Royal Navy was not signing on any new personnel at that time, but that a notice would be printed in the Evening Post notifying all those wanting to enlist in HM forces where to apply, dates, times etc.

The notice did not appear in the Evening Post till July 1945. The recruiting office where we had to report to enlist was at the old Falle's drapery store in Beresford Street. This store was used during the Occupation as the German Field Post Office 1941-1945. Hundreds of young men and women signed on thinking they were going to fight the Japs. My pals and I were some of the first to sign on.

The ship that took us to England also carried a large group of German officers who were on their way to prisoner of war camps in England. It was so strange because the German officers had to line up with us on the ship to collect a cup or mug of tea. When we docked at Southampton they were escorted to a waiting train bound for the prisoner of war cages just outside London. We, the volunteers for the British army, were transported by train to Bodmin in Cornwall for six weeks of primary training. I and two other Jersey lads were posted to our regiment, Gloucesters, at Colchester, Essex. After infantry training the next posting was Germany. We were transported by ship from Hull to Cuxhaven, then by slow troop train to Hanover. Then we moved around all over the place. Brussels Belgium, Hamburg, Train Guard to Berlin Operation, 'Seagull', the Hartz Mountains Operation, 'Woodpecker', Warsaw Poland Operation 'Slavic.' The last place that I was based in was the Hook of Holland with trips to Denmark and Vienna.

On Liberation Day in Jersey the Royal Navy destroyer HMS Beagle (H30) was anchored in the roads between Noirmont Point and Elizabeth Castle in St Aubins Bay. Six young Jersey people, Frank, John, Florence, and Marie Le Pennec, and two friends, Geoffrey Poole and Harry Bardin, wanted to visit the Beagle.

Harry Bardin borrowed a small rowing boat from St Aubin's harbour. He picked up the other five friends off the beach at First Tower. As they were rowing towards the destroyer they met other local people rowing towards the ship. They were in a ship's lifeboat which they had taken from St Helier harbour. It had been in the water and secured alongside the ship that it belonged to, the S. S. Eskwood.

The two rowing parties agreed to exchange boats, as the bigger lifeboat could take the six people and as there were six oars on board. The small rowing boat could be handled better by having only three people on board. Once more the six young people rowed towards the Beagle. Five manned the oars and one on the tiller. Having reached the Beagle, they climbed the rope ladder, all except Frank who was so seasick that he remained in the lifeboat. Once on board the Beagle, they were greeted by the crew and taken down to the ships galley for a hearty meal of fried eggs, bacon and sausages, followed by spotted dick and mugs of hot tea. They gave the sailors whatever German mementoes they had with them. The crew in turn gave them chocolate and cigarettes.

The Captain, Douglas Williams, went down to the ships galley and shook hands with them. He also kindly arranged for a parcel of food for each to take home with them. They thanked everyone, got back into the lifeboat and rowed back to the beach at First Tower. All the six were seasick with all the rich food inside them, the like of which they had not seen or eaten for five years.

On the Liberation anniversary 9 May 1995, the ex-captain of HMS Beagle, and his wife were staying with a friend at Maison Charles at Bel Royal. The Commander said that he would like to meet Marie Le Pennec, now Mrs Mière and her husband, Joe. Marie and I had morning tea and cakes with the charming Commander and his lady wife, and their very kind host, Commander P.C. Gibaut, ex-Royal Navy. Commander

Williams did remember local people rowing out to his ship but after so many years he had forgotten who.

The lifeboat that the six young people used belonged to a coal boat Eskwood, a ship with an interesting history. When the German commandos from Jersey raided Granville, 8th March 1945, they captured the Eskwood and sailed her to St Helier harbour, 9th March 1945. She only had a few tons of coal in her bunkers, having only a short time before discharged her cargo in Granville. After the Liberation of Jersey she was towed back to Swansea, refitted and renamed Kilworth in 1946. She had been built in 1911, and was scrapped in 1957.

JERSEY LOYALIST PETITION 1945

The Jersey Evening Post   Monday 18 June 1945

Deal with Quislings
Petition to be presented to the States.

A few weeks ago two organisations which worked underground during the Occupation, checking up on collaborators with the enemy, joined forces; they were the Jersey Auxiliary Legion and the Loyalist.

Contact was later established with similar organisations in the country parishes, and meetings and representatives of all organisations took place at which a strong central committee was formed. Major J.C.M. Manley was elected president; Major H. P. Lamy vice-president; Captain C.G. Poole Hon Secretary and Treasurer; and it was decided that the title of the central organisation shall be the Jersey Loyalist.

At a meeting held on Saturday afternoon (16 June 1945) it was decided to take steps to have a petition presented to the States of Jersey praying that a special court be set up to deal with persons accused of having collaborated with or assisted the German war effort during the Occupation of this Island. It is hoped to have the petition presented at the next Thursday assembly (21 June 1945).

In every country that had been occupied by the Germans there were trials of collaborators set up by special courts of justice - all except the Channel Islands. The Jersey Loyalist presented a petition to the States of Jersey, Thursday 21 June 1945. The Jersey Loyalist was an organisation which worked underground during the German Occupation of Jersey 1940-1945. The petition was headed 'Deal with Quislings.'

The Jersey Loyalist Petition

The following is a petition presented to the States of Jersey yesterday (Thursday 21st June 1945) by the Jersey Loyalists:- to Alexander Moncrieff Coutanche Esquire, Bailiff of Jersey, President, and to the Members of the Assembly of the States of Jersey.

This Memorial and humble petition of loyal and faithful subjects of His Majesty, residing and domiciled in the Island of Jersey sheweth:-

1.   That the Channel Islands, of which Jersey forms an integral part, are the oldest overseas possession of the Crown of England, and throughout the centuries the inhabitants of Jersey have manifested and shown their loyalty and devotion to the Crown and to the Mother Country to such an extent that reigning sovereigns have from time to time granted to the Island charters, conferring privileges and rights in recognition of the service and loyalty of the inhabitants, the charters forming part of the constitution of which the Islanders are justly proud.

2.   That your petitioners deplore and beg to report that during the military Occupation of the Island of Jersey, commencing 1st July 1940, a number of the inhabitants, both male and female, having varying forms and degrees, either deliberately or otherwise collaborated, consorted with, assisted, associated or traded with the King's enemies, or materially increased and assisted their war effort against His Majesty's and Allied Governments, and this to the sorrow, disgust and humiliation of all loyal subjects of His Majesty residing in the Island.

3.   That your petitioners consider that the actions and doings of such persons constitute acts of disloyalty and treason, and that any charges proved render the guilty persons liable to punishment appropriate to meet the degree of offence committed;

4.   That the various ways in which offences have been committed may be summarised as follows:-

A.   Engaging in the transportation to and from the Island of enemy arms and ammunition, the discharge or embarkation of such, the transportation of same within the Island, and the construction of works of military importance.

B.   Assisting the German authorities in their attempts to coerce the inhabitants by acting as informers.

C.   Sustaining the morale and the physical well-being of the enemy armed forces by selling to them, by means of 'Black Market,' trading food and, or other articles which should have been sold to their fellow Islanders who were sorely in need.

D.   Consorting, and, in certain cases, co-habiting by women with members of the German forces, and some while in receipt of allowances made to them by His Majesty's government on behalf of husbands serving in the British forces.

E.   Engaging voluntarily in work for the enemy, and this, particularly when done by men receiving allowances or pensions from His Majesty's government.

F.   Entertaining in their homes, by local residents, of officers and men of the armed forces of a nation with which their own country was at war.

G.   Assisting or collaborating in any way with the enemy.

5.   That your petitioners are of the opinion the conduct of offending members of the population indicted under the above headings, warrants minute and careful investigation by an independent Tribunal or Court of Inquiry.

6.   That it is likely that many of such guilty persons will attempt to leave Jersey as soon as possible, and try to settle in some part of the mother country or of the British Dominions, where their infamous behaviour and conduct during the war will be unknown and where they hope to escape the shame which they would justly reap in the Island of Jersey.

7.   That there is good reason to suggest that members of the female population (quite apart from common prostitutes) who have consorted and in instances co-habited with members of the enemy armed forces are so affected in health and perverted in mind by enemy propaganda, as to render them dangerous to be allowed to mix with male British persons who will come to be in the Island after the end of the Occupation. Your petitioners deplore to relate that in a number of cases the women in question are mothers of young children and or wives of loyal and patriotic members of His Majesty's forces.

Your petitioners therefore humbly pray

A.   That immediate legislative action should be taken for the constitution of a Tribunal or Court of Inquiry (military or other) before which Tribunal or Court shall be brought all such members of the population indicted and charged with the commission of treasonable or other criminal acts as here in before described, and that the said Tribunal be empowered to inflict on offenders such punishment as the degree of guilt of each individual case may be deemed to merit; that in the interests of the community, part of the punishment to be inflicted shall be the withdrawal of civil rights, depriving the guilty from exercising the right of franchise in public and municipal affairs.

B.   That adequate steps be taken in order to prevent the immigration of guilty persons into the United Kingdom or the British Dominions except on such conditions as the competent British Authority may impose.

C.   That in order to afford protection to members of His Majesty's forces contemplating marriage, adequate means and measures be taken to create a distinction between female members of the population who have been loyal to British interests and those who have consorted with the enemy.

D.   That proper legal and constitutional procedure orders and exactments be made by the Competent Authority in order to cause to be inscribed in the rolls of the criminal records of the Royal Court of Jersey, the findings of the Tribunal in cases where guilt has been established.

E.   Finally that such measures be taken as the Competent Authority may deem just and equitable. And for which your petitioners as in duty bound, will ever pray.

For and on behalf of the Central Organising Committee of the Jersey Loyalists.

Unfortunately the reception of the 'Loyalist's Petition in the States can hardly be termed a friendly one; in fact, this is what one member of the States, Deputy Richardson, had to say; 'That the spirit of lawlessness was about was illustrated by the fact that the Petition was signed by people actually serving in the civil service of the Island' and he added, 'It was the duty of the authorities to inform such officials that their action was contrary to the principles of justice, and that unless they desisted they themselves might be the first to suffer.'

My Comment:
In plain words, if any civil service person signed the Jersey Loyalist Petition they would lose their jobs. These Jersey civil service people wanted the inquiry, they had nothing to hide, and the inquiry would have cleared them of any suspicion of collaboration.'

'Most States Members were against the Jersey Loyalist's Petition. It was the same States Members who were against the petition that sat in the States in the Occupation years. If they had nothing to hide what was their reason for not wanting a full inquiry?'

Many of the loyal old Jerseymen in 1945 stated that; Without a full inquiry now in 1945-46, it would all come back to their grandchildren in the years to come - the finger of suspicion of collaboration. And how right our old people were.

The Evening Post, Wednesday 27 June 1945.

What our readers think. (letters to the editor)

Are Loyal Servants to be penalised?

Dear Sir,

I do not think that many people will agree with the speaker at the States Assembly on Thursday last who was reported to have said that the spirit of lawlessness was illustrated (not by the fact of burglaries now taking place, which cannot be blamed on the German troops) but by the fact that civil servants (amongst others) were signing a petition to the States asking that informers, collaborators and other disloyal persons, whether in the employ of the States or others, should be brought to justice. Are such loyal British citizens to be penalised for their praiseworthy attempts to get something done? It is certainly not the spirit of justice, nor the duty of the authorities to inform such officials that they may have to be the first to suffer for their actions. It would be strange, in the year of our Lord 1945, if loyal servants of the States which, after all, is the servant of the people, not the master - should be made to suffer for their patriotism in trying to bring to justice the disloyal ones, as has been done in the other occupied countries - France, Belgium, Denmark and Norway. I might add that the Jersey Loyalist are a non-political and non-religious body whose members are of many shades of politics and creeds, united by their loyalty to the British Crown.'

Signed; W. Gladden
Gleneatrn
St Martin
Jersey
24 June 1945

Helping the enemy

Dear Sir,

When are we going to hear that the Islands' quislings and collaborators are to be arrested and punished. If you are making a list, I can give you the name of one evil specimen to add to it.

I am truly yours,
A. Godfray.'

Acknowledgments to the Jersey Evening Post

My Comment:

The Evening Posts of 1945 were full of letters to the editor about collaborators and quislings in Jersey. God help us, if any English or other newspaper journalist looked or read through the old Evening Posts from May 1945 to May 1946. They would get the wrong impression of our very loyal Jersey people. The British Government did not want to get involved with any scandal, or back biting in the Channel Islands.

In May 1945, the British press were full of stories about collaboration in the Islands. The States of Jersey should have held the inquiry on this subject. This would have put paid to all the rubbish printed in the British press. Many historians in England and the Islands think that's why Winston Churchill did not visit the Islands in 1945. He was invited to the Islands, and he wrote a charming letter saying he was sorry, but could not accept the invitation, due to other engagements. In the British army in August 1945, I was asked if I was one of those Jersey collaborators from the Islands. I was so offended and angered with this insult that I knocked the officer down. I was placed on a charge but got away with a warning.'

JERSEY SERVICEMEN RETURNING TO JERSEY, 1945

The Mière brothers, Bill & Mark.

The returning thousands of ex-servicemen and women (among them my two brothers and cousins) were stopped from voting in the first post-war Jersey elections. They were refused the vote by the very poor excuse that they had not registered in 1945. But how could they have registered in 1945? Most of them were still in the forces, or held up in England. After Liberation many Jersey servicemen and women missed their leave (after waiting 5 years to come home to Jersey) because the British Government and States of Jersey would not give them permits to travel to the Island. The mailboats leaving England for the Islands were mostly not even half full, sometimes only forty people on board.

The Evening Post in 1945-46 was always full of letters from Jersey servicemen and women, complaining and asking why they were not allowed to travel home to their families in Jersey after fighting for five long years in the British forces. The British Government and our Jersey States made excuses, but many ex-servicemen thought the reason was that the States did not want them to return in 1945; the ex-servicemen and women returning to Jersey would have voted for a change in our States and would have demanded a public inquiry into collaboration. I think they could have been wrong, but they also had a good point, the British Government and States of Jersey giving such poor excuses to these ex-servicemen and women and their families in Jersey.

Here is one sample of a Jersey Serviceman trying to return to his family in Jersey.

The Evening Post, Tuesday 21 August 1945.

Letter from a sailor - a true mother's son

Dear Sir,

I came over to Jersey without a permit and was not allowed to land to see my mother, brothers and sisters, after fighting for over six years to liberate the Islands. I tried to get compassionate leave but was told it was not urgent by two welfare officers. When I arrived in Jersey I was told that I had to stay on board the mail boat till I got back to England. I saw my mother, she came down to the boat to speak to me, after a true Jerseyman delivered my letter on a motorcycle to her. But my brothers and sisters were not allowed to come down and speak to me after seven years in the Royal Navy.

There are other servicemen like me. Don't you think it is time we came back, instead of some people taking a holiday to England while I am waiting to get over to help my mother. She had no money and was actually in debt. All I had was 30/- she only had what she stood in, her shoes had great holes in and took water on wet days. Is there some way in which we can get over?'

The Evening Post, Thursday 23 August 1945.

What our readers think.

He travelled without a permit.

Dear Sir,

You told how my son came down to Jersey on the mail steamer without a permit and how I was permitted to see him on board the 'Hantonia' before he was taken back. He could not obtain a permit to cross because I could not forward a medical certificate. The doctor whom I saw, told me that I was not dying so he couldn't give me one, and he added that he also wanted to see his people whom he had not seen for six years. Since then this doctor has left the Island. My daughter who came to the Island on the same boat as my son - she had a permit - has been on active service. My son, who was only 17 when I last saw him, has six years service. I have been in bad health for two years and I needed my son home on important business, yet he was not even allowed ashore to see his brother and other sisters. I know there must be many other mothers waiting to see their boys, yet day after day we hear of persons going from and returning to the Island whose reasons were surely not as urgent as those of us who, fortunate enough to have been spared, would like to see our loved ones. I am only a poor woman and have no influence, but I wish you could give my case the publicity of your columns.'

Violet M Ozouf
(Mother of the boy without a permit)

The Evening Post. Friday 24 August 1945

Restriction on travel to Channel Islands.

Home Secretary answers questions in the House.

Mr Chuter Ede said that control of travel to the Channel Islands was imposed at the request of the Military Governor and the Island authorities (States of Jersey).

In reply to a supplementary question as to whether he was satisfied that attempts were being made by some Islanders to delay the return of their professional rivals Mr Chuter Ede said it was the first time he had heard such a suggestion. He had seen the Bailiffs of Jersey and Guernsey, and the Lieut Governors and knew they were exceedingly anxious that the flow of repatriation should go on as uninterruptedly as possible. The object of a slow return was to ensure the orderly return of the residents.'

Channel Island soldiers and leave. It is a scandal ..... Lord Portsea'

Question to be asked in the Lords.

Soldiers and sailors from the Channel Islands on leave from overseas in England, cannot get home to see their families, from whom they had been parted through the years of war.

Unless some arrangement is made for them, many may soon be in drafts bound for other foreign lands without having seen their dear ones. Lord Portsea, who has done so much to help his fellow Channel Islanders, is to ask a question on the subject in the House of Lords. I am going to ask why all these men have been given leave, after four or five years service, and are not allowed to go home. There is not enough transport to take them. It's a scandal. All these men are volunteers. At present there is only one small boat sailing to the Channel Islands three times a week. It can accommodate about 380 passengers which is entirely inadequate. Why can't they give us more ships? We used to have daily boats from Weymouth, Southampton, London and Plymouth. Many hundreds of civilian Channel Islanders are still in this country with little prospect of returning until shipping facilities improve. 'At present,' said Lord Portsea, 'only those who could plead strong compassionate grounds such as a wife or husband in the Islands, seriously ill, could get permission to sail. 'The whole treatment has been gross,' he said. 'A good many people could afford to wait until October or November, when there may be more room, but it is the plight of these servicemen with whom I am most concerned.'

This is a question which has been frequently raised in our columns (of *The Evening Post*) and when Lord Portsea was interviewed by an *Evening Post* reporter while in Jersey some time ago he expressed much the same sentiments as he has done in the above interview. Editor *The Evening Post*.

Acknowledgments to the Jersey Evening Post

HEINZ C WOELFE - German Secret Field Police

In 1945, I was undergoing infantry training at the 15 I.T.C. at Colchester, Essex. One day I heard through the Jersey grapevine that some of the ex-German Secret Field Police were at the big prisoner of war camp, camp number 9 at Tiptree, Essex near Colchester. I got myself an appointment to see our colonel and gave him a short version of my Occupation history, and requested if it was possible for him to arrange for me to interview some of the ex-German policemen who had been based in Jersey in 1940-1945. The colonel informed me that he already had my war and personal details in his files. He also stated that he could see no problem in arranging with the officer in charge of the prisoner of war camp a meeting or interview with the ex-German policemen.

On the appointed day, a Saturday morning in October 1945 - I took a bus from Colchester to the POW camp at Tiptree. At the main gate of the POW camp the guard checked my army pass, and my soldiers service book No. 64. I was then escorted into the camp adjutants office. Seated at the desk was a major, grey headed and about 45 years old. I came to attention and saluted, gave my name and rank and number. 'Sit down, soldier,' he said. 'There has been new correspondence from London since I last spoke to your commanding officer.' The major started to read from a paper or letter. 'The War Office states that a private Mière, Gloucester Regiment has no written authorisation to interview or interrogate any POWs that are under our jurisdiction, and the POW camp commanding officer has no authority except in writing from the War Office to grant any interviews or interrogations with prisoners of war.' The Major informed me briefly that the letter also stated that my request to see and interview these POWs was refused on the grounds that these prisoners war records or any personal details came under the British Government War Department, and were covered under the Secrets Act of etc.

I later discovered that Woelfe and the staff of the German Secret Field Police had been very helpful to British Intelligence officers and had supplied them with very useful information when they were being interrogated by British Intelligence at the POW holding camp outside London. I did intend to follow up my request with a letter to the War Department. But before I could proceed any further in this matter, I was posted for advanced infantry training on Salisbury Plain, then posted to Germany where much later on I tried to discover the whereabouts of Woelfe and his ex staff.

Paul Mulbach, a German army corporal who headed a committee of anti-Nazi soldiers in Jersey, was trying to incite other soldiers to mutiny against their officers in the Island. If the mutiny had been successful the mutineers would have handed over the Island to the British. He approached one of the local Resistance groups in Jersey which was headed by Norman Le Brocq and Les Huelin, and asked them if this local Resistance group would help by duplicating anti-Nazi leaflets in English and German.

The local Resistance thought at first this could be a German police trap. But after checking they found that Paul Mulbach who had strong socialist views was genuine. Norman and Les were already printing BBC war news pamphlets with the use of an old flat bed duplicator. They started printing copies for Paul, who then passed them around among the German garrison in Jersey. But by March 1945 Paul Mulbach knew he was being watched and followed by the German Secret Field Police. So he deserted from his army unit and went underground with the help of Norman Le Brocq and his group.

They organised civilian clothes, ID cards, and undercover accommodation, even an old bicycle and food. The German Secret Field Police organised a search for him and Woelfe led one of the hunting parties to find him. But Paul, having been given an excellent disguise by a Spaniard, Senen Equisabal - with dyed hair etc was never captured. If Paul had been caught his fate would have been sealed and, after a quick court martial, he would have been executed.

When Jersey was liberated Paul Mulbach gave himself up to the British forces. And with an excellent reference from Norman Le Brocq, Les Huelin and the Resistance group he was repatriated back to Germany. But life can be strange. Paul never even thought he would ever meet the man who was trying to hunt him down in Jersey. At a camp where British Army Intelligence staff were classifying returning German servicemen, sorting out the Nazi from the anti-Nazi personnel, Paul arrived. After being interviewed, he was told that the camp interpreter would show him to his sleeping quarters. What a surprise Paul had, for the camp interpreter was none other than Woelfe the German Secret Field policeman.

Paul returned to the office he had just left, and gave the British Intelligence officers a full report and history of the camp interpreter. Heinz Woelfe was transferred to another British army camp. Later Woelfe was in the American zone of Germany. The Americans gave him a job as a security officer (arresting his own people). Heinz Woelfe (known as the Wolf in Jersey) was going to publish his war diary. This would have been very interesting as it would have cleared up a few points in our Occupation history. He did leave behind in Jersey in 1945 a daughter, now living in London.

INTERVIEW WITH LORD COUTANCHE

Like many old Jersey people I knew Lord Coutanche and had many good old chats with him when he retired as Bailiff of Jersey. After he retired he became a different man, more relaxed after his years in office. I suppose the stress of the German Occupation years took its toll on him. When he was in office and you spoke to him he was very sharp, as if he did not want to bother with you. Those that knew me well did not blame Lord Coutanche's attitude. When talking to me we did not always see eye to eye about certain parts of the Occupation. Many times I have had a good old chat with him at Belcroute. On a fine day you saw him having a chat with locals and visitors with his old straw hat on and dressed in very casual clothes.

One day when having a long conversation with him about my days in the German prison in 1944-45, he said, 'it was all right for you young hot heads, you were very young and only saw your side of the German Occupation but, every time you got in trouble with the Germans it was I who had to go to College House and face the full anger for your actions. It made it very difficult for me to negotiate with the Kommandant to ease restrictions on our people. In your case, I remember your mother came to see me at my chambers one morning. She informed me that the German police were treating you in a very brutal manner, with beating and had knocked your front teeth out.'

'I do remember your mother but I do not remember the rest of the conversation I had with her - it was so long ago. You have reminded me that I said to your mother that I would look into the matter and see what I could do. You know you were a very foolish young man. My intervention on your behalf must have born fruit because as you have just said the ill-treatment stopped. You have also reminded me that when you were on leave from the army, Christmas 1945, you came to see me and thanked me for stopping the Germans from ill-treating you. I do not remember meeting you then. I was very busy at that time trying to get the Island back on its feet with no time for chit-chat, there was so much to do. Yes I do remember very well going to the prison on the evening of 7 May and releasing you political prisoners, that was one of my most pleasurable duties that day.' I was very impressed and amazed at Lord Coutanche. Here was a retired man still very sharp minded and nothing wrong with his memory box. Fancy him remembering my mother after all those years, all the more so because he must have met thousands of people over the years of his long and distinguished service to Jersey.

Going back to those Occupation years, I can understand that some of our anti-Nazi activities would have caused trouble for our Jersey authorities as it did for the Germans. The following is from an old Evening Post of the time.

Warning by the Bailiff of Jersey.

On several occasions recently military sign posts in the Island have been either damaged or turned in the wrong direction, in a manner clearly calculated to mislead the military forces.

I urgently warn the inhabitants to avoid such foolish actions and ask them to do all in their power to prevent such senseless acts on the part of irresponsible persons.

Otherwise severe penal measures must be expected from the military authorities - measures which will affect the whole population including its innocent members.

It is in the interest of the whole population to assist in the prevention of the recurrence of similar acts.

Signed: A.M. Coutanche
Bailiff of Jersey
21 May 1941

My Comment:

The German signposts were made of very dry wood, they burned very well in our fireplace and in the fireplaces of our loyal friends.

The Germans were very annoyed. When reaching a cross road they had to drive round and round to get their direction route. In one night (1941) alone the 12 German signposts at the crossroads at Robin Hood disappeared.

Acknowledgement to The Evening Post.

GERMAN MILITARY UNDERGROUND HOSPITAL

Cap Verd entrance of HO 8 (now The Jersey War Tunnels) 1944 with German servicemen and civilian workers.

Excavating and drilling work began on 21 October 1941 at the Cap Verd entrance with troops from German army construction and pioneer engineers units in Jersey. One of the German pioneer soldiers returned to Jersey in 1976. He visited the Underground Hospital and I interviewed him. His name was Guenter Kornec, and was born in East Prussia. He was in No. 3 section, No. 2 Company pioneers and was billeted at the Aberfeldy Hotel, St Helier.

He informed me that one morning in October 1941 his unit engineers placed chargers at what was to be the Cap Verd entrance of Artillery Quarters No. 8 but as the rock was soft (Briowerian Shale) the whole bank collapsed. That's why at the top of the Cap Verd entrance it is very flat for about 200 feet. Guenter Kornec also stated that the small flat valley at Cap Verd was to be a workshop to service the big artillery guns. Concrete pillars were to be built all around the workshops, and camouflage nets placed over the workshops to hide the site from the air. His unit also built the concrete magazine to hold the explosives. It was built alongside the Cap Verd entrance and is still there.

The Meadowbank entrance was started in February 1942. By this date, construction was handed over to the OT Organisation Todt, the German contracting firm of Gremmich working at Meadowbank. The German contracting firm of Karl Plotner was at Cap Verd. The first forced labour men were Spanish Republicans, Alsatian Jews, Poles and Algerians. The Spanish, Alsatian Jews, and Poles were billeted at West Park Pavilion.

Later, in August 1942, Russian and Ukrainian slave workers were brought over to Jersey. But by the time these slaves started work at what is now called The Jersey War Tunnels, the open galleries were well advanced. The forced labour workers and the Russian and Ukrainian slaves worked under appalling conditions. They were underfed, received brutal treatment from the OT overseers, many had no boots or shoes. No wonder they were in poor health. Many accidents occurred and there were deaths, due mostly to rockfalls. But we must not forget the fact that voluntary well paid and well fed Jersey, British, Irish, French, Dutch also worked at the tunnel which was later to become the Underground Hospital.

The States of Jersey by German orders were permitted to pay its work force only £2.50 to £3 per week. But on the other hand the Germans paid their voluntary workers between £10 and £12 per week. The German OT overseers worked alongside the other workers in the tunnel. They also had many accidents, and some were also killed by rockfalls. The bodies of the slave workers were not buried in the walls and floors of the tunnel. The rumours of bodies thrown into the wet concrete were started by people who should have known better. Bodies were removed from the tunnel and taken to the Strangers' cemetery at Westmount and buried in graves marked out in sections of nationality. Mind you, there are very strong rumours that slave workers are buried in unknown graves. That does not surprise me at all, because bodies were found at the Strangers' cemetery in unmarked graves and no records of these were made.

One Sunday morning in 1980, at my request, Arthur Bassett who had been one of the voluntary workers for the OT at Meadowbank (Underground Hospital) told us how the work of lining the tunnel walls, roof, floor etc. was done and how the railway trucks were pulled/pushed by a small diesel locomotive on 60cm gauge railway lines. The trucks brought the wet concrete to the entrance of the tunnel, the side tipping trucks were then unchained and pushed to the working site. The concrete was tipped onto the floor of the tunnel. The workers then shovelled the concrete up and behind the wooden shuttering to line the walls and clay draining pipes were placed in the concrete.

For lining the roof of the tunnel curved roof formers were used, planks fixed across the formers and then the concrete was shovelled up from the floor onto a wooden stage. Two men working on this stage then shovelled up the concrete onto the next wooden stage where two more men shovelled up the concrete into the box section of the roof formers. Long handled tampers were used to taper the concrete. Before the box section was half full of concrete clay draining pipes were bedded in the wet concrete. These clay pipes connected with the draining pipes in the vertical walls, and again connected with the draining pipes in the tunnel floor. Water drained into the wooden covered concrete lined gully channels that even today convey the drainage water down to the Cap Verd entrance then out to the brook that runs under the small Cap Verd valley. All the water channels slope towards Cap Verd.

Arthur also pointed out the only known place where there are bodies in the tunnel. He went on to state the following facts. One morning towards the end of 1942, three Polish face workers were drilling in a side tunnel when the whole rock roof collapsed. Arthur remembers that all the lights in the tunnel went out. For six days the OT workers tried to reach the three Polish face workers but the more rock they took out the more came down. The OT left the air compressors running in the pipe so that the trapped men had a safe pocket till help arrived but after seven days the OT and army engineers and a German army geologist recommended that as this side tunnel was not safe and a major fault in the rock was identified so they gave orders for this side tunnel to be sealed.

Arthur worked at the tunnel for two years. One could go on and on about the construction of the Underground Hospital tunnel. There is no better book to read about the tunnels in Jersey than 'German Tunnels in the Channel Islands' by Michael Ginns MBE in archive book No 7. Michael, to my mind, has made a first class work on this subject. The Germans never used the so called Underground Hospital. See letters from German Medical Orderly Richard Wessel, who worked at the Underground Hospital whose correct name was "Casualty Receiving Station."

When I first worked at the German Military Underground Hospital in 1976, I was very surprised by the amount of distorted information on big display boards placed on the walls around the tunnel complex. One large board stated that women and little children had worked in this tunnel and had died or were killed and are buried where they fell in this tunnel. Another large notice stated prisoners working in this tunnel are buried where they fell. Please respect this tunnel as the underground is their grave. Visitors used to ask me to point out these graves because they wanted to photograph the spot.

After a lot of argument and debate with the curator and company directors the false and distorted worded boards were removed. All this was replaced with the Joe Mière Collection giving the true history with photographs of the Occupation. An entire chamber was devoted to my collection recalling the courage of Islanders who resisted and suffered for their heroism. I was also pleased that the so called 'Kommandant's Office' was changed to its real name "The Storeman's Quarters." A notice 'Mortuary' was also removed and replaced by a notice "Unfinished Corridor." There was no officer's mess in the Underground Hospital. At one time the small scrub up room was called the dispensary. This was the scrub up room for the operating theatre. We also changed the name on the orderly's quarters. There were no female nurses in the Underground Hospital, only male medical orderlies.

At war's end the lavatories had not even been connected to any main drain or soak away pit. There was and still is a big water sump 30 feet deep that holds 16 thousand gallons. A third entrance was planned, so was another escape shaft to the east of the tunnel. Years ago you could see the outline was to be dug out on top of the tunnel but partly filled in only. In the unfinished parts of the tunnel you can still see the level markers in the floors encased in concrete with a metal peg and code number scratched on the cement top.

If you believe in ghosts or not, I can only state what I have seen while I was at the Underground Hospital.

I have seen what I take to be the ghost of an OT overseer walking the corridors. Visitors to the Underground Hospital have reported to me what they have seen. Many think it is a British army ghost because of the Khaki uniform, but the OT overseers wore the same Khaki. I always kept an open mind on this subject. One evening a young Jerseyman and his girlfriend parked their car right in the Meadowbank entrance to the Underground Hospital. Something made them look towards the gate. They had quite a shock when they saw a man in a Khaki uniform coming through the steel bars. They thought he was smoking because all around him there was white smoke or mist. He went right through their car, and as he passed they felt very cold. They did not hang around after seeing him but drove off at speed. They told Joe Le Saint who was the young man's foreman where he worked. Two weeks later, Joe Le Saint told me the story.

One lady visitor reported to me that she had seen a man in a Khaki uniform bending down as if looking through a door keyhole. But the double doors to the ward were wide open. The following year the visitor lady returned to Jersey. She repeated to me once again what she had seen. An old school friend of mine working with me at the Underground Hospital, Leslie Keeping, was a doubting Thomas. He could not be convinced that there were any apparitions in the Underground Hospital. Then one morning he heard footsteps in the corridor outside the ward where he was cleaning the display units. He looked out into the corridor, but the footsteps stopped. He returned to his work but once he was back in the ward the footsteps started again. Once more Leslie looked out into the corridor and again the footsteps stopped. Leslie was alone in the Hospital at about 7.30am - the staff and I did not arrive till 8am. Now Leslie does not doubt anymore about ghosts in the Underground Hospital.

When I went on a TV programme 'The Time and the Place' I was very surprised at how many people on the programme spoke about what they had seen at the

Underground Hospital. One lady who had lived at Cap Verd, right facing the rear entrance of the Hospital, told the TV programme that as a young child she and her father had seen many times a man in a uniform come from the tunnel entrance and walk right through their garden wall. I spoke to her and tried to get her and her children to visit the Underground Hospital. The look in her eyes told me that she would not go even near the place, and she never did .

I know nothing of psychic phenomena but have had experiences of ghosts. At a house we bought in Green Road I had an experience I will never forget. I was working at night from 6pm to 1am in the morning to try and get it ready for my family to move in. I was painting the staircase late one evening when the door bell rang. But after opening the front door no one was there.

The next evening the round connecting box on the wall started to smoke. I opened the box and disconnected the points. It was getting very late so thought I had better go home.

The next evening as I was painting in this house I thought someone was watching me from the top of the staircase, I knew that a child was looking at me as I worked, I could not see the child clearly but this child was about 3 years old. The next day I checked with the people next door, the Bevis family who had lived there for years. I told Mrs Bevis what I had seen. She went quiet then a little pale and seemed upset. She told me a little girl had died in the small room at the top of the stairs only a few years before.

I knew the son of the people who had lived in the house before we had bought it. I told him what I had seen and he told me that the little girl I had seen had been his little sister who had died in the small room at the top of the stairs. He told me she often stood at the top of the stairs and looked over the stair rail. He asked me not to tell his father or mother (whom I knew) because they would be very upset. I do not know why some of us see things. I don't know anything about the subject of psychic phenomena, and I do not want to know. I keep an open mind on what I have seen.

Herr Frans Knemayer. Organisation Todt.

Ex-OT officer in Jersey 1941-1944. He worked in the planning office as a draftsman/architect (one of the then draftsman/architects employed by the OT at their Midvale Road headquarters in Jersey. He was born at Dresden, Germany, March 1905. His father was killed in the 1914-18 war. Most of his family were missing when Dresden was bombed in 1945. He now lives just outside Mannheim, West Germany.

Herr Frans Knemayer was posted to Jersey from Lorient, France, in 1941. Before his posting to Lorient he was stationed in Paris, working on plans for A A gun sites and air raid shelters and bunkers, etc. I was on duty in the Underground Hospital one summer day in 1979 and spotted this tall elderly visitor who was pointing out different parts of the wards and corridors to a fine looking lady and a younger couple. The lady was Herr Knemayer's wife and the couple - his daughter from his first marriage and her husband. The four of them were conversing in German, the tall man who was doing all the explaining seemed to know his way around and, with the little German that I could understand, it seemed that he had been in this tunnel complex before.

Towards the end of their visit I saw my chance and approached the tall German visitor. I had a little chat with him, then asked him if he had been in Jersey during the war years. I explained to him that we were very interested in any information that would bring to light any history in the planning and building of this tunnel complex. At first he was very evasive but eventually he agreed to answer a limited number of my questions on the understanding that they were not political questions (Thought better not ask him about the slave workers. Germans are very touchy on this subject. If you want to end a conversation quickly with the Germans, just mention the Russian slave workers).

We sat on the wall at the end of the car park. After lighting up a cigarette Herr Knemayer spoke. 'What do you want to know?' 'Firstly,' I said, 'do you have any objections to my taking down notes?' 'No,' he replied. 'Go right ahead - but no photographs, please.' I told him that he spoke better English than I did. He smiled. 'My knowledge of English was very limited when I was last in Jersey in 1944 but since the war I have worked for the Americans in Germany - that polished up my English.'

My next question was aimed at finding out what he did in the Island during the German Occupation. Was he in the forces? A pause from him and then he said: 'Yes and no. Our firm did work for the German military forces in Germany from 1937 to 1939 - and then I was transferred to the Organisation Todt, the O.T. In 1940 I was posted to Paris. We had a lot of planning on hand. Then I was posted to the planning office outside Lorient and was on the inspecting staff. Then we went on to St Malo and then to Jersey. This was in July 1941. In other words, I was a civilian in uniform. We had extra pay because we were away from home.

I next asked him if he remembered his OT headquarters in Midvale Road. He replied: 'Oh, yes, I do remember our offices in Midvale Road. Now we are over here for only two days - my wife, my daughter and son-in-law. We were touring around France and we looked in on St. Malo. That's where the headquarters for these Islands was - all changed now - looks better and cleaner since the rebuilding. I could not find my way around from what I remembered of it. But I do remember the offices in Midvale Road - went there this morning. It's now a hotel but the outside has not changed. I used to share a room at the back overlooking a very long garden. Then they moved our sleeping quarters to a house at the top of Queen's Road but I could not find it again.'

I asked him if all his planning had been worked out in Midvale Road or whether the plans had come from the St Malo headquarters. 'Not all the plans were drafted in Jersey,' he replied. 'Many came from St Malo, sometimes Paris. We worked for the army, navy and air force and also civilian contractors - all very secret in those days. One of our staff got drunk one night and spoke about our work at a party given by a well known Jersey business man who lived in Midvale Road. The very next day this staff man was posted away from Jersey for having said too much about our planning work.'

My Comment:

Yes, we knew this business man and his family. They lived opposite our house in Midvale Road. They often entertained the OT. It was the Le Poidevin family, chemists in Bath Street. And to think old man Le Poidevin had a son in the RAF.

As I have already explained, in 1943 our group blew out his chemist shop fronts with home made bombs. The Germans and even the local Jersey police were trying to find out who did this deed. The Le Poidevin family informed on us to the police who passed it onto the Attorney General's office. We think he passed the information on to the German police. Among the official Jersey documents are a number of letters informing the Bailiff of Jersey of the identity of people who were responsible for acts against these collaborators. The Jersey authorities have decided that these letters should remain classified (closed files) until 2045, as some of the informers are still alive and living in Jersey.

Years later the rough sketch-plan by Herr Frans Knemayer of the tunnel complex was re-drawn by me so as to have a copy in hand. In his rough sketch Frans Knemayer did not show any water tanks (well) or any air conditioning or any WCs or washrooms, or any stores or staff quarters or fuel store or operating theatre but just the outline of the tunnel complex.

He stated that this tunnel complex was to be an A.A. artillery barracks/shelter for the Luftwaffe A.A. Gunners who were based on the opposite hill facing this tunnel complex. Luftsperr Abteilung A.A. Barrage Unit. or Artillerie -Unterschlupf/Shelter.

Top right: Meadowbank entrance. **Bottom right:** German servicemen & O.T. workers with Jersey Cow outside Cap Verd entrance 1944. From left to right, First German: Hans Müller. Blond young man: S.Lowdobik (Polish). German in white overall trousers: Herman Gnutzmann. Fourth man: German NCO, Karl Witteman. Fifth man: (Spanish worker) Antonio Flores. **Inset:** "Lunch Time."

Richard Wessel

4803 Steinhagen (Westf.)
~~Lärchenstraße 45~~ · Telefon (05204) 3667
Erfurter Str. 20

⁓r. Joe ⁓ière
86 Les Cinq Chênes
Fire Oaks
St. Saviour
J e r s e y
Channal-Islands

Steinhagen, den 1. 6. 81

Sehr geehrter Herr Joe ⁓ière at ,,Sunny Jersey!"

Ich danke Ihnen für Ihren Brief vo⁓ 24. 5. 81, den ich erhielt und
sage ⁓einen besten Dank ⁓ür! Ich bin gern bereit, Ihnen Ihre
Frager zu bea⁓t⁓⁓⁓⁓⁓⁓⁓r Fa⁓ilie geht es ⁓ut, und ⁓ir sind
alle⁓⁓⁓⁓⁓⁓⁓⁓⁓⁓e alt und leide unter Blut-Kreislauf-
⁓⁓⁓⁓⁓⁓⁓⁓ngen ⁓it den Augen. ⁓enn Sie ⁓ir einen
⁓⁓⁓⁓⁓nnen Englisch schreiben, ich kann
⁓⁓⁓⁓⁓ut schreiben.

⁓⁓⁓ben, ⁓ährend der Zeit als ich in
⁓⁓⁓⁓⁓ch ka⁓ i⁓ ⁓är⁓ 1⁓42 aus Frankreich
⁓⁓⁓s ⁓erton Hotel. Dies Hotel war
⁓⁓⁓⁓t beschlagnah⁓t. Ich blieb dann
⁓⁓⁓⁓ical Orderly) i⁓ ⁓erton Hotel.
⁓⁓⁓⁓l versetzt, weil wir i⁓ ⁓erton
⁓⁓⁓⁓hatten. I⁓ General Hospital
⁓⁓⁓ster und Dr. Schütz. Als i⁓
⁓⁓⁓r und A⁓erikaner angefangen
⁓⁓⁓nicht fertig. Die gesa⁓te
⁓⁓⁓r Insel Jersey abgezogen,
⁓⁓⁓sorgen. De⁓zufolge wurden
⁓⁓⁓⁓⁓ten, ⁓elche Bauhandwerker
⁓⁓⁓⁓⁓nker befol⁓len. Stabsarzt
⁓⁓⁓⁓ertigstellung übertragen.
⁓⁓⁓bin und ich das Vertrauen
v⁓⁓⁓⁓⁓⁓⁓⁓⁓⁓⁓⁓arung der Holzarbeiten
mi⁓⁓⁓⁓⁓⁓⁓⁓⁓en. Unsere Arbeit ging bis
zu⁓⁓⁓⁓⁓⁓45. ⁓eines ⁓issens nach wurde nie

284

1066/146   Steinhagen, 1.6.81

Dear Mr. Joe Mière in "Sunny Jersey,"

Thank you for your letter of 24.5.81, which I received and for which I am very grateful! I will be glad to answer your questions for you. My family is well, and we are all in good health. I am 76 years old and suffer from trouble with the circulation. Hence the disturbed vision with the eyes. If you want to write me a letter, you can write in English, I can read English, but I cannot write it so well.

I will now tell you about my life, during the time when I was in "my beloved sunny Jersey." I came to the Merton Hotel in Jersey in March 1942 from France (Fontainebleau). This hotel was requisitioned by the German armed forces at the time. I then stayed at the Merton Hotel for 1 year as a medical orderly. Then I was transferred to the General Hospital because we had no opportunities for surgery at the Merton Hotel. At the General Hospital, I was the theatre nurse for Dr. Köster and Dr. Schütz. When in the summer of 1944 the invasion of the English and Americans began, the Underground Hospital was not finished. The whole O.T. (Organisation Todt) was withdrawn from the island of Jersey, and every unit had to see to itself. Consequently from our medical squadron all soldiers who were in the building trade were ordered to work on the half-finished bunker. Medical Officer Dr. Köster was granted the power to give orders for completion. As I am a carpenter and joiner by trade and I was in the confidence of Dr. Köster, I was ordered to carry out the woodwork with other skilled workers. Our work went on until the capitulation on 8.5.1945. To the best of my knowledge, no wounded or sick person was ever delivered to this bunker (hospital). On 9.5.1945 we were relieved by a British medical unit. Thus the war was over for us.

It was from this time that the friendship with Herbert Dallein arose, which has continued till now by correspondence. Up to the end of my imprisonment at the end of November 1946, I was then a medical orderly in an English field hospital. It was in the Ladies' College.

I hope my comments are enough for you. If you have any further questions, you can ask your questions in English. Unfortunately I can no longer reply to your letter in English due to my age.

Yours sincerely,

Richard Wessel

Ex-German serviceman, Richard Wessel's letter to Joe and translation. He worked at The Underground Hospital in 1944 -1945.

Richard Wessel outside the Merton Hotel where he was stationed in 1942.

LIST OF ESCAPEES FROM THE CHANNEL ISLANDS 1940-1945

As there are no official lists of people who escaped from the Channel Islands in 1940-1945, this is the unofficial list of escapees from Jersey and Guernsey. Researched and compiled by me from 1948 to 2003. Guernsey and Alderney were researched and compiled by David Krecheler.

The letters before the names denote which is their Island of origin. J for Jersey. G for Guernsey. A for Alderney.

J. Abraham	M.S.	September	1940	Dartmouth
J. AhierRichard		17 October	1944	Captured
J. Allo Alain Jean		14 November	1944	Port Bail
J. Allo Helene Marie		14 November	1944	Port Bail
J. Amy Hedley Thomas		25 February	1945	Surville
J. Audrain	Dennis Desiré	3 May	1942	Drowned
J. Avare	Mark	21 February	1945	Carteret
G. Beck	Clarence	2 July	1940	Dartmouth
G. Best George		1 July	1940	Falmouth
G. Best Majory		1 July	1940	Falmouth
G. Bichard	Herbert Le C.	6 September	1940	Dartmouth
G. Bichard	Herbert	15 September	1940	Portland
J. Bisson	Madeleine	13 September	1944	Drowned
J. Bisson	Ronald	13 November	1944	Drowned
J. Blandin	David	9 October	1944	Hauteville-sur-Mer
J. Boisnante	Jacque	September	1940	Dartmouth
J. Bondis	Charles	20 September	1944	Blainville-sur-Mer
J. Bonney	Frank George	25 October	1944	Granville
G. Bougourd	Alfred	14 August	1943	Dartmouth
G. Bougourd	Mrs E. J.	1 July	1943	Dartmouth
J. Briard	Garnet	9 September	1944	Captured
G. Broche	Miss Jeanne A.	15 September	1944	Portland
J. Carter	Ian	4 July	1940	Portland
J. Cavey	Bernard E.	20 September	1944	Blainville-sur-Mer
J. Clarke	Captain Edward	18 January	1945	Blainville-sur-Mer
G. Claybourne Mr R		1 July	1940	Falmouth
G. Claybourne Mrs R		1 July	1940	Falmouth
J. Clayton-Greene May		3 July	1940	Dartmouth
G. Cohu	Frederick	1 July	1940	Dartmouth
J. Collins	Kenneth	10 October	1944	Captured
G. Corbert	Gertrude	14 August	1943	Dartmouth

G. Corbert	William H.	14 August	1943	Dartmouth
J. Costard	Alan	22 October	1944	Captured
J. Costard	Herbert	29 September	1944	Beauville
J. Cotillard	Phil (Cot)	3 July	1940	Dartmouth
J. Couillard	James Terence	20 September	1942	Dartmouth
J. Craigie-Burnet	F.W.	August	1940	Portland
J. Crill	Peter Leslie	11 November	1944	Coutainville
J. Curwood	Peter	20 September	1944	Captured
J. Davey	Douglas George	20 September	1944	Blainville-sur-Mer
J. Davies	Dorothy Cath	July	1940	Dartmouth
J. Davies	Thomas James	July	1940	Dartmouth
G. Despointes	Harold	1 July	1940	Start Point, Devon
J. Desverges	Pierre	9 October	1944	Hauteville-sur-Mer
J. Deveau	Florance M.	September	1940	Portland
J. Deveau	June F.	September	1940	Portland
J. Deveau	William H.	September	1940	Portland
J. Dobson	Harold	July	1940	Dartmouth
G. Dorey	William	6 September	1940	Brixham
G. Duport	Percy	6 September	1940	Brixham
A. Duquemin	Arthur	8 April	1944	Weymouth
G. Duquemin	Wilfred	1 July	1940	Start Point, Devon
G. Enticott	William	3 November	1944	Cherbourg
G. Falla	Clifford J.	1 July	1940	Start Point, Devon
J. Floyd	John	11 November	1944	Coutainville
G. Fryer	Reginald	1 July	1940	Falmouth
G. Golivet	Xavier	23 January	1945	Carteret
J. Gorval	Andre L	13 November	1944	Drowned
J. Goudre	Valentin	9 October	1944	Hauteville-sur-Mer
J. Gould	Maurice Jay	3 May	1942	Captured
J. Gruchy	Edward	10 October	1944	Carteret
G. Guille	Mrs	1 July	1940	Start Point, Devon
G. Guille	Horace	1 July	1940	Start Point, Devon
G. Guille	Violet	1 July	1940	Start Point, Devon
G. Guille	Winston	1 July	1940	Start Point, Devon
G. Guille	Zoe	1 July	1940	Start Point, Devon
J. Haas	Lieut George	18 January	1945	Blainville-sur-Mer
J. Hamon	Eric	8 October	1944	Carteret
J. Harvard	Rene W	23 February	1945	Granville
J. Hassall	Peter	3 May	1942	Captured
J. Hoar	John Wymark	25 September	1944	Beauville
G. Hockey	Frederick	6 September	1940	Brixham
G. Hockey	Frederick Jnr	6 September	1940	Brixham

G. Hockey	George	6 September	1940	Brixham
G. Hockey	Harold	6 September	1940	Brixham
J. Horman	Oscar	20 September	1944	Blainville-sur-Mer
J. Houghton	George	22 October	1944	Bricqueville-sur-Mer
G. Hubert	Jack	14 August	1943	Dartmouth
J. Huelin	Victor	9 October	1944	Surville-sur-Mer
J. Hutchings	Barbara	8 October	1944	Carteret
J. Jennings	Peter Stanley	September	1940	Portland
J. Jesty	Kenneth	22 October	1944	Bricqueville-sur-Mer
J. Journeaux	Colin Robert	14 May	1943	Axmouth
J. Killer	Francis	20 September	1944	Captured
J. Kleinstein	Arthur Samuel	18 March	1941	Drowned
J. Kleinstein	Marther Helga	18 March	1941	Drowned
J. Koster	Sieba	16 September	1944	Drowned
J. Kyte	Harry	3 July	1940	Dartmouth
J. La Cloche	Hugh	20 September	1944	Captured
J. Langley	John	8 October	1944	Carteret
J. Langlois	Marquerite	September	1940	Dartmouth
J. Larbalestier	Bernard	27 November	1944	Drowned
J. Larbalestier	John	27 November	1944	Drowned
J. Lawrence	Richard R.	October	1944	French Coast
G. Lawrence	William	15 September	1942	Portland
J. Laurens	Olive Marie	20 September	1942	Dartmouth
J. Le Brun	Basil	21 September	1944	Carteret
Le Chavetois	Desiré	1 July	1940	Start Point, Devon
Le Cornu	Martin	13 November	1944	Captured
Le Corre	Edward	20 September	1944	Blainville-sur-Mer
J. Le Couteur	George	10 November	1944	Les Salines
J. Le Cuirot	Dennis	July	1944	St Malo
G. Le Farge	Brian	1 July	1940	Start Point, Devon
J. Le Feuvre	A	18 September	1944	Captured
J. Le Feuvre	Donald	17 October	1944	Captured
J. Le Gallais	Joe	23 February	1945	Granville
J. Le Gallais	Philip	23 February	1945	Granville
Le Gallez	Irene	1 July	1940	Falmouth
Le Lierre	Frank	8 October	1944	Hauteville-sur-Mer
J. Le Lievre	Donald	9 October	1944	Hauteville-sur-Mer
J. Le Marquand	Douglas V.	10 October	1944	Shot/killed
J. Le Marquand	Stanley	September	1944	French coast
J. Le Marquand	George	10 October	1944	Captured
J. Le Masurier	Edward (Snipe)	11 November	1944	Granville
J. Le Mière	Paul Andre	18 September	1944	Carteret

J. Le Monnier	Edouard	18 September	1944	Carteret
G. Le Morellec	Grace	14 August	1943	Dartmouth
G. Le Page	Frank	1 July	1940	Start Point, Devon,
G. Le Page	John	23 January	1945	Start Point, Devon
G. Le Page	Herbert	14 August	1943	Start Point, Devon
G. Le Page	Leonard	1 July	1940	Start Point, Devon
G. Le Page	Mrs	14 August	1943	Dartmouth
G. Le Page	Thomas	23 January	1945	Carteret
G. Le Parmentier	Doris	1 July	1940	Falmouth
J. Le Poidevin	Lenard	25 October	1944	Granville
G. Le Provost	Miss M	1 July	1940	Falmouth
J. Lerouille	Roger	21 September	1944	Carteret
J. Le Sueur	Francis (1st)	11 September	1944	Captured
J. Le Sueur	Francis (2nd)	10 November	1944	Les Salines
J. Le Sueur	Max	10 November	1944	Granville
J. Le Sueur	Robert	18 October	1944	French coast
J. Love	Robin	25 September	1944	Beauville
G. Lowe	Frederick	1 July	1940	Start Point, Devon
J. Lucienne	Roy	13 November	1944	Drowned
J. Luxton	C. A.	23 February	1945	Granville
J. MacFarlane	Harry	9 October	1944	Surville-sur-Mer
J. Machon	Basil W.	22 October	1944	Bricqueville-sur-Mer
G. Mahy	William	6 September	1940	Brixham
J. Malatesta	Salvadore	18 September	1944	Carteret
J. McLintin	Dennis (Mac)	22 October	1944	Captured
G. Mann	Arthur	1 July	1940	Start Point, Devon
G. Mann	Claude	1 July	1940	Start Point, Devon
J. Marett	Arthur	3 July	1940	Dartmouth
J. Mourant	Roy	11 November	1944	Coutainville
G. Mueller	Helga	1 July	1940	Devon
J. Neil	Michael X.	10 October	1944	Captured
J. Newey	John F.	20 September	1942	Dartmouth
J. Nicholle	Frank, Henry	20 September	1942	Dartmouth
G. Noel	Miss J.	1 July	1940	Start Point, Devon
J. Noel	Peter	27 November	1944	Captured
G. Noyon	Captain Frederick	3 November	1944	Cherbourg
J. O'Connor	Captain James	September	1940	Dartmouth
G. Ogier	Arthur	2 July	1940	Dartmouth
G. Ogier	Frank	2 July	1940	Dartmouth
G. Olliver	Mr A	1 July	1940	Start Point, Devon
G. Olliver	Mrs J	1 July	1940	Start Point, Devon
G. Olliver	Peter	1 July	1940	Start Point, Devon

J. Palewski	Maurice Georges	18 September	1944	Carteret
J. Parris	Kenneth	10 November	1944	Les Salines
J. Penkov	Vitaly Michael	18 September	1944	Carteret
J. Perrin	Rosanna June	27 October	1944	Bricqueville
G. Pike	Herbert	1 July	1940	Budleigh Salterton
G. Pike	Monica	1 July	1940	Budleigh Salterton
J. Pinel	Francis	10 October	1944	Carteret
J. Pinel	John W	10 October	1944	Carteret
J. Prain	Eric	10 November	1944	Les Salines
J. Price	Michael G.	10 November	1944	Les Salines
J. Queripel	Richard	15 November	1944	Port Bail
J. Querree	William	15 November	1944	Port Bail
J. Rault	Denis	25 October	1944	Granville
J. Rault	John Francis	24 September	1944	French coast
J. Raymonds	Marie	15 September	1942	Portland
J. Renouf	Albert R.	8 October	1944	Denville
J. Ridley	Charles Stanley	September	1940	Dartmouth
G. Rive	Ernest	1 July	1940	Start Point, Devon
J. Roe	Denis	7 October	1944	Frenchcoast
J. Rogers	Ronald G.	10 October	1944	Carteret
J. Rumball	William	11 November	1944	Granville
G. Savident	Cyril	1 July	1940	Budleigh Salterton
G. Savident	John (3 years)	1 July	1940	Budleigh Salterton
G. Savident	Joseph	1 July	1940	Budleigh Salterton
G. Savident	Mr J.	1 July	1940	Budleigh Salterton
G. Savident	Mrs J.	1 July	1940	Budleigh Salterton
J. Sinclair	Olga Mary	September	1940	Dartmouth
J. Siouville	Jean-Claude	18 September	1944	Carteret
J. Smith	Patrick	9 October	1944	Hauteville-sur-Mer
J. Storr	Gaston	18 September	1944	Carteret
J. Sullivan	Jospeh Pat	July	1940	Portland
G. Talbot	Mrs E	1 July	1940	Falmouth
J. Talmas	Luis Juan	22 October	1944	St Germain Plages
J. Taylor	Graham	25 September	1944	Beauville
G. Taymon	Raymond	15 September	1942	Portland
J. Touzel	Roseanna	22 October	1944	Bricqueville
J. Touzel	Frank	22 October	1944	Bricqueville
J. Turner	Belza	16 September	1944	Captured
J. Turner	George	September	19040	Dartmouth
J. Vibert	Dennis	21 September	1941	Dartmouth
J. Volant	Tony	October	1944	Captured
J. Voisin	Edward B.	September	1943	Plymouth

J. Voisin	John R.	September	1943	Plymouth
G. Waymouth	Frank	1 July	1940	Start Point, Devon
G. Waymouth	R.H.	1 July	1940	Start Point, Devon
G. Waymouth	Mrs N.	1 July	1940	Start Point, Devon
J. Webb	Dennis (Pat)	22 October	1944	Captured
G. Wheaton	James G.	1 July	1940	Falmouth
J. Wheeler	Charles	20 September	1940	Falmouth
J. Whithy	George	11 September	1942	Sidmouth
J. Woods	Robert	9 October	1944	Surville-sur-Mer

ESCAPEES FROM THE CHANNEL ISLANDS NAMES UNKNOWN 1940-1944

G. Austrian girl	1 July	1940	Start Point, Devon
G. father and son	1 July	1940	Devon
J. British sea captain	July	1940	
J. British sea mate	July	1940	
J. British seaman	July	1940	
G. British seaman	July	1940	
J. British sea cook	July	1940	
J. British sea captain	September	1940	
J. Irish sea captain	September	1940	
J. Dutch sea captain	September	1940	
J. Dutch seaman	September	1941	
J. Dutch seaman	September	1941	
J. French barge skipper	21 September	1944	Carteret
J. French seaman	25 September	1944	
J. French fisherman	25 September	1944	
J. French woman	25 September	1944	
J. German soldier	December	1944	Captured
J. German seaman	December	1944	Captured
J. German seaman	December	1944	Captured
J. German seaman	December	1944	Captured

The German soldier and the three German seamen above were held under sentence of death in the German Military wing of the prison in Gloucester Street, St Helier. I spoke to these four German servicemen when I was being held in the same wing of the prison while I was serving time in solitary confinement. One spoke good English. I cannot remember their names, but I remember one of them came from Hamburg. They were all very anti-Nazi. There were about 70 German servicemen in the Military wing Block C in 1945. Most of them were under sentence of death, or waiting to be sentenced. The war ending in May 1945, saved them from being shot. I would like to meet them again and have a good old chat about those days. And get their names for our records.

CHANNEL ISLANDERS IN ALLIED FORCES - 1939-1946

Research work in military records has produced these unofficial and incomplete lists of Channel Islanders who served in the 1914-18 and 1939 World Wars and Channel Islanders who were killed/died in the 1914-18 and 1939-45 World Wars.

Please note: the totals include the Channel Islanders who served in the Allied and Commonwealth forces of Australia, Canada, Newfoundland, New Zealand, South Africa etc. The lists also include French residents from the Channel Islands and Channel Islanders who died in German concentration camps 1940-45.

The Channel Islands' records are to be proud of and show the loyalty of the Islanders. I have researched the world records (war records) for many years, with the great help of good friends who live in the Commonwealth. Having lost many of my family in the two World Wars, my interest started many years ago. We must never forget our loyal and brave Channel Island men and women who served. We owe them a debt that we can never repay. Thanks to the Royal British Legion which keeps our Islander's memory green and honours the service they rendered for our freedom.

I have been waiting for many years for someone to step forward and contradict or correct my research totals. I would welcome any updating of them. I am just an old Jersey countryman who loves his people.

Contact:-
Joe Mière
No. 4 Warren Court
La Folie Estate
Millbrook
St Lawrence JE3 1JX

The Channel Islands are very proud of the fact that no fewer than ten thousand four hundred and eighteen (10,418) Channel Islanders, men and women, served on all fighting fronts in the 1939-1945 war. One must not forget that their loved ones and homes were under Nazi rule for five long years.

In the 1914-1918 war the Channel Islands sent twelve thousand four hundred and sixty (12,460) of their sons to the battle fronts.

Total of Channel Islanders who served and died in two world wars
1939-45 war. Served: 10,418. Killed/died on active service: 870
1914-18 war. Served: 12,460. Killed/died on active service: 2,298.

1914-18 war Served:		1914-18 war killed/died	
Jersey	6,292	Jersey	862
Guernsey	5,109	Guernsey	1,112
Alderney	116	Alderney	43
Sark	48	Sark	17
French	895	French	264
Total	12,460	Total	2,298

1939-45 war Served		1939-45 war Killed/died:	
Jersey	5,978	Jersey	516
Guernsey	4,011	Guernsey	252
Alderney	204	Alderney	25
Sark	27	Sark	1
French	198	French	48
Total	10,418	Total	842
		Concentration camps	28
		Total	870

The totals include the Channel Islanders who served in the Allied and Commonwealth forces, Australia, Canada, Newfoundland, New Zealand, South Africa.
Research work by: Joe Mière, Jersey, Channel Islands

H.M.S. Hood sunk in the North Atlantic ocean close to the Denmark strait near Greenland. 24 May 1941 after a 15 inch shell fired from the Bismark penetrated her magazine which exploded.

There were only three survivors out of over 1,400 officers and men:

Signalman Ted Briggs RN
AB R.E. Tilburn   RN
Midshipman Dundas RN

Among the 1,400 crew of the H.M.S. Hood were five Channel Islanders.

Edward Owen de St George of 15 Hue Street, St Helier
AB Donald Guille Benoist of Guernsey
Marine Wallace Ablett   (35) of 5 Commercial Buildings, St Helier
AB Ronald Makin (19) of Jersey
Francis J. Thomas (43) of Jersey

Sadly the five Channel Islanders went down with the Hood. I should be very grateful for any new information relating to them. We have been researching on and off for many years for the names and ranks etc. of our Jersey servicemen and women who served in HM Forces 1939-1946. It seems that no local authority, club, or organisation has ever recorded a full list. The ex-service lists would run into thousands of names. If anyone knows of a Jersey list of ex-service personnel 1939-1946 we would be grateful for the information.

Besides being very proud of our ex-servicemen and women we find it so interesting to research and so far have found the following sets of brothers and sisters who served in the forces in 1939-1946

5 sets of 6 brothers who served.
3 sets of 5 brothers who served
1 set of 5 brothers plus 2 grandsons that served.
10 sets of 4 brothers who served
2 sets of 4 brothers plus 2 sisters that served.
20 sets of 3 brothers who served
58 sets of 2 brothers who served.

There must be many more to research as the years go marching along. We hope and pray that on 9th May, Liberation Day, our people in the Island will spare a thought for our ex-servicemen and women and for those who did not return. Without them there would be no Liberation Day. I often think of the words in a young soldier's last letter home to his loved ones; (two days later he was killed).

'I love the warm sunshine that shines on our love'
'I love the wind in the trees that brings your love to me'

Ma Cabine

Many of us ex-servicemen will never forget 'Mr Vibert' who during the war years 1939-1945 ran 'Ma Cabine' the centre for Channel Islanders serving in His Majesty's forces. You could leave a message for family or friends, or a note to contact pals or brothers or sisters in the services. Mr Vibert rendered a great service to our Channel Islanders in the armed forces who were cut-off from their homes in the Channel Islands for five long years. I am sure many ex-servicemen and women still remember that 'Ma Cabine' was that link with home. Unofficially known as 'Ma Cabine,' it was at 26 Gideon Road, Battersea, London SW11. From Liverpool Street you took the 11 bus to Trafalgar Square, then the 77 bus to the Town Hall, you asked for Grayshott Road, 'Ma Cabine' was at the bottom of the road.

Send to:
Joe Mière
No 4 Warren Court
La Folie Estate
Millbrook
St Lawrence JE3 1JX
Tel: 01534 727592

Salerno Memorial to the Men of the Hampshire Regiment.Cut into the memorial stone are the words of testament.

**In memory of the men of The Hampshire Regiment
who fell on the beaches of Salerno September 1943**

Here dead we lie because we did not chose to live and shame the land from which we sprang. Life to be sure is nothing much to lose, but young men think it is, and we were young.

**2nd Battalion   The Hampshire Regiment
2/4th Battalion The Hampshire Regiment
1/4th Battalion The Hampshire Regiment
5th Battalion   The Hampshire Regiment**

Many Jersey boys served in one or other of the many battalions of the Hampshire regiment. Quite a number of these gallant lads fell in Italy on the beaches of Salerno, when no less than four Battalions of the Hampshires took part in this hazardous operation. It will surely be of great interest to all the members and ex-members of the Regiment, and to relatives and friends of the fallen to know that a memorial to the men of the four battalions who lost their lives at the Salerno landings and the subsequent fighting in September 1943 has been placed in the chapel at St Martin and St George in Ponteagnano, about six miles east of Salerno on route 18. The memorial which is on the left of the altar, is a plaque bearing the above inscription underneath the regimental badge. Beneath the memorial is a book containing the roll of honour. A dedication service was held on 19 July 1945 and was attended by a large number of members of the regiment. Many of the Hampshires are buried in the large cemetery about two miles beyond the chapel. (C.C. No 5 Section Imperial War Graves Commission C.M.F.'s)

Please note: the above information is from the The Evening Post, 13 August 1945.

Acknowledgments to the The Evening Post

THE ROSE OF NO MAN'S LAND (a song)

Verse:
I've seen some beautiful flowers grow in life's garden fair,
I've spent some wonderful hours lost in their fragrance rare;
But I've found another flower wondrous beyond compare,

Chorus:
There's a rose that grows in no man's land
and it's wonderful to see.
Although it's sprayed with tears it will live with me for years
in my garden of memories.
It's the one red rose that the soldier knows.
It's the work of a master's hand.
Amidst the war's great curse stands the Red Cross nurse.
She's the rose of no man's land.
Out of the heavenly splendours to the trail of woe.
God in his mercy sent her cheering the world below.

Music composed by James A. Brennan, with words by Jack Caddigan.

The song was one of many popular wartime songs sung by Charles Hart and Elliott Shaw, and was released by Leo Feist Inc, in 1918. It was later dedicated to Jane Delano (1862-1919) founder of the American Red Cross Nursing Service and the nurses who died during the Great War.

Monday 12th January 2004.
....

Being that there is no Official lists of Channel Islanders who were arrested and deported by the German Occupation Forces to German Penal Prisons and German Concentration Camps in France and Germany 1940-1945, this is the unofficial and incomplete lists. Researched by Joe Miere, from 1948 to 2004.

These lists are incomplete, and may contain some erros. These lists do not constitute a complete record of those deported from the Channel Islands. The Jersey lists are close to being completed, but there does not seem to be a complete Guernsey list to check - up on.

The enclosed lists have been up-dated, 12 January 2004.
....

4000, Channel Islanders were arrested and imprisoned by the German Occupation Forces, 1940 - 1945.
Jersey ; 2,600. Guernsey and Sark 1,400.
....

Between August 1940, and August 1944, over 620 persons were arrested, and deported to France and Germany, by the German Occupation Forces. In Jersey 22 did not return from the German Concentration Camps or Penal Prisons in France and Germany.
....

Some of the deported persons, were sent to special holding internment Camps in Germany. These specified categories of individuals were arrested and deported on the 13th and 25th of February 1943.
....

Plus;; 2,200 United Kingdom born Channel Islanders were deported by force to German Internment Camps in Germany, in 1942 - 1943. 45 of these United Kingdom Channel Islanders did not return, they lay buried in Germany.
....

THESE CHANNEL ISLANDERS MUST " NEVER BE FORGOTTEN "
....

No 4 Warren Court. La Folie Estate. Millbrook. St Lawrence. Jersey. Channel Islands. J E 3 -1JX. Tel; 01534 - 727592.

Joe Miere

Joe Mìere.

299

J.	Abraham.	Edward.	
G.	Addam.	Arthur	James.
G.	Addicott.	Henry	Alan.
G.	Allen.	William.	
J.	Alexander.	Joseph	Thomas.
G.	Allo.	Marquérite.	
G.	Amedroz.	Reginald.	
G.	Amy.	Bernard	J.
J.	Amy.	Geoffrey	Arthur.
J.	Amy.	John	Paul.
J.	Angell.	Richard.	
G.	Arrowsmith.	William	Bertram.
G.	Ashcroft.	Sidney.	
G.	Aubert.	Madelaine.	
J.	Auffret.	Robert	Arthur.
J.	Auffret.	Francis.	
G.	Auffret.	Arthur	Herbert.
G.	Auger.	Marcel	Jules.
J.	Aumonier.	Raymond.	
J.	Aune.	Jacques.	
G.	Bachmann.	Emile.	
G.	Baker.	William	Alfred.
G.	Bailey.	Donald.	
G.	Bailey.	Kingston	George.
G.	Bailey.	Robert	Philip.
J.	Banovich.	Irene.	
J.	Barbier.	Emile	Flavien.
J.	Barette.	Philip	Reginald.
J.	Barette.	Thomas.	
J.	Bartlet.	Bertram.	
G.	Barry.	Julia.	
G.	Bataille.	George	Kenneth.
J.	Baudains.	Philip	John.
J.	Bedford.	Arthur	Edward.
J.	Beer.	Ronald.	
J.	Begot.	Camile	Marie.
G.	Bell.	Robert.	
J.	Bennett.	Robert.	
J.	Berezay.	Desire	Auguste.
J.	Berry.	William	Henry.
G.	Bessin.	Rene.	

G.	Beuzeval.	Frank.	
J.	Bird.	Arthur	John.
J.	Bird.	Edward	Touzel.
G.	Bird.	Gerald.	
G.	Bird.	Mary.	
G.	Bird.	Walter.	
G.	Bird.	Wilfred.	
J.	Blandiam.	Marcel.	
J.	Blandioux.	Adozphone.	
J.	Bonass.	Dermot.	
J.	Bond.	Denis	Royston.
J.	Boukerka.	Hockiner.	
J.	Boudin.	Alfred.	
J.	Boudin.	Philip.	
J.	Bowditch.	Lawrence	William.
J.	Bower.	Herbert.	
G.	Brehaut.	Gordon.	
J.	Breleche.	Janet	Claire.
J.	Brettel.	Peter.	
G.	Breton.	Nelson.	
J.	Breuilly.	George	Thomas.
J.	Breuilly.	Sidney	Charles.
G.	Brichta.	Jean.	
J.	Brum.	Klara	Claire.
G.	Brouard.	Osmond.	
J.	Bruton.	Edward	John.
J.	Burley.	Charles	Gordon.
G.	Burton.	Cyril	Peter.
G.	Burton.	Edward	Walter.
J.	Burton.	William	John.
J.	Caindeau.	Rene	Marcel.
J.	Capron.	Bernard.	
S.	Carré.	Hedley.	
G.	Carré.	Reginald	Thomas.
G.	Carey.	Cecil	William.
G.	Carey.	Cederick	O'Donoghue.
J.	Carson.	George.	
J.	Cartwright.	Sydney.	
J.	Cary.	Hamilton	Southwell.
J.	Cary.	George.	
J.	Ceuleman.	Emilien.	
J.	Chapion.	Maurice	Marcel.
J.	Chapman.	Arnold	Edward.
G.	Chauvel.	William	Charles.

J.	Chevalier.		Henri	Jean.
G.	Chick.		Albert	Edward.
G.	Chilcott.		Robert	John.
J.	Clarke.		Edward	Arthur.
J.	Cleary.		Denis	Patrick.
J.	Cohu.	Rev	Clifford	John.
G.	Collivet.		George	Philip.
J.	Connor.		Alfred	James.
J.	Connor.		Patrick	Joseph.
J.	Corbel.		John	Francis.
J.	Coutanche.		John	Charles.
G.	Cox.		George.	
G.	Cox.		Robert.	
J.	Craig.		Percy	John.
J.	Craig.		Stanley	Arthur.
J.	Cretonier.		Eugene	Marcel.
J.	Czechouna.		Helena.	
J.	Dale.		James	Cyril.
J.	Daly.		Thomas	Peter.
G.	Damarell.		William	Alfred.
J.	Dauny.		Edward	Alfred.
J.	Dauny.		John.	
J.	Dauny.		Walter	Alan.
J.	Davey.		Clarence	James.
J.	Dawson.		Charles	David.
J.	Dean.		Harry	Ste Claire.
J.	Delauney.		Geoffrey	Ernest.
J.	Delque.		Marie	Therese.
G.	Dextor.		Leslie.	
J.	Dextor.		Norman.	
J.	Dimmery.		Arthur.	
G.	Domille.		Gerald.	
G.	Dodd.		Arthur.	
G.	Dodd.		Harold.	
J.	Downer.		Arthur	Richard.
G.	Downs.		James	Henry.
J.	Draper.		John.	
J.	Drelaud.		Evelyn.	
J.	Drumond.		James	Edward.
J.	Dubois.		Emile	Marcel.
G.	Dumont.		Jack	Collings.
G.	Dumont.		Robert	William.
G.	Dumont.		William	Francis.
J.	Dupré.		Ernest	George.

G.	Duquemin.	Cyril	Oliver.
J. G.	Duquemin.	Elizabeth.	
G.	Duquemin.	Henry	Edward.
G.	Duquemin.	Frederick.	
J.	Duquemin.	Francis	Graham.
G.	Duquemin.	Stephen	John.
J.	Durand. Rev	Raymond	Albert.
J.	Durant.	Edward.	
G.	De Bertram.	Francis	Harold.
G.	De Carteret.	John	Charles.
J.	De Ste Croix.	Philip	Charles.
J.	De Gourdan.	Paul.	
G.	De La Chapelle.	Jean (John)	
J.	De La Haye.	Cyril.	
J.	De La Haye.	Gerard	Colin.
J.	De La Houge.	Clement	Joseph.
J.	De La Mare.	Francis	Arthur.
G.	De Lisle	Nicolle.	
J.	De Pauw.	Adelphine.	
G.	Edalson.	Reginald.	
G.	Edison.	Andrew	James.
J.	Edwards.	Thomas	Charles.
G.	Edwards.	William	David.
J.	Egre.	Standley	Hedley.
J.	Elliott.	John	Peter.
G.	Elliott.	Frank.	
J.	Evans.	Thomas	Alan.
J.	Evere.	Joseph	William.
J.	Eveson.	Joseph	Mark.
G.	Falla.	Arthur.	
G.	Falla.	Francis	Walter.
G.	Falla.	Frank.	
G.	Falla.	John	Hocart.
G.	Falla.	Robert.	
J.	Falle.	Arthur	Stanley.
J.	Falle.	Edmond.	
J.	Falle.	Jannine	Josette.
J.	Falle.	John	James.
G.	Falle.	Percy	Edward.
G.	Falle.	Thomas	William.
J.	Faramus.	Anthony	Charles.
J.	Featherstone.	Harry.	
J.	Federle.	Jacqueline.	
J.	Ferbrache.	Dora.	

G.	G.	Ferbrache.	George	Albert.
	J.	Ferrand.	Francis	William.
	J.	Ferey.	Harold	Albert.
	G.	Ferris.	Charles.	
	J.	Ferris.	Vyvian.	
	J.	Ferron.	Albert	Thomas.
	G.	Feugeris.	Lucien.	
	J.	Finkelstein.	John	Max.
	G.	Flambard.	Rene	Ernest.
	J.	Fox.	Edward	Robert.
	J.	Fox.	Georges	James.
	J.	Fraser.	Ian	Alexander.
	G.	Friend.	Charles	Albert.
	J.	Fromage.	Emile	Rena.
	J.	Gallichan.	George.	
	J.	Gallichan.	Herbert.	
	J.	Gallichan.	John	William.
	J.	Gallichan.	Walter	(Sonny)
	G.	Gallienne.	Harold.	
	G.	Garland.	Elvina.	
	J.	Gates.	Reginald	Charles.
	G.	Gaudion.	Thomas.	
	J.	Genty.	Camile	Louise.
	J.	Gibaut.	Eldon	Stanley.
	J.	Gideon.	Marie	Evette.
	G.	Gillingham.	Joseph	John.
	G.	Girard.	Hedley.	
	G.	Giraud.	John.	
	J.	Giron.	Raymond.	
	J.	Godfray.	William	Joseph.
	J.	Gosselin.	Alexander.	
	G.	Gosselin.	Ernest.	
	G.	Gosselin.	Maurice	Lionel.
	J.	Gosset.	Clarence.	
	J.	Gould.	Louisa	Mary.
	J.	Gould.	Maurice	Jay.
	J.	Green.	Gordon.	
	J.	Green.	Robert	Charles.
	J.	Green.	Stanley.	
	G.	Green.	Winifred	Elizabeth.
	G.	Greenway.	William.	
	J.	Grihaut.	Charles	Victor.
	J.	Grimshaw.	William	Edward.

G.	Guillebon.	Louis	Xavier.
G.	Guillemet.	Charles.	
G.	Guille.	Edgar	John.
J.	Guille.	Edward.	
S.	Guille.	John.	
J.	Guille.	Ronald.	
G.	Guimart.	Albert	Thomas.
J.	Guiton.	Emile	Frederick.
G.	Guiton.	Serge	Georges.
G.	Gulbert.	Ronald	Arthur.
J.	Hacquoil.	Alfred	George.
G.	Hadge.	Benjamin.	
G.	Hamel.	Clarence	Walter.
J.	Hamon.	George.	
S.	Hamon.	John	Peter.
J.	Hamon.	Louis.	
J.	Hamon.	Walter.	
S.	Hamon.	William	James.
J.	Hannaford.	Raymond.	
G.	Hannis.	Arthur	John.
G.	Hardy.	Warren	Norman.
G.	Harper.	Jack.	
J.	Harricot.	Harry	Francis.
J.	Harris.	John	Ronald.
G.	Harris.	winfred	Mary.
J.	Hassall.	Peter.	
S.	Hathway.	Robert	Woodward.
G.	Hayes.	John	Crossley.
G.	Haywood.	Edward.	
J.	Healy.	William	Peter.
G.	Heaume.	Aubrey	Langlois.
J.	Henry.	Alfred	Emile.
G.	Henry.	Ernest	John.
G.	Herring.	Henry.	J.
J.	Hervé.	Marcel	Eugene.
J.	Hervé.	Yvenous.	
J.	Heuze.	Ernest	Bienaime.
J.	Heuzo.	Ernest.	
G.	Hill.	Marion	Francis.
J.	Hill.	Maurice	Victor.
G.	Hockey.	Cyril.	
G.	Hockey.	Dennis.	
G.	Hockey.	Stanley	George .

G.	Hotton.	Albert.	
J.	Houillbecq.	Frank	Gordon.
J.	Houillbecq.	James	Edward.
G.	Howe.	Reginald	Charles.
G.	Howlett.	Albert	William.
G.	Hurford.	Ronald.	
G.	Hutchesson.	Charles	Le Marchant.
G.	Illatimer.	Anthony	Timothy.
G.	Illet.	Francis	Edward.
J.	Illton.	Edward.	
J.	Impines.	Albert	Louis.
J.	Ingram.	Peter.	
G.	Ingrouille.	John	Henry.
J.	Irine.	George	Thomas.
G.	Izacard.	Maurice	Georges.
G.	Jackson.	Raymond	Mark.
G.	Jackson.	Colin	Robert.
J.	Jackson.	Frank	Stanley.
G.	James.	Crotius	Alexander.
G.	Jenkins.	Arthur	Clarence.
J.	Jestin.	Louis.	
J.	Jesty	William	James.
J.	Johnson.	Peter	Bruce..
J.	Jolliffe.	Frank.	
J.	Jones.	Harry	Thomas.
G.	Jones.	John	Henry.
G.	Jones.	Audrey	Ann.
G.	Keighley.	George	Stanley.
G.	Kelly.	Andrew	Sean.
J.	Kelly.	Patrick	Timothy.
J.	Kennedy.	Anthony.	
J.	Kenfocci.	Berkail	Michael.
J.	Kent.	Joseph	Philip.
J.	Kent.	Ronald.	
G.	Kent.	Stanley	George.
G.	Kibble.	Eric.	
J.	Kinard.	Lillian.	
J.	King.	Edward.	
G.	Knight.	Charles.	
J.	Knight.	Simon	Francis.
J.	Kirwan.	Patrick.	
J.	Kowlack.	Thomas.	
J.	Kuenze.	Stephen.	
J.	Lafoley.	Arthur	James.

G.	Lainé.	Walter	Henry.	
G.	Langlois.	Edwin	Mauger.	
J.	Langlois.	Geniveve.		
G.	Langmead.	Arthur	John.	
G.	Lanyon.	Hubert	Henry.	
G.	Lawson.	Douglas.	James.	
G.	Legg.	Ernest	Stanley.	
G.	Legg.	Reginald	Cyril.	
J.	Leister.	Dennis	John.	
G.	Lempriere.	Florance	Marie.	
J.	Lempriere.	Gordon	Edward.	
J.	Lempriere.	Harold	Edward.	
J.	Lempriere.	John.		
J.	Lewis.	Francis.		
G.	Lihou.	Stanley	du Frocq.	
J.	Lingshaw.	John	George.	
J.	Lock.	Frederick	John.	
J.	Loister.	John.		
J.	Lloyd.	Esther	Pauline.	
J.	Lorre.	Jean	Marie.	
G.	Losch.	Franzeph.		
J.	Louis.	Albert	Louis.	
G.	Lowe.	Cyril	George.	
G.	Lowe.	Theodore.		
J.	Lucas.	Ronald	Dennis.	
J.	Luce.	George	Martin.	
J.	Luciennes.	Francis	Marcel.	
G.	Luciennes.	Francine	K.	
G.	Luffman.	William	George.	
G.	Lynch.	William	Mark.	
J.	Le Blancq.	Thomas.		
G.	Le Blond.	Leona.		
J.	Le Borgne.	Arthur	George.	
J.	Le Boutillier.	John.		
J.	Le Boutillier.	Raymond.		
J.	Le Breton.	Edward	Charles.	
J.	Le Breton.	Nelson.		
G.	Le Caer.	John	Joseph.	
J.	Le Calvez.	Alfred	Jean	Desire.
J.	Le Cornu.	Philip	Edward.	
J.	Le Cornu.	Walter	Martine.	
J.	Le Druillenec.	Harold	Osmond.	
J.	Le Duff.	Francois.		
G.	Le Gallez.	Alfred	Thomas.	
G.	Le Gallez.	Thomas	Albert.	

G.	Le Gallez.	William	Edward.
J.	Le Gastelois.	Henry.	D.
G.	Le Goff.	Francis.	
J.	Le Fevre.	André.	
G.	Le Fevre.	Eugene	Henri.
G.	Le Fevre.	Harold	Francis.
J.	Le Feuve.	Maurice.	
J.	Le Feuve.	Robert.	
J.	Le Flock.	Francis	John.
J.	Le Huquet.	Alain	Rene.
J.	Le Huquet.	Marcel.	
J.	Le Jehan.	Roland	Andre.
J.	Le Kercheval.	Emile	Francis.
J.	Le Lerre.	Alfred.	
J.	Le Lievre.	Eugene.	
G.	Le Lievre.	Edward.	E.
J.	Le Luyer.	Marcel.	
J.	Le Main.	Thomas	Edward.
J.	Le Maistre.	Alice.	
G.	Le Maistre.	Eric	Stanley.
J.	Le Maistre.	John	Henry.
J.	Le Marquand.	Gordon.	
J.	Le Masurier.	Addele.	
J.	Le Mercier.	Wilfred	George. (Billy)
G.	Le Moigne.	Alexis	F.
J.	Le Monnier.	Albert	Alfred.
G.	Le Nourty.	Osmond	Ernest.
J.	Le Page.	Clement.	
J.	Le Page.	Edward.	
G.	Le Page.	Frank.	
G.	Le Page.	Norman.	
G.	Le Page.	Thomas	Charles.
G.	Le Page.	Stanley	Edmond.
G.	Le Provost.	Ernest.	
G.	Le Provost.	Nicholas	John.
G.	Le Provost.	Thomas	Herbert.
J.	Le Provost.	Thomas	William.
J.	Le Put.	Edward	Armand.
J.	Le Put.	Georges	Yves.
G.	Le Quesne.	Edward	George.
J.	Le Quesne.	Francis	Charles.
J.	Le Quesne.	Francis	Walter.
J.	Le Riche.	Andrew	John.
J.	Le Riche.	John	Mark.

J.	Le Roux.	Dennis.		
G.	Le Tissier.	Hedley	Cecil.	
G.	Le Tissier.	George	Philip.	
J.	Le Vesconte.	Alan.		
J.	Le Villio.	Frank	Rene	Julien.
G.	Machon.	Charles	Nicholas.	
G.	Machon.	Roy.		
J.	Magan.	Dennis.		
J.	Mallett.	Albert	John.	
J.	Mallett.	Arthur.		
G.	Mallett.	Frank.		
J.	Manghan.	Maurice	Joseph.	
J.	Mansell.	Thomas.		
J.	Marie.	Edward	Paul.	
G.	Marriette.	Arthur.		
G.	Marriette.	Jessie.		
G.	Marriette.	Joan.		
J.	Marshall.	Emma	Constance.	
J.	Marsh.	William	Howard.	
J.	Martin.	Roger.		
J.	Marzin.	Georges.		
J.	Masse.	Frank.		
J.	Mathurin.	Therese	Marie.	
J.	Melon.	Roger.		
G.	Menez.	Rene.		
G.	Michael.	Anne.		
G.	Michael.	Dorothy.		
G.	Miller.	Percy	William.	
J.	Mogot.	Albert	Louis.	
J.	Moignard.	John.		
J.	Moisan.	Alphonse.		
J.	Molina.	Antonia.		
J.	Morel.	George	John.	
J.	Morel.	Stanley.		
J.	Morin.	Raymond.		
J.	Moss.	Sidney	Albert.	
J.	Motie.	Richard	Francis.	
J.	Moulpied.	Andrew	Charles.	
J.	Muels.	Edward	Peter.	
G.	Mulholland.	M.		
J.	Murphy.	Timothy	Patrick.	
J.	Mylne.	Vivienne.		
J.	Mc Callen.	Philip	James.	
J.	Mc Closky.	Patrick	Joseph.	
J.	Mc Gratin.	Michael.		

G.	Mc Gugan.	Andrew	Sean.	
G.	Nant.	Henry	John.	
J.	Neilson.	Brian	Ian.	
J.	Neilson.	John	Birkmyre.	
G.	Nicholas.	Frank.		
G.	Nicholas.	Frederick	John.	
J.	Nicholle.	Emile.		
G.	Nicholle.	Geffrey	Stanley.	
J.	Nicholle.	Jack.		
G.	Nicholle.	John.		
J.	Nicholle.	John	Whitley.	
G.	Nicholle.	Mary.		
G.	Nicholle.	Walter	John	Ernest.
J.	Norrise.	Mark	William.	
J.	Norman.	Kathleen.		
J.	Norton.	Edward.		
J.	O' Callagan.	Denis	Patrick.	
J.	O' Callagan.	Cyril.		
J.	O' Connell.	Maurice	Mossy	
J.	O' Connor.	Frederick	Albert.	
J.	Ogier.	Leonce	L'Hermitte.	
J.	Ogier.	Richard	L'Hermitage.	
J.	O' Hesrn.	Patrick	Joseph.	
J.	Oldron.	Jacques.		
J.	Oliver.	Stanley.		
G.	Oliver.	William	Thomas.	
J.	Olivier.	Eugene	Paul.	
G.	Olivier.	Ernest	Paul.	
J.	Olivier.	Arthur	Richard.	
G.	O' Meara.	Bryan	John.	
J.	O' Shea.	Joseph	Patrick.	
J.	Page.	Frederick	William.	
J.	Paignell.	John	Edward.	
J.	Painter.	Clarence	Claude.	
J.	Painter.	Peter	Edward.	
J.	Paisnel.	Emile	John.	
J.	Palistra.	Peter.		
J.	Pallot.	Amelia.	Marie.	
J.	Pallot.	Garnet	Edward.	
J.	Palmer.	Stanley	Henry.	
G.	Parry.	William	Edward.	
G.	Parsons.	Frank.		
J.	Perrot.	Lester	Marcel.	
G.	Piesing.	Harold	Edward.	

J.	Pinchon.	August	Andre.	
J.	Pinchon.	Jules.		
J.	Pinwell.	John	de Carteret.	
J.	Pittard.	Francis.		
J.	Pitolet.	Marie.		
J.	Pleasants.	Eric.		
J.	Poole.	Harold	Claude.	
G.	Pomeroy.	Alfred	Edward.	
G.	Potts.	Frederick.		
J.	Preston.	Harry.		
G.	Priaulx.	Lawson	George.	
J.	Prigent.	Gordon.		
J.	Proteau.	Theodore.		
J.	Quemard.	John	Charles.	
J.	Quereé.	Albert	Reginald.	
J.	Querré.	Arthur	Wilfred.	
J.	Querré.	Clifford	Bond.	
G.	Quick.	James	Thomas	William.
J.	Quinn.	Thomas	Patrick.	
J.	Quinn.	Walter.		
G.	Quinn.	William	George.	
J.	Rabet.	Henry	Yves.	
G.	Randall.	Charles	Russell.	
J.	Rault.	André	Louis.	
J.	Rault.	Eugene	Marcel.	
J.	Rebour.	Francis	John.	
J.	Reilzen.	Emile.		
J.	Reubens.	Edward	Charles.	
J.	Richardson.	Robert	Thomas.	
G.	Rich.	Alfred.		
J.	Riches.	Richard.		
G.	Robilliard.	Harold	Mauger.	
G.	Robin.	Harold	John.	
J.	Ross.	Anne	Muir.	
J.	Ross.	Edward	Oliver.	
J.	Rossi.	Marcel	Jean Marie.	
J.	Rossi.	Marcel (Jnr)	Fortune.	
J.	Routier.	Mabel.		
J.	Rowe.	Adelene	May.	
G.	Rowe.	Edward	James.	
J.	Rowe.	Michael.		
G.	Russell.	William	Charles.	
G.	Rutter.	James.		
J.	Ryn.	Michael	Andrew.	

J.	Ryn.	Timothy	Joseph.
G.	Ryn.	Thomas	Patrick.
J.	Samson.	Kevin	Cyril.
J.	Sandeman.	Basil.	
J.	Sangan.	Anthony	Robert.
J.	Sangan.	Gladys.	
J.	Sarre.	Richard	William.
G.	Sarre.	Ronald	Herbert.
J.	Schornmacher.	Leon.	
J.	Scimmer.	Louis	Henri.
S.	Sharp.	George.	
G.	Sherwill.	Ambrose	James.
G.	Short.	Frederick	Winter.
J.	Sinclair.	June	Mary.
J.	Smith.	Charles.	
J.	Smith.	Claud	Martin.
J.	Smith.	Herbert	Percival.
G.	Smith.	William	Edward.
J.	Soyer.	John	(Jack)
G.	Spitz.	Augusta.	
G.	Stranger.	Philip.	
J.	Staples.	Ronald.	
J.	Staples.	Colin	William.
G.	Steiner.	Therese.	
J.	Stephen.	Louis.	
J.	Still.	Alfred	B.
J.	Still.	Michael	Lewis.
J.	Still.	Ruby.	
J.	Streader.	Jean.	
J.	Streader.	Marcia.	
J.	Streader.	Phyllis.	
J.	Streader.	Sidney.	
J.	Sugdury.	Georges.	
J.	Sutton.	Charles	Royston.
G.	Symes.	Francis.	
G.	Symes.	Henry.	
G.	Symes.	Louis.	
G.	Symes.	Mary.	
G.	Symes.	Rachel.	
G.	Symes.	William.	
J.	Symons.	Reginal	James.
G.	Tanguy.	Albert	Louis.
J.	Tanguy.	Douglas	Walter.

J.	Tanguy.	Louis.	
G.	Tardiff.	Frank	Archibald.
G.	Tardivel.	James.	
G.	Taylor.	Sidney	James.
J.	Thoma.	Rene	André.
J.	Thomas.	Edouard	Pascal.
J.	Thomas.	Frederick	Cyril.
J.	Thomas.	Harold	William.
G.	Thomas.	Philip.	
J.	Thorne.	James	Edward.
J.	Tierney.	Joseph	(Joe)
G.	Timms.	Sidney	Henry.
J.	Torode.	Kenneth	William.
J.	Tostevin.	Douglas	George.
J.	Tostevin.	Lenard	Percy.
G.	Travers.	Richard	Michael.
J.	Travert.	Emile	Eugene.
J.	Traylen.	Alfred	Ernest.
G.	Tuck.	Frank	Hubert.
J.	Turner.	Walter	Albert.
J.	Turpin.	Colin	Francis.
J.	Turpin.	Coritin	Julian.
J.	Turpin.	Howard	Herbert.
J.	Tyrell.	Frederick	Charles.
G.	Tyrell.	George	Edward.
G.	Tyrell.	Percy	Thomas.
J.	Van Van Oostroom.	Cornelius.	
J.	Vasse.	Frederick.	
J.	Vasselin.	Jean -Pierre.	
GG.	Veron.	Marcel	Yves.
J.	Vincent.	Douglas	Charles.
J.	Voisin.	Francis	Mark.
G.	Voisin.	Kenneth	Brian.
J.	Voisin.	Peter	Ronald.
J.	Wakeham.	George	Bennett.
J.	Wakeham.	Stanley	Cyril.
J.	Walling.	Jack.	
G.	Ware.	Frank	William.
J.	Wellborne.	Cyril	de Montfort.
J.	Wilkinson.	Henry	Reginal.
J.	Williams.	David	Harold.
J.	Williams.	Gerald	Thomas.
G.	Williams.	George.	
J.	Williams.	Percy	William.

J.	Woods.	Anthony	Robert.	
J.	Woods.	John	Edward.	
J.	Woods.	John	Ernest	Frederick.
G.	Woods.	Reginald	James.	
G.	Woods.	Stanley	George.	
G.	Wondsor.	Albert	Edwin.	
G.	Worth.	Charles	Edward.	
G.	Worthington.	Basil	Arthur.	
G.	Wyzacks.	Paul	Stanlas.	

People deported from Jersey by the German Occupation forces to German concentration camps and penal prisons in Germany and France, 1940-1945 and did not return, they were killed or died in the camps and prisons.

COHU	Canon Clifford	Died.	February 1945	Spergau
DAUNY	Walter Allen	Died/Missing		Germany
DIMMERY	Arthur	Died	4 April 1944	Laufen
FOX	George James	Died	11 March 1945	Naumburg-on-Saale
GOULD	Louisa	Died	February 1945	Ravensbruck
GOULD	Maurice Jay	Died	10 October 1943	Wittlich
HOUILLEBECQ	James	Died	29 January 1945	Neuengamme
JOHNSON	Peter Bruce	Died	Missing 1945	Dora-Mittelbau
MARSH	William Howard	Died	March 1945	Naumburg-on-Saale
MUELS	Edward Peter	Died	1945	Liegenhelm
NICOLLE	John Whitley	Died	1944	Dortmund
OGIER	Leonce L'Hermitte	Died	1 August 1943	Biberach
PAGE	Frederick William	Died	5 January 1945	Naumburg-on-Saale
PAINTER	Clarence Claude	Died	February 1945	Dora-Mittelbau
PAINTER	Peter	Died	27 November 1944	Gross-Rosen
PAISNEL	Emile	Died	29 August 1944	Naumburg-on-Saale
QUEREE	Clifford Bond	Died	1 May 1945	Naumburg-on-Saale
ROSSI	Marcel Fortune	Died	February 1945	Flossenburg
SINCLAIR	June	Died	1943	Ravensbruck
SOYER	John (Jack)	Died	29 July 1944	Brehal
TIERNEY	Joseph (Joe)	Died	April 1945	Celle
LE VILLIO	Frank Rene	Died	26 September 1946	Nottingham

POPULATION TOTALS OF CHANNEL ISLANDS 1940-1945

Total population of the Channel Islands. Census taken 10 August 1940.

Jersey population	Census taken 10 August 1940;	41,101
Guernsey population	Census taken 10 August 1940;	24,429
Sark population	Census taken 10 August 1940;	470
Total population		66,000

Gender totals of Jersey Population. Census taken 10 August 1940.

Males;	18,773
Females	22,328

Total Jersey population 1940;   41,101

Left Jersey during the evacuation to England 1940.	10,798
Left Guernsey during the evacuation to England 1940.	20,202
Total population evacuated to England.	31,000
Total balance of population left in the Islands.	66,000

United Kingdom born population living in the Channel Islands 1941;

Jersey

Men 18 to 45	1,305	1,305
Men 46 to 60	700	2,005
Men over 60	728	2,733
Boys under 18	213	2,946
Women over 18	2,391	5,337
Girls under 18	189	5,526

Jersey total: 5,526

Guernsey

Men 18 to 45	432	432
Men 46 to 60	359	791
Men over 60	444	1,235
Women over 18	1,525	2,760
Children 5 to 18	70	2,830

Guernsey total: 2,830

Total UK born population living in the Channel Islands   8,356

The Germans deported 2,200 in 1942-43 to internment camps in Germany this left a balance of 6,156 UK born people still living in the Islands. (These totals do not allow for births and deaths)

Ref: Red Cross Supplies to the Channel Islands 1944-1945

Civil Population of the Island of Jersey. 14 February 1945.

Up to 18 years of age =	males	4,797
Up to 18 years of age =	females	4,690
Over 18 years of age =	males	12,667
Up to 18 years of age =	females	16,591

Total   38,745

Foreign Civilian Workers receiving Red Cross Parcels, not included in the population total = 156

Certified approximately correct:

Signed; A Coutanche
Bailiff of Jersey
February 14 1945

The Evening Post, 26 August 1940

Guernsey's census figures. 20,000 left the Island in 1940.
1939 Guernsey population 42,000-45,000

1940 Census Guernsey.

Males: 65 years and over	1,807	
64 years to 19 years	8,067	
18 years to 14 years	865	
13 years to 6 years	460	
5 years to 1 year	446	Total: Males 11,645
Females: 60 years and over	2,931	
59 years to 19 years	7,322	
18 years to 14 years	843	
13 years to 6 years	551	
5 years to 1 year	469	Total: Females 12,116
Babies under 1 year	220	

Total Guernsey Population August 1940;   23,981

Acknowledgement to the ***Jersey Evening Post***

German Occupation of the Channel Islands 1940-45
Lists of totals of births in Jersey, Guernsey, Sark 1940-45

Jersey
Births	1940	723	Illegitimate	35	4.8%
Births	1941	458	Illegitimate	28	6.1%
Births	1942	404	Illegitimate	29	7.2%
Births	1943	444	Illegitimate	35	7.9%
Births	1944	527	Illegitimate	58	11.0%
Births	1945	475	Illegitimate	34	7.2%

Guernsey
Births	1938	834	Illegitimate	45	5.4%
Births	1939	744	Illegitimate	40	5.4%
Births	1940	568	Illegitimate	35	6.2%
Births	1941	243	Illegitimate	15	6.2%
Births	1942	261	Illegitimate	49	18.8%
Births	1943	337	Illegitimate	55	16.3%
Births	1944	395	Illegitimate	86	21.8%
Births	1945	393	Illegitimate	80	20.3%

Sark
Births	1939	7	Illegitimate	1
Births	1940	7	Illegitimate	1
Births	1941	3	Illegitimate	1
Births	1942	6	Illegitimate	0
Births	1943	3	Illegitimate	0
Births	1944	3	Illegitimate	1
Births	1945	4	Illegitimate	0

Note: One must bear in mind that the Channel Islands were not occupied by the Germans till (Guernsey) Sunday 30 June 1940, (Jersey) Monday 1 July 1940. So one must discount any German births in 1940, also the British men and forced labour men from Spain and France did their share of making the local women pregnant- and the young Jerseymen were not asleep when it came to casual sex. I often wonder how many illegitimate American servicemen's children (black and white) were born in England- also how many German prisoners of war became fathers to children in the United Kingdom.

A debt we cannot repay. The loyal and proud record and history of our dear Channel Islands.

1914-18 war   12,460 Channel Islanders served in forces.
1914-18 war   2,298 Channel Islanders killed.
1939-45 war   10,418 Channel Islanders served in forces.
1939-45 war   870   Channel Islanders killed.

Out of a Channel Island population of 66,000 (1940-45) 4,000 Channel Islanders were arrested by the Germans and imprisoned. (Jersey 2,600) (Guernsey 1,400)
Over 620 Channel Islanders were taken from the Islands to German concentration camps and penal prisons in France and Germany 1940-1944.
Plus; one must add to the lists the 2,200 UK born Channel Islanders. Deported by force to internment camps in Germany 1942-1943.

There were 225 Channel Islands men, women, boys and girls that either escaped from the Channel Islands 1940-1945 or were drowned, shot or arrested in the attempt to escape to England or France.

When the Germans in 1942-1943 deported the UK born Channel Islanders, thousands of us in Jersey demonstrated against the Germans deportation of our English people. The Germans had a great surprise and many of us were arrested and put in prison, some were deported to camps in Germany. And please remember we are not English but British and proud of it. I am now 77 years old and still love our country. This old simple Jerseyman feels very sad of what's happening in dear old England. We in Jersey still love our British way of life and still think that our Norman laws are the best.

GIBRALTAR   population 1940

In the summer of 1940 the British, concerned for the safety of the population of Gibraltar and the need to strengthen their base there, evacuated 25,000 people from Gibraltar to England. Many of these evacuees were billeted in Kensington, London. Some of them in small hotels in Kensington. Some of these evacuees found work at the Post Office Savings Bank headquarters in Blythe Road, West Kensington.

Some stayed on after the war and became established civil servants. Some were still there in the late sixties when the Government moved the Savings Bank headquarters to Glasgow. They were evacuees rather than refugees and they were displaced British subjects.

Channel Islands.Population 1940.   97,000

Evacuated to England June 1940   Jersey   10,798
                                    Guernsey and Alderney   20,202
Total Evacuated   31,000

Total population remaining in Channel Islands
                                    Jersey   41,101
                                    Guernsey   24,429
                                    Sark   470
Total remaining in Islands   66,000

UK born population living in Channel Islands in 1941

                        Jersey = 5,526
                        Guernsey = 2,830
                        Total 8,356

Jersey Evening Post. Saturday 18th February 1995

Occupation lectures

CONTINUING the series of lunchtime lectures about different aspects of life in Jersey during the Occupation, Joe Mière is the guest speaker this Thursday when his subject will be 'Political Prisoners'.

Mr Mière, 69 in July, was himself a political prisoner in the former prison in Gloucester Street, one of 2,600 people arrested by the Germans for contraventions of their rules of occupation.

He will be speaking of the living conditions, the German and Jersey guards, the accommodation and his experiences during the six months that he was imprisoned from the end of 1944.

Mr Mière had various jobs, including engineering, hairdressing and clothing retail, during and after the Occupation, before he eventually became the curator of the German Underground Hospital.

Although retired now, he still maintains his Occupation collection at the hospital.

The talks begin at 1 pm and 2 pm both lasting 30 minutes. They will be held in the Members Room of the Société Jersiaise.

Joe Mière

FORGOTTEN PEOPLE. BAILIFF UNVEILS THE PLAQUE TO POLITICAL PRISONERS

In memory of political prisoners

A LIFETIME commitment to the memory of political detainees imprisoned at the Newgate Street jail during the Occupation has finally paid off for veteran Joe Mière.

Mr Mière, a detainee during the last six months of the Occupation, has campaigned tirelessly for years to establish some form of lasting memorial to the local and foreign men and women who were imprisoned by the occupying forces because of their actions against the Nazi regime.

Crystal radio set

'If you were caught with a crystal radio set or defacing Nazi posters, or disregarded the orders of the authorities in some other way, you could have found yourself in one of the 10 ft by 8 ft cells, usually holding four detainees each. People from all walks of life found themselves in there. Often many members of one family spent a spell at the jail,' he recalled.

Mr Mière (67), along with many other surviving detainees, believes that a lasting memorial would make a fitting tribute to those who survived the internment as well as those who died during their time in the prison, known to all at the time as 'the Gloucester Street jail'.

Such was Mr Mière's determination that he wrote to the Lieut-Governor, Air Marshal Sir John Sutton, to ask for his assistance in the matter. With the Lieut-Governor's support, Mr Mière approached the Occupation and Liberation Committee, who are now

Joe Mière wants a lasting memorial to the political detainees

planning to erect a polished granite plaque at the old jail's site in remembrance of the detainees.

Mr Mière is thrilled that the tribute is finally going ahead, having amassed a great deal of support through publicising the campaign.

'Through my letters on the subject of "our forgotten people", as I refer to them, I've had a flood of calls and many touching letters from detainees and family of those who were imprisoned at some time or other. The news of the plaque has been welcomed by us all and I am personally thrilled,' he said.

In Memory of Political Prisoners The Jersey Evening Post, Saturday 11 March 1995

Acknowledgments The Jersey Evening Post

Occupation and Liberation Committee

States Greffe, Jersey, JE1 1DD, Channel Islands

Tel: 0534 502000   Fax: 0534 502098

314/5/6(1)

18th April 1995.

Dear Mr Gray,

Thank you for your letter of the 8th April received today, the 18th April 1995. I am sorry that you do not like my reply but I am afraid that there is not much that we can do about it at this stage. The plain and simple fact is that it has taken a considerable amount of effort both by myself and by Joe Miere to get the political prisoners recognised at all. As no doubt you are aware, in the past, there has been considerable reluctance by the Government of Jersey to recognise political prisoners at all. I am not party to the reasons for this but I did sympathise with Mr Miere when he made his approach and so steered this particular issue through my Committee to its successful conclusion. Therefore you will get recognition at last. However, there will not be large social event surrounding this Official recognition although both the Lieutenant Governor and the Bailiff will be present at the unveiling on the 27th April.

I am afraid that we had to choose a date. I asked Joe Miere for his advice on a suitable date, one that would not clash with other events. It was he that chose April 27th. He did so because, as I explained before, this was the date of the last piece of real savagery by the German occupying forces ie; the shooting of one of their own for attempting to escape. It is certainly significant to Joe Miere and as he has been the driving force behind this whole scheme I felt that it was only right that we accede to his advice on this occasion. Again the date is set and that is it.

Your last paragraph referring to dedicating a memorial to the Escapees has me confused. You say that ' a number failed to make it and were arrested '. Those who failed to make it, and there were nine who died, are recognised by having their names on the plaque which will commemorate the bravery of all those who escaped or who attempted to escape. Again as I explained to you there will be a Book of Remembrance which will be placed in the Town Hall which you can look at next time you are over.

Thank you for your letter. I am sorry if you are still disappointed but I am afraid that there is little that I can do about it at this stage.

Yours sincerely,

Bruce Willing,
Co-ordinator,
Occupation and Liberation Committee.

Mr P.Gray,
La Campagne,
50190 Nay,
France.

The Bailiff unveils the plaque.

During the period of the German occupation of Jersey, from 1st July 1940 to 9th May 1945, many inhabitants were imprisoned for acts of protest and defiance against the Occupation Forces in H.M. Prison, Gloucester Street which stood on this site. Others were deported and held in camps in Germany and elsewhere from which some did not return. This Plaque is placed in their memory with grateful thanks from the people of Jersey on the 50th Anniversary of the Liberation of Jersey, 9th May 1995.
This Plaque was unveiled by Mr. Philip Bailhache, Bailiff of Jersey on 27th April 1995.

When the States of Jersey placed the plaque to the memory of the political prisoners outside the old prison wall in Gloucester Street on 27 April 1995, I am sure the ghosts of many of the old political prisoners watched and nodded in satisfaction. And the spirit of the brave young Frenchman, François Scornet, taken from this prison and shot at St Ouen's Manor 17 March 1941, was also there.

Also the spirits of the German servicemen who were also taken from this prison and executed at Fort Regent, Queens Valley, La Moye, St Saviours, Grouville, etc. Without shame I will think of them and the days and months we spent under the same prison roof. Although our countries were at war, we shared a common enemy - the brutal Nazis.

What about the Island's 'forgotten people'?

From Joe Mière.

HOW pleased we were to read the article by Leigh Petters (JEP,16 July) on the 50th Liberation Anniversary plans that a memorial will be unveiled to those who escaped or perished trying to escape during the German Occupation.

This memorial to the brave escapees was very long overdue, and I am pleased that the courage of the escapees will at last be recognised officially.

But what about our 'forgotten people'?

There is no memorial to the 4,000 political prisoners of the Channel Islands Occupation who were arrested and imprisoned by the Germans.

It seems they are always overlooked or not recognised by the States of Jersey and Guernsey, or even the British government.

Many served their sentence in Channel Islands prisons but some were sent to French and German prisons, and even to German concentration camps.

I do know what the States attitude during the Occupation was — and here I quote my old friend, political prisoner, the Guernseyman Frank Falla: 'It was made very clear that anyone who stepped out of line with the Germans could expect no sympathy, understanding or help from our local government.

'If you offended the Germans and got punishment for it that was your own fault, and the local authorities had no intention of helping you in your troubles.'

This was the right impression to give the Nazis — but it should not have been practised by the authorities on their own people.

So, is this the reason why our own States of Jersey have never recognised the Occupation political prisoners? And why have no States Members have even brought forward a petition, on behalf of our 'forgotten people', to place a memorial plaque outside the old prison wall in Gloucester Street?

States Members, please prove to me you did, or do, care about our forgotten people, then I will have faith in you.

The Dower House,
Parkinson Drive, Millbrook, St Lawrence.

From Joe Mière Monday 25th July 1994.

*Acknowledgement to **The Jersey Evening Post***

Bailiff unveils plaque to the prisoners of the Occupation

TRIBUTE was paid yesterday by the Bailiff, Mr Philip Bailhache, to the courage of those imprisoned during the Occupation for their resistance to the German force.

Unveiling a granite tablet set in the wall in front of the Hospital, near where the old prison stood in Newgate Street, Mr Bailhache said: 'The prison itself has gone and the people incarcerated behind its walls are a diminishing band. The site beyond these forgotten walls holds hundreds if not thousands of stories of courage and resilience, most of which will never now be told.

'But enough stories have been told to make it right and timely that the Island should now honour those who protested against the rule of the invader and who defied, often at enormous personal risks, the occupying force.'

Among the stories which have been told are those of Joe Mière, Peter Gray, Jurat

BY DENA JEUNE

Mr Mière, who campaigned for a memorial to be established and eventually sought the help of the Lieut-Governor, endured two sentences, one of them for protesting as English people were deported. He explained that people were sent to the German prison for acts ranging from defacing German signs, disobeying orders and passing around news, to helping escaped Russian prisoners of war.

'Some were here only for a day before they were sent on to camps and prisons in France,' he said.

Mrs Renouf, who at the age of 17 was imprisoned because she would not denounce her father to the Germans for keeping a wireless at the family farm at Bel-Val, St Martin, said that she would do the same thing again.

She served nine weeks, initially in a single cell. Her father was sentenced to two years and her mother to ten months in 1944, their crime of secreting a wireless made worse by the fact that

by sending him to the German court wearing short trousers did not work, however, and he spent several weeks in prison.

'It was pretty grim, certainly not a holiday camp,' he reflected. 'But you can always bend regulations, and we got up to some stunts.'

One evening he got his door open and released two German soldiers imprisoned in neighbouring cells so that they could play cards together.

In his speech, Mr Bai made special mention

Bailiff unveils plaque to the prisoners of the Occupation
The Evening Post, Friday 28 April 1995

Tribute was paid yesterday by the Bailiff, Mr Philip Bailhache, to the courage of those imprisoned during the Occupation for their resistance to the German forces. Unveiling a granite tablet set in the wall in front of the hospital, near where the old prison stood in Gloucester Street, Mr Bailhache said: 'The prison has gone and the people incarcerated behind its walls are a diminishing band. The site beyond these forgotten walls holds hundreds if not thousands of stories of courage and resilience, most of which will never now be told.

But enough stories have been told to make it right and timely that the Island should now honour those who protested against the rule of the invader and who defied, often at enormous personal risks, the occupying forces. Among the stories which have been told, are those told of Joe Mière, Peter Gray, Jurat Gruchy. Mr Mière who campaigned for a memorial to be established and eventually sought the help of the Lieutenant-Governor, endured two sentences, one of them for protesting as English people were deported. He explained that people were sent to the German prison for acts ranging from defacing German signs, disobeying orders and passing around news, to helping escaped Russian prisoners of war. Some were here only for a day before they were sent on to camps and prisons in France and Germany.

Not to be forgotten Mr Bailhache said were the people whose offences against the Germans were considered too serious for a sentence to be served in Jersey, particularly those who had harboured Russian prisoners and other slave workers. Often they were sent to Germany, where many languished in prisons and camps never to return', Mr Bailhache said. He unveiled the plaque, watched by the Lieutenant-Governor, Sir John Sutton, by members of the Occupation and Liberation Committee, and by a small crowd of about ninety people, many of whom had been imprisoned during the Occupation.

'On the face of it, there is something unusual about erecting a plaque in honour of prison inmates, but during war time and especially in territory occupied by an enemy force, there are many ambiguities' he said. 'Is the taking of a German revolver or helmet to be classified as stealing? From a contemporary German viewpoint the answer is obviously yes – in the petty regulations and edicts of an occupying force but they were not criminal in the true sense of the word. We salute the courage of all who defied the invaders and showed the sturdy spirit of independence which beats in every true Jersey heart.

Acknowledgement to The Jersey Evening Post

THE START OF THE JOE MIERE COLLECTION

The Joe Mière Collection was born in the German Occupation of Jersey 1940-1945. Having been arrested by the Germans firstly in 1941, then in 1942, then in 1944 and imprisoned with many of the people whose photographs are now on display in the Joe Mière Collection at The Jersey War Tunnels Museum. I often thought to myself these people will be forgotten so will most of our Occupation history, to be lost forever if some person or other does not start to record this Occupation history-but not just words but in photographs.

I could not find anyone who wanted to undertake this research work or to spend many hours, days and even years to record and collect personal photographs and personal Occupation histories and to spend their own cash in buying writing material and, most of all, the expense of buying stamps and recorded delivery letters to be sent all over the world. No person I asked was even interested or ready to put a hand in their pocket or take that very lonely road of research work. Many told me that I should undertake the task. They said that I had first hand experience and knowledge of most of the people who were arrested and imprisoned by the Germans 1940-1945.

So the Joe Mière Collection of photographs and personal Occupation histories started in a serious way after I was demobbed from the British Army in 1948.

Friends and people of the Occupation years were very kind to me, always ready to tell me their war history, and give me photographs to copy. The trust they placed in me was wonderful and they were only too pleased that some one was recording their experiences or those of their family. Even after fifty years we still keep in touch. As the years went by I added more material and details to the collection, when my pocket and availability allowed. As a family man with a wife and three little children to support I found it very hard to make ends meet - but bit by bit the collection grew.

The hours and days spent interviewing people seemed to never end. But it was a labour of love and a great satisfaction to me - which was my own reward. There was no thought or hope of a financial compensation for all the years of hard work. I took it as a great honour that trust placed in me by all those loyal and brave people who gave me their time and photographs and recollections. Many have now passed on but their families keep in touch with me. They all know that I am honour bound to protect their photographs and personal memories. They also know that I will always guard and make sure that what they have given me will not fall into the wrong hands.

By the time I started work at the German Military Underground Hospital Museum as Deputy Curator in March 1976 the collection was quite large.

AT LAST THE END OF MY BOOK

So at last I have come to the end of my book. I really have enough information in my archives to write ten books but one has to stop somewhere.

At war's end in May 1945, I was nearly 18 years old. My birthday was on 27th July 1945. So in July, 1945, I joined the British army - Gloucester Regiment. We all thought we were going to fight the Japs. I was posted to Germany (of all places) I served in Germany, Austria, Denmark, Belgium even had a few trips to Warsaw in Poland. I also served in Holland where I was engaged to a lovely Dutch girl, but in the end it did not work out. I left the army at the end of 1948 and returned to Jersey again. I got engaged to a very nice and kind Jersey school teacher. She was my sister's friend. But we were not meant to be.

Now and again I went out with my best friend's sister, Marie, but we were only good friends. She was lovely, not only in looks but a very kind girl. I did not know it at the time but really she was my dream girl with her lovely smile. After going out one evening in December 1953, it all came to me-I was in love with her. That evening I asked her to marry me. She made me very happy when she said 'yes.' We got married on the 19th of April 1954.

At the church she looked so lovely. What a lucky chap I was to have such a lovely girl as my wife. Even after Fifty years we still love one another dearly. Without my Marie there would be no point in living. We have three fine children - a lovely daughter, Martine, two big handsome sons, John and Michael, seven wonderful grandchildren, five granddaughters, Marie-Clair, Donna, Jade, Chelsea and Rochelle and two fine grandsons, Joshua and James. There are two very nice and kind daughter-in-laws, Cheryl and Angela, and a very supportive son in law, Alain. What more could anyone want from life? We are a close-knit little family and we have friends all over the world.

The year 2000 was very upsetting for my dear Marie and our family as I was diagnosed with prostate cancer. My blood count was over 600 and the normal blood count is 10 to 14. But with our family doctor, Dr Perkins, and Mr Ingram and his team at the William Knott Day Hospital I am not doing so badly. One gets days that are very bad, but with the care of the doctors and my dear Marie (she is wonderful) I think I will make it for our golden wedding in 2004.

What a surprise we received in April 2003 when the Jersey Heritage Trust invited me to lunch and informed me that they were going to have my portrait painted which will be hung in the Barreau Le Maistre Art Gallery at the Jersey Museum, as Jersey Citizen of 2003. What an honour for me and my family. The artist is an award winning portrait painter Andrew Tift. He is a great guy and we get on so well. His work is so wonderful and very true to life as you can see on the back cover of this book. The Jersey Heritage Trust certainly picked a real top portrait painter. My Marie and I cannot still get over the fact that I am getting honoured in this way by our own Jersey people.

Then another surprise, on Liberation Day, 9th May 2004, I was again truly honoured when I was presented with a medal by the Russian Government for the role I have played as a researcher and archivist of Occupation related material about Russian nationals, and other activities. This is something for which I am very grateful and will always cherish - I still can't get over it.

Marie is so proud of her big Joe and I am a proud old Jerseyman who loves his wife and family, and loves his Jersey people.

A Beintôt, A La Préchaine.

Joseph Arthur Mière

Golden Wedding

To Dear Mum and Dad
and Dear Grandpere and Grandmere

Joe and Marie Mière

We wish you a very Happy
**Golden Wedding Anniversary Day
19th April - 2004**

Thank you for all your understanding,
your patience through the years,
For sharing every happiness
as well as the tears,
For loving with open hearts
and open arms as well,
You are loved, treasured and
appreciated more than words can tell.
With Love from all your loving family.

„СОРОК ЛЕТ ПОБЕДЫ
В ВЕЛИКОЙ ОТЕЧЕСТВЕННОЙ ВОЙНЕ
1941—1945 гг.“

УДОСТОВЕРЕНИЕ

MR JOE MIÈRE.

ВРУЧЕНА ЮБИЛЕЙНАЯ МЕДАЛЬ

„СОРОК ЛЕТ ПОБЕДЫ
В ВЕЛИКОЙ ОТЕЧЕСТВЕННОЙ
ВОЙНЕ 1941—1945 гг.“

Президент
Российской Федерации

9 - may 2004 года

Joe Mière with his medal. 'This is a great honour,' he said

Russian honour is a surprise for Occupation hero

BY PAULA THELWELL

OCCUPATION historian Joe Mière has been honoured by the Russian government for his lifetime's research and for helping wartime slave workers.

The surprise presentation was made at the Liberation dinner at the Jersey War Tunnels on Sunday.

For once the talkative Mr Mière admitted that he had been lost for words. Speaking the next day, he said: 'I was called forward by Bob Le Sueur, who announced that I was to be presented with a medal from the Russian government.

Research

'The assistant naval attaché in London, Captain Andrei Vanchugov, then presented me with the Russian Medal, with thanks for all my research work on the people, those who escaped, political prisoners, and for helping Russians with their research on their compatriots who died in the Channel Islands between 1942 and 1945.'

Mr Mière's family were also mentioned in the citation. During the Occupation they sheltered escaped Russian slave workers at their Midvale Road home.

The presentation is the latest accolade for Mr Mière, whose work was honoured last year by Islanders when he was chosen by popular vote as the subject for the Jersey Heritage Trust's Citizen of the Year portrait. This summer will see the publication of Mr Mière's 50-year research, entitled Never to be Forgotten.

'This medal is a great honour for my family,' he said. 'We have only just got over the surprise and shock of having my portrait painted.'

Sunday evening's event was the second major celebration at the War Tunnels for Mr Mière and his wife, Marie, because last month they were joined by 100 family and friends to celebrate their Golden Wedding. The tunnels are also home to the Joe Mière Collection, which tells the story of Islanders during the Occupation.

Jersey Evening Post

O P I N I O N

An honour richly deserved

NOW that the Island has celebrated yet another Liberation Day, the events of the Occupation, now six decades in the past, will once more fade into the background. Reminders of the war years in the shape of everything from bunkers and anti-tank walls to museums and memorabilia will still exist, but many Islanders take them more or less for granted throughout much of the year.

There are, however, still those who were touched personally and deeply by the Occupation, its shortages, its uncertainties and the challenges of conscience and courage it presented. And, as the historian Paul Sanders pointed out during his recent visit to the Island, we should remember that a majority of those who endured the oppressive presence of a foreign power did so with fortitude and remarkable bravery.

Among those who fall into this category is Joe Mière, whose activities in helping slave workers escape from their Nazi masters were recognised on Sunday when he was presented with a medal by the Russian government. Significantly, the award also recognised the role Mr Mière has played over many years as a researcher and archivist of Occupation-related material.

Mr Mière can feel justifiably proud of his honour, which is richly deserved. As an Island, we too can take pride in it, for the medal is symbolic of the generally exemplary conduct of a community which suddenly found itself the victim of a global clash of power and a collision of ideologies.

In an ideal world there would be a medal for every Islander who listened to the BBC on a concealed radio set, who sheltered slave workers on the run, or who engaged in acts of defiance against the occupying power. In the real world, this is obviously not possible, but all those acts of courage or selflessness are worthy of continuing respect.

Too much has been written in recent years about the deficiencies of some of those who lived through the Occupation. We Islanders — not to mention increasing numbers of the educated British public — know that the truth, as exemplified by Mr Mière's medal, lies elsewhere.

Item reference number	Registration card photograph
D/S/A/4/A12340	Jack Frede Harry Walling
D/S/A/14/A56	James Colgan
D/S/A/4/A12412	Leonard Washington
D/S/A/11/A1688	Alfred Paul Le Huquet
D/S/A/4/A2896	Philip Le Cornu
D/S/A/13/A320	Harry Ferguson
D/S/A/13/A548	Walter Holman Kennett
D/S/A/11/A3247	Frank Tregear
D/S/A/4/A2582	George William Le Cocq
D/S/A/13/A920	Jenny Thomas
D/S/A/13/A919	Fred Thomas
D/S/A/4/A2692	Alfred James Connor
D/S/A/4/A680	Alexandrienne Juillet Baudains
D/S/A/4A2588	Kevin John Le Cocq
D/S/A/4/A7937	Kenneth Alfred Mathew
D/S/A/4/A5610	Ronald John Harris
D/S/A/11/A1795	Ronald Bernard Kent
D/S/A/4/A3394	David Thomas Dawson
D/S/A/4A2812	Kenneth James Corfield
D/S/A/4/A696	George Baudains
D/S/A/13/A371	Eldon Stanley Gibaut
D/S/A/13/A473	Maurice Victor Gamble Hill
D/S/A/13/A430	Raymond Hannaford
D/S/A/4/A9238	Florence Marquerite Le Pennee
D/S/A/13/A594	John George Lingshaw
D/S/A/4/A7163	José Lillicrap
D/S/A/7/A1043	Marjory May Robins
D/S/A/13/A746	Eric Pleasants
D/S/A/4/A9063	Frederick William Page
D/S/A/4/A9064	Nellie Winifred Page
D/S/A/11/A871	James Clarence Davey
D/S/A/4/A3510	Owen Joseph Dore
D/S/A/5/A820	George Louis Sty
D/S/A/13/A583	Denis Leister
D/S/A/4/A9113	Philip Charles Pallot
D/S/A/11/A2822	Mary Erica Richardson
D/S/A/4/A817	Albert Gustave Bedane
D/S/A/4/A9513	John de Carteret Pinwell
D/S/A/3/A881	Edward Peter Muels
D/S/A/3/A928	Emile John Paisnel
D/S/A/4/A9876	Clifford Bond Queree
D/S/A/4/A11238	John Soyer
D/S/A/11/A2373	John Whitley Nicolle
D/S/A/11/A2464	Clarence Claude Painter
D/S/A/11/A2463	Peter Edward Painter
D/S/A/4/A12248	Francois Rene Julien Le Villio
D/S/A/11/A897	Arthur Dimmery
D/S/A/11/A2131	William Howard Marsh
D/S/A/10/A335	Walter Allen Stanley Dauny
D/S/A/11/A681	Clifford John Cohu
D/S/A/4/A4290	George James Fox
D/S/A/11/A927	Harold Osmond Le Druillenec
D/S/A/9/A433	Louise May Gould
D/S/A/11/A829a	Dennis Philip le Cuirot
D/S/A/13/A978	Cyril de Montford Wellborne
D/S/A/4/A4975	Michael Peter James Aloysius Gray
D/S/A/4/A10462	Joan Maingay Robin
D/S/A/11/A/2917	Marcel Fortune Rossi

Reference numbers for photographs kindly supplied by the Jersey Heritage Trust.